11+ Non-Verbal Reasoning

When it comes to 11+ preparation, nothing beats practice — and this CGP book is packed with the best practice you'll find, all at the perfect level for ages 10-11.

It starts with questions that focus on one concept at a time, so children can really get to grips with each key skill. Once they're confident, there's a selection of mixed-topic Assessment Tests to help them get used to the style of the real 11+ papers.

We've also included detailed, step-by-step answers. Everything you need!

How to access your free Online Edition

This book includes a free Online Edition to read on your PC, Mac or tablet. You'll just need to go to **cgpbooks.co.uk/extras** and enter this code:

3741 7742 1062 0449

By the way, this code only works for one person. If somebody else has used this book before you, they might have already claimed the Online Edition.

Practice Book – Ages 10-11

with Assessment Tests

How to use this Practice Book

This book is divided into three parts — Spotting Patterns, 3D Shapes and Spatial Reasoning, and Assessment Tests. There are answers and detailed explanations at the back of the book.

Spotting Patterns

- Each section contains practice questions focusing on one of the main concepts your child will need to understand for the Non-Verbal Reasoning part of the test.
- These pages can help your child build up the different skills they'll need for the real test.
- Your child can use the smiley face tick boxes to evaluate how confident they feel with each topic.

3D Shapes and Spatial Reasoning

- Your child may have to answer questions on 3D Shapes and Spatial Reasoning in the Non-Verbal Reasoning part of the test. This section concentrates on the skills your child would need for this.

Assessment Tests

- The third part of the book contains eight assessment tests, each with a mix of question types.
- You can print multiple-choice answer sheets so your child can practise the tests as if they're sitting the real thing — visit cgpbooks.co.uk/11plus/answer-sheets or scan the QR code. →

Answer Sheets

- Use the printable answer sheets if you want your child to do each test more than once.
- If you want to give your child timed practice, give them a time limit of 30 minutes for each test, and ask them to work as quickly and carefully as they can.
- The tests get harder from 1 to 8, so don't be surprised if your child finds the later ones more tricky.
- Talk your child through the answers to the questions they got wrong. This will help them understand questions that work in a similar way when they come up against them in later tests.
- Your child should aim for a mark of around 85% (39 questions correct) in each test. If they score less than this, use their results to work out the areas they need more practice on.
- If they haven't managed to finish the test in time, they need to work on increasing their speed, whereas if they have made a lot of mistakes, they need to work more carefully.
- Keep track of your child's scores using the progress chart on page 118.

Published by CGP

Editors:
Michael Bushell, Emma Clayton, Sammy El-Bahrawy, Alex Fairer, Duncan Lindsay, Hannah Roscoe, Ben Train.

With thanks to Glenn Rogers for the proofreading.

ISBN: 978 1 78908 806 9
Printed by Elanders Ltd, Newcastle upon Tyne
Clipart from Corel®

Based on the classic CGP style created by Richard Parsons.

Contents

Tick off the check box for each topic as you go along.

Spotting Patterns

3D Shapes and Spatial Reasoning

Assessment Tests

Shapes

Most questions will be based around shapes, so you need to get to know them.

Warm Up

1. The two shapes in each figure will be **joined** along the **dotted lines** to make a new shape. How many **sides** will each new shape have?

a. 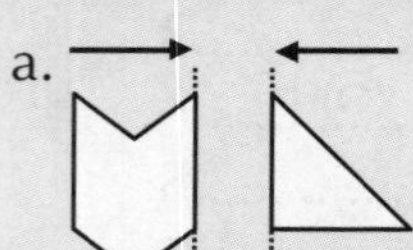 b. 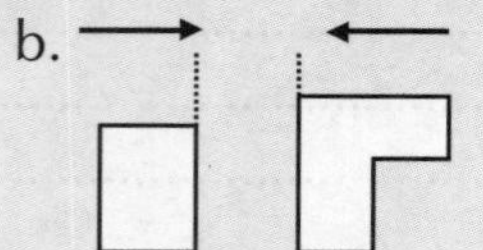 c. 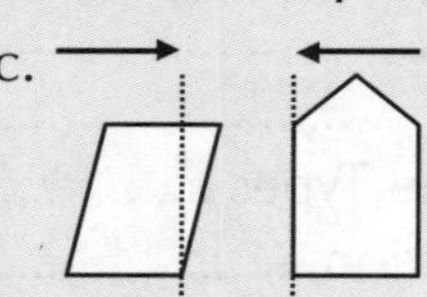 d. 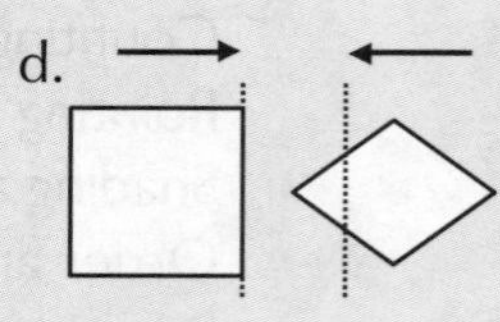

2. In each pair, circle the shape that has **more lines** of **symmetry**.

a. 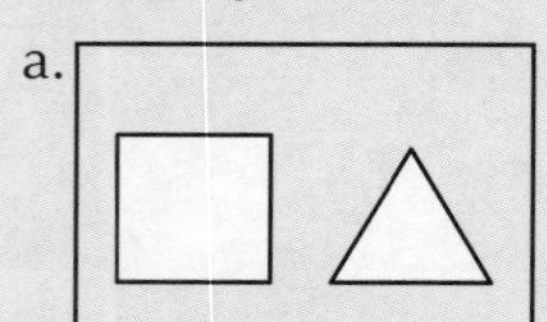 b. 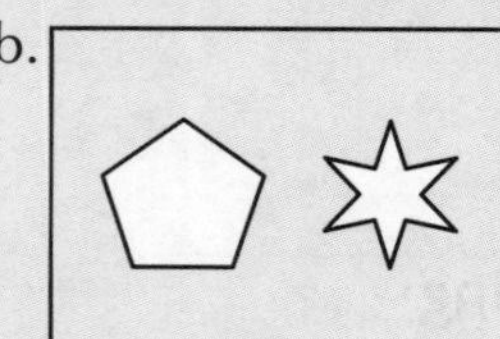 c. 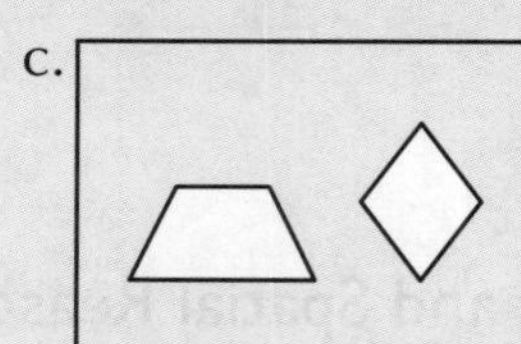 d. 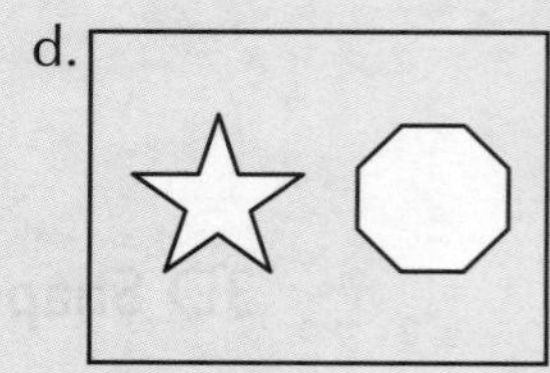

Find the Figure Like the First Two

Work out which option is most like the two figures on the left.

Example:

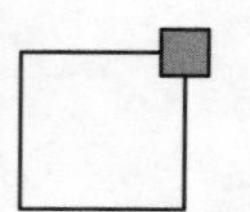 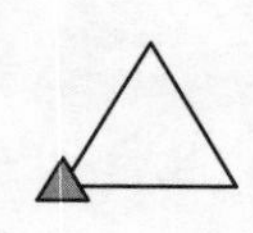 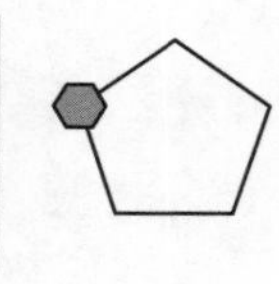 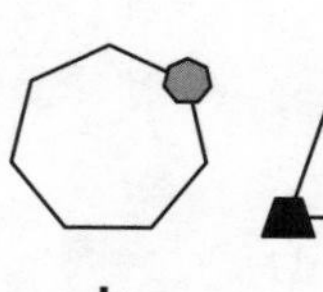 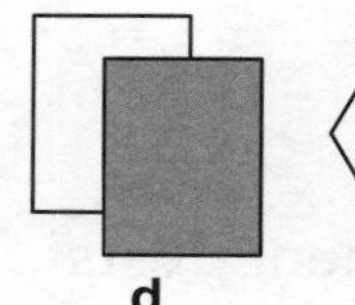 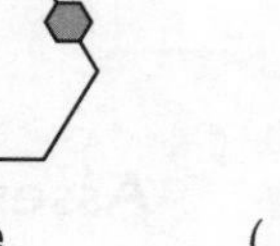

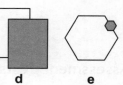

a b c d e (b)

In all figures, there must be a small grey copy of the large white shape on one of the corners of the white shape.

3.

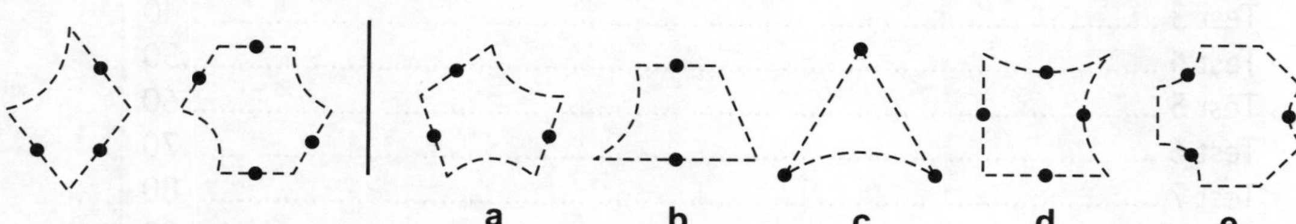

a b c d e (____)

4.

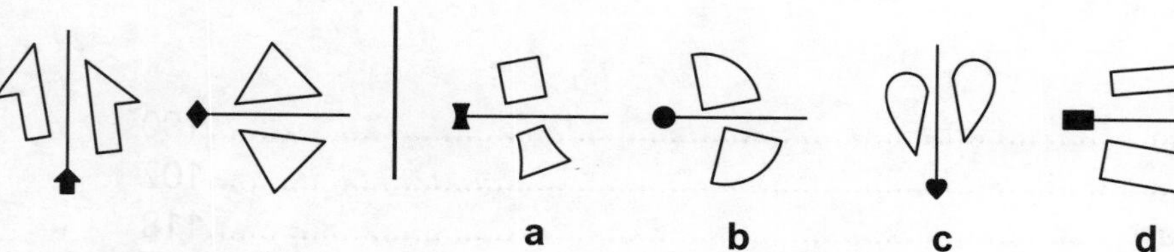 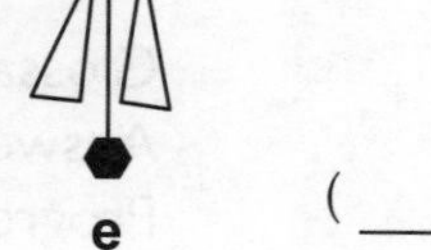

a b c d e (____)

5.

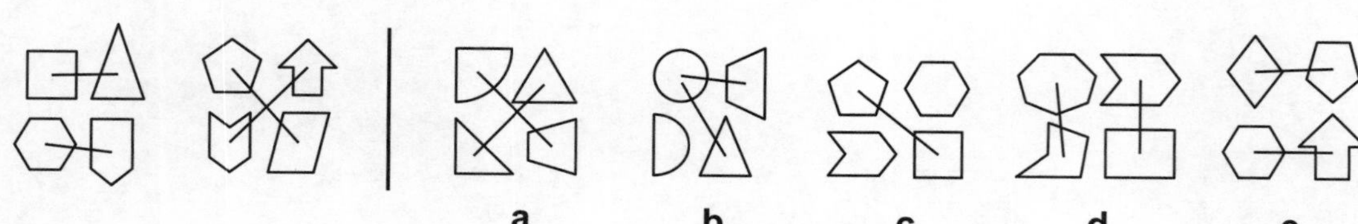

a b c d e (____)

Counting

If in doubt, count everything — shapes, sides or lines. It might give you a clue to the answer.

Warm Up

1. Are there more **squares** (S) or **circles** (C) in each of the figures below?

a. 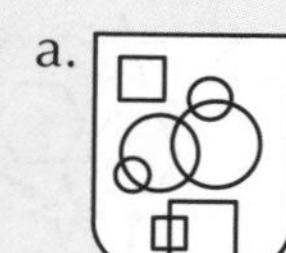 ______

b. 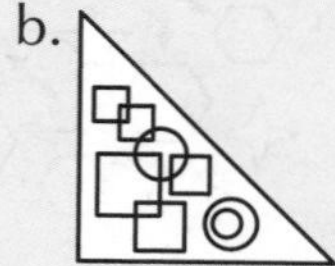 ______

c. 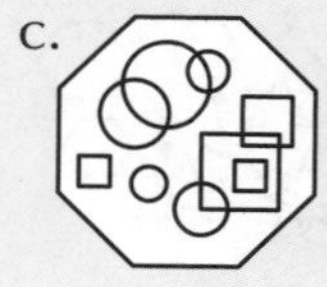 ______

d. 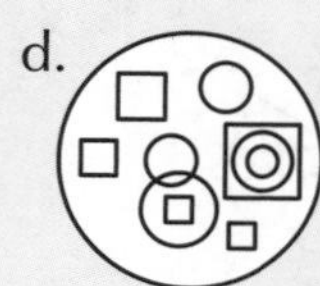 ______

e. 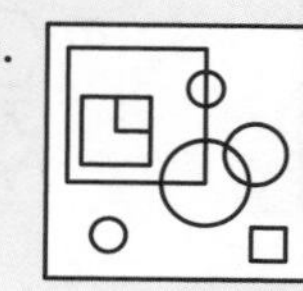 ______

2. In which options below do the number of circles **match** the number of triangles?

a. 

b. 

c. 

d. 

e. 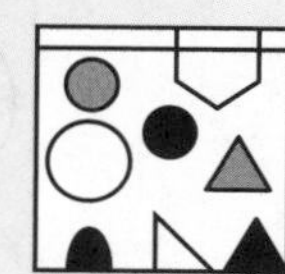

Options: ______________

Odd One Out

Find the figure in each row that is most unlike the other figures.

Example:

a

b

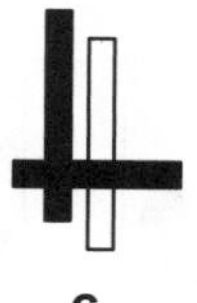
c

d

e

(a)

In all other figures, there are two black rectangles and one white rectangle.

3.

a

b c

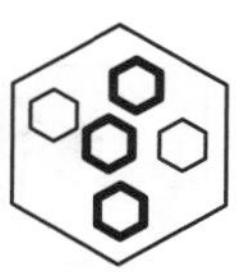
d

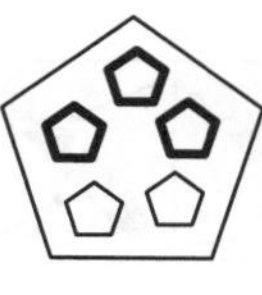
e

(____)

4.

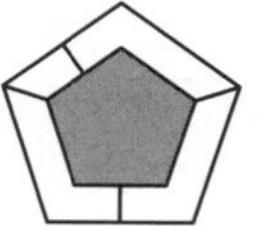
a

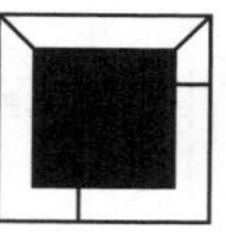
b

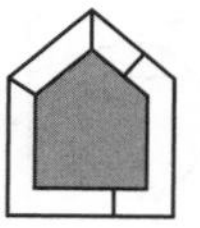
c

d

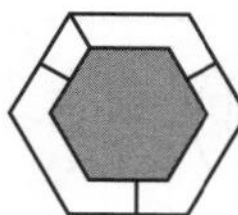
e

(____)

5.

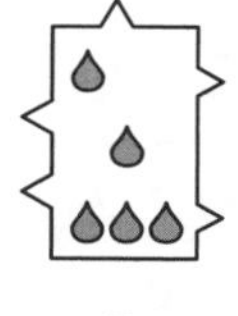
a

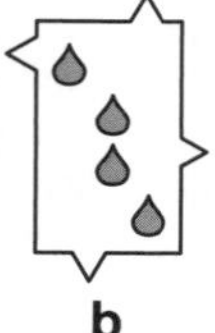
b

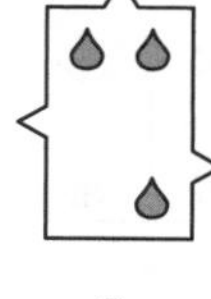
c

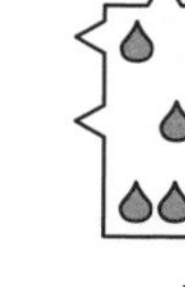
d

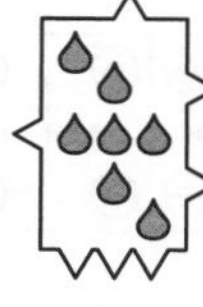
e

(____)

Pointing

You should always check what an arrow is pointing at, and in which direction it's pointing.

Warm Up

1. In each figure, are there more arrows pointing to **stars** (S) or **hexagons** (H)?

a. ______

b.  ______

c. 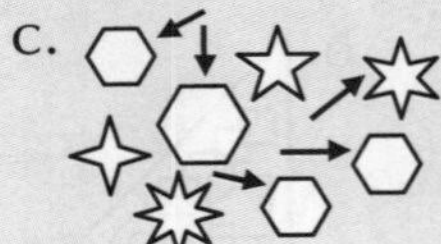 ______

d.  ______

2. In each figure, are there more arrows pointing **clockwise** (C) or **anticlockwise** (A)?

a. 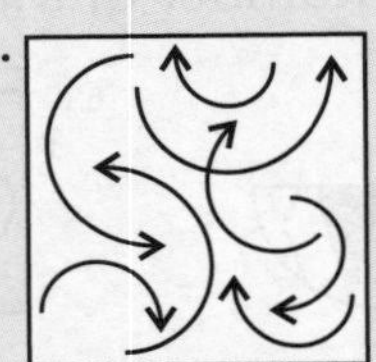 ______

b. ______

c. 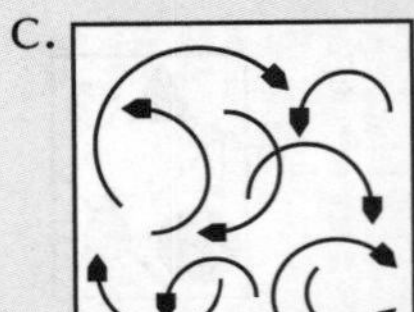 ______

d.  ______

Complete the Series

Depending on which test you take, you might get five squares on the left instead of four — see p.20-21.

Work out which of the options best fits in place of the missing square in the series.

Example:

 a 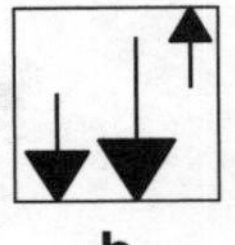 b 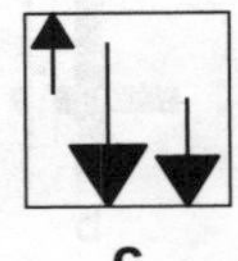 c  d

(C)

Each arrow alternates between pointing up and down.

3. 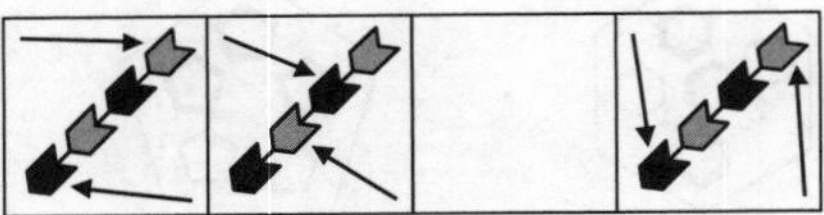

 a  b  c  d

(____)

4. 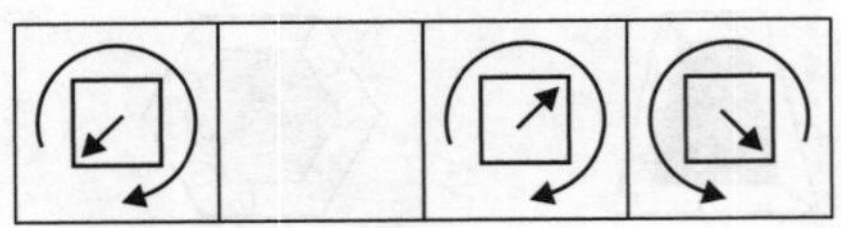

a 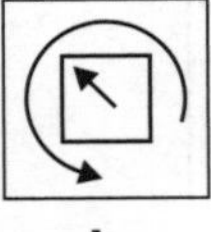 b 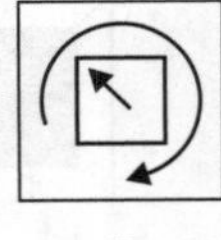 c  d

(____)

5. 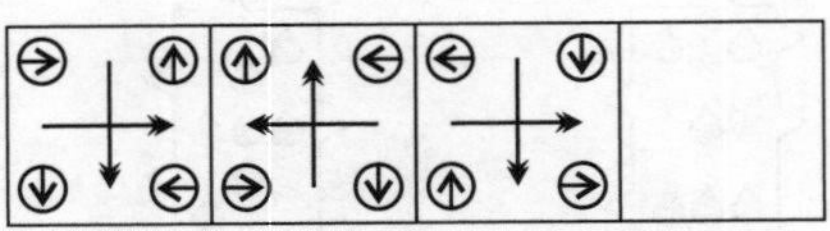

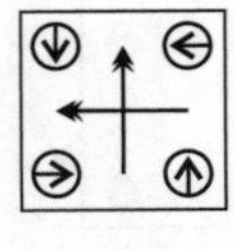 a  b 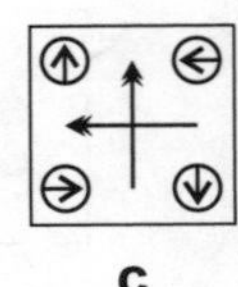 c 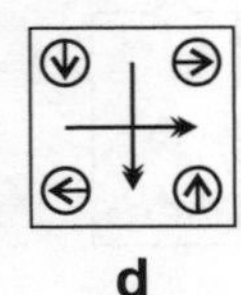 d

(____)

Shading and Line Types

There are lots of different shadings and line types you need to look out for.

Warm Up

1. What is the most **common shading** in each of the figures below — black, white, grey, spotted or hatched?

a.  b.  c.  d.

__________ __________ __________ __________

2. In each figure, circle all the shapes that have the **same type** of **outline**.

a. 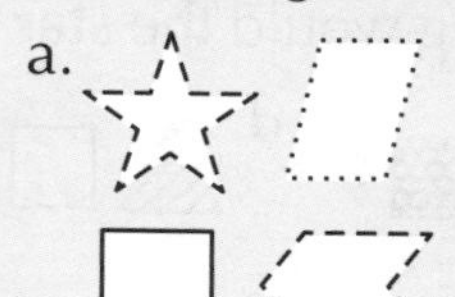 b. 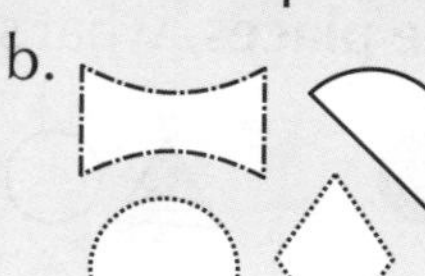 c. 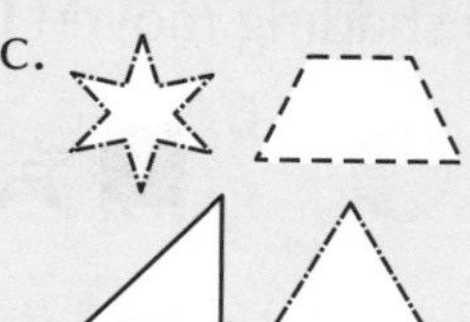 d. 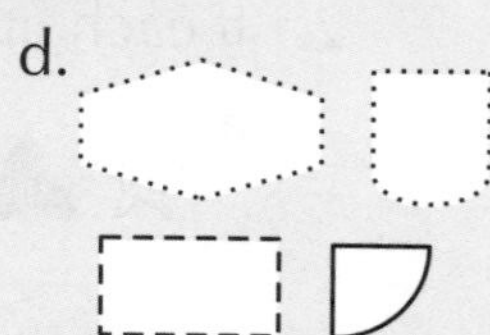

Complete the Pair

Depending on which test you take, you might get two example pairs to look at instead of one — see p.34-35.

The first figure below is changed in some way to become the second. Choose the figure on the right that relates to the third figure in the same way that the second relates to the first.

Example:

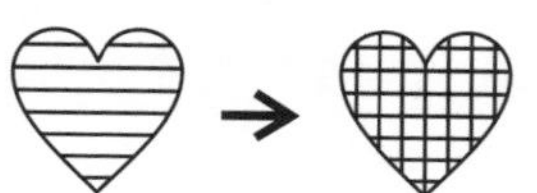 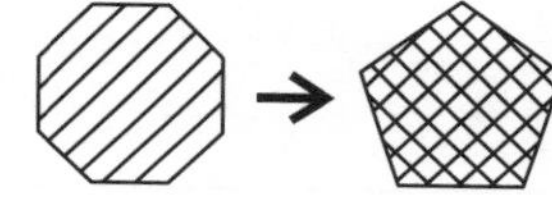 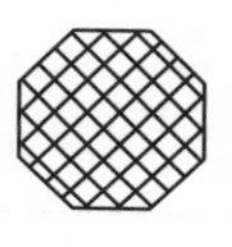 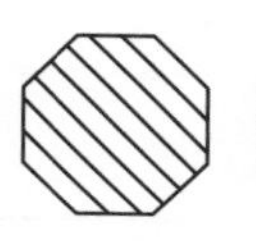 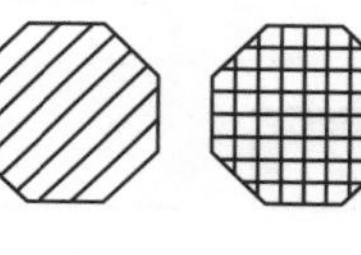

a b c d e (b)

A second layer of hatching that is rotated 90 degrees to the first layer appears inside the shape.

3.   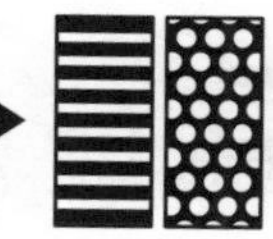    

a b c d e (____)

4. 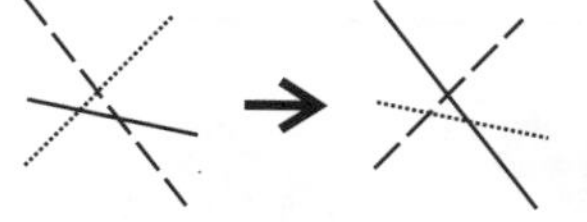 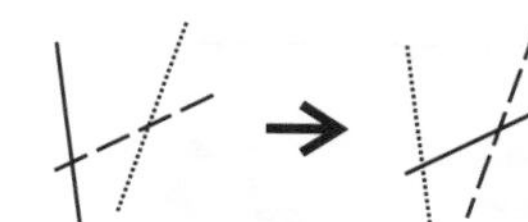 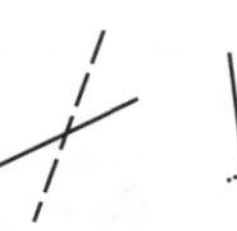 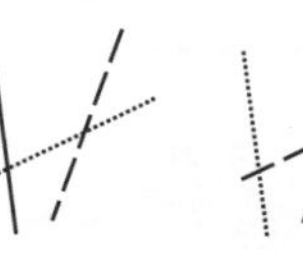 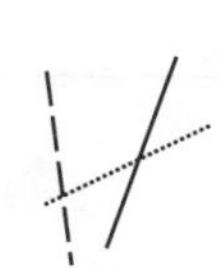 

a b c d e (____)

5. 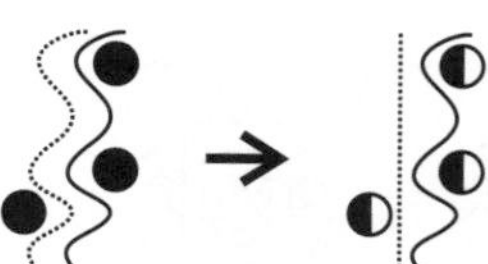 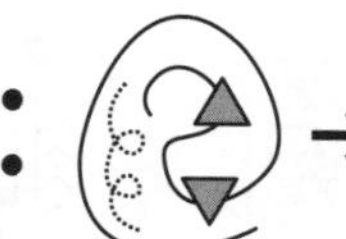 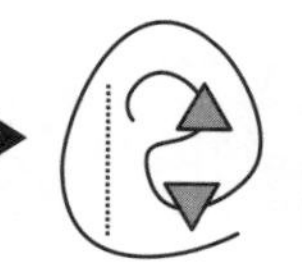 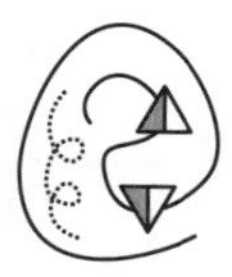 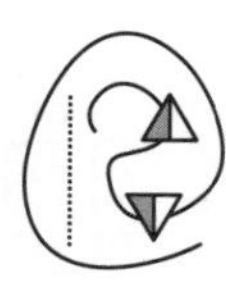   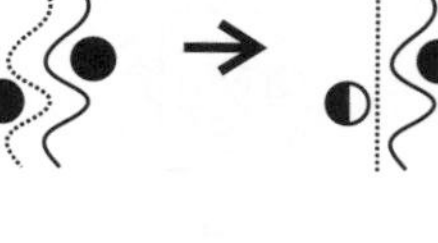

a b c d e (____)

Order and Position

You should always look at where an object is positioned in relation to other objects.

Warm Up

1. In each figure, **shade in** the circle that the **square** will replace once it has **moved** in the way shown by the number and the arrow. If the square reaches the end of a row or column, it will move back to the other end.

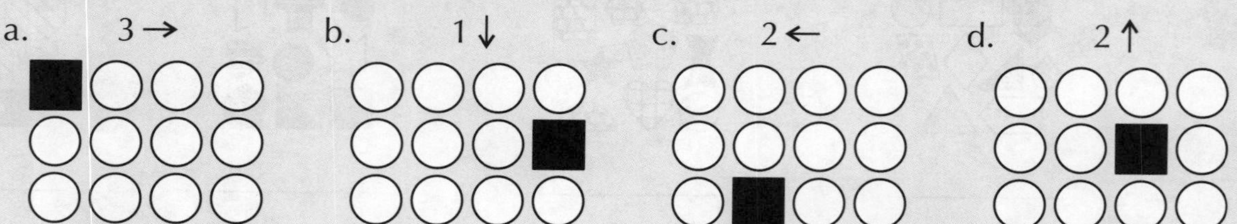

2. If each figure's shading moved **left three places**, what shading would the **star** have?

3. Do the shapes move **clockwise** (C) or **anticlockwise** (A) in each figure?

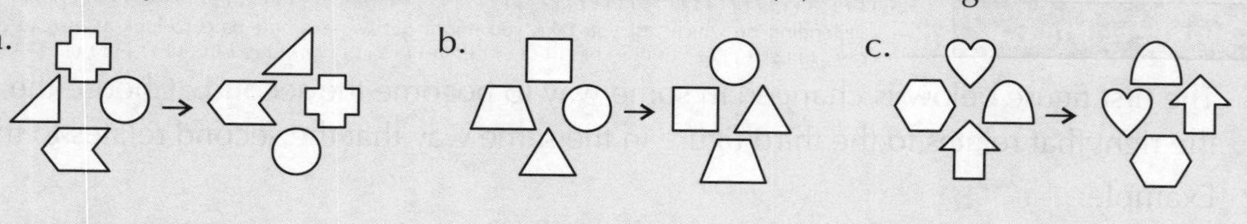

Changing Bugs

Look at how the first bug changes to become the second bug. Then work out which option would look like the third bug if you changed it in the same way.

Example:

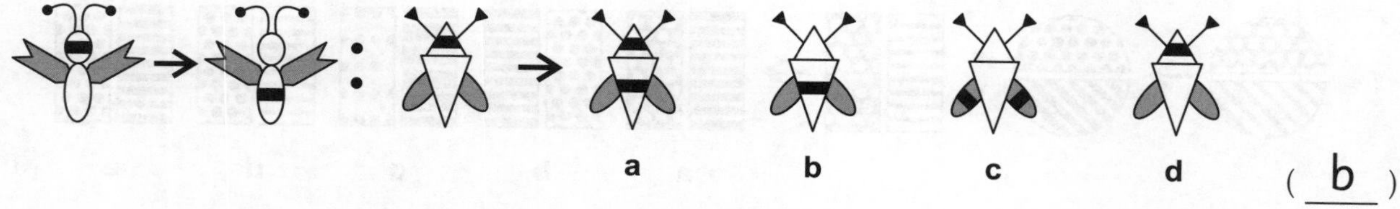

(b)

The black band on the bug's head moves down onto the bug's body.

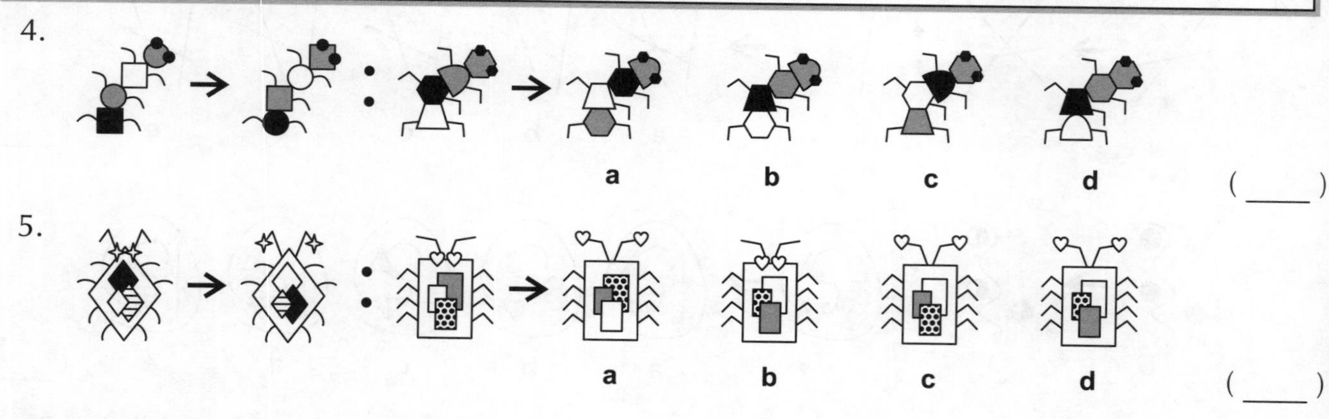

6.

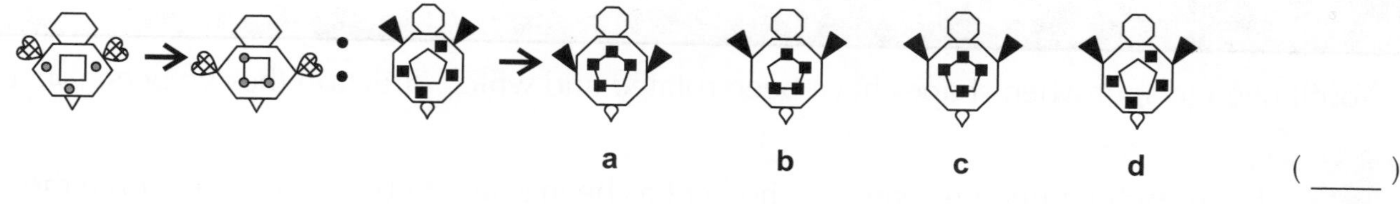

(____)

7.

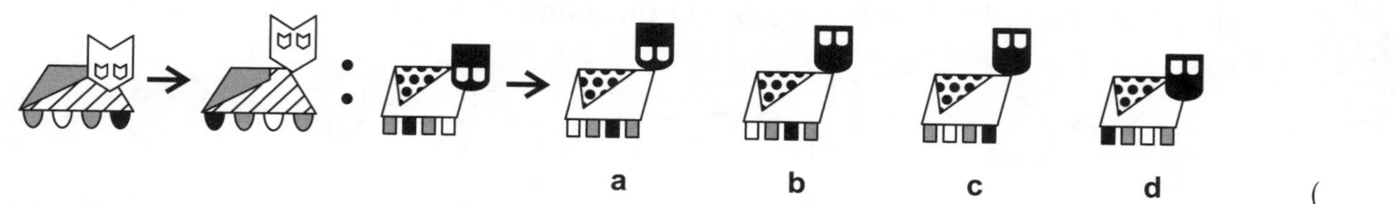

(____)

Complete the Square Grid

On the left of each question below is a big square with one small empty square.
Find which of the five squares on the right should replace the empty square.

Example:

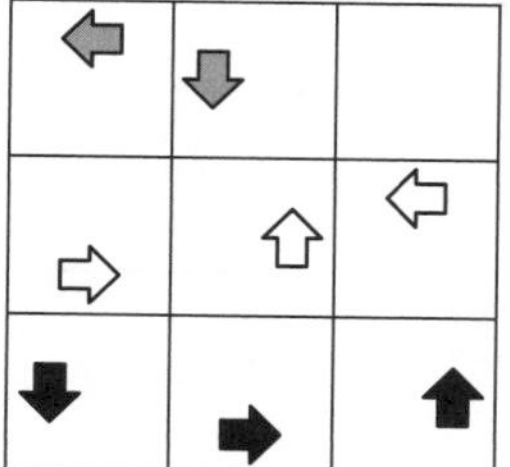

a

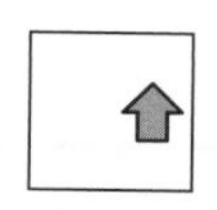
b

c

d

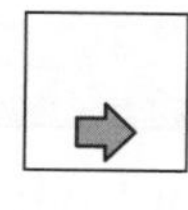
e

(*e*)

Working from left to right, the arrow moves to the next side of the grid square in an anticlockwise direction.

8.

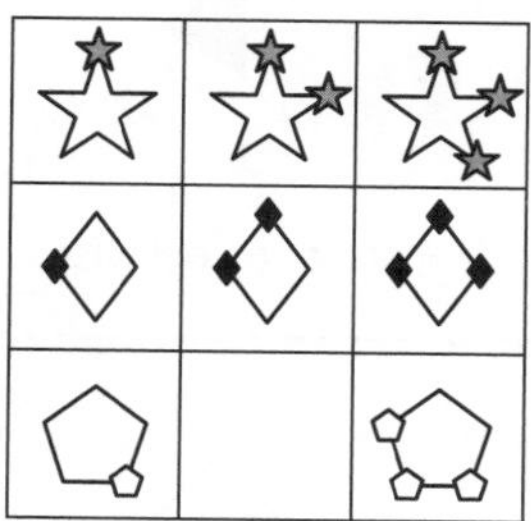

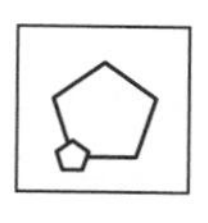
a

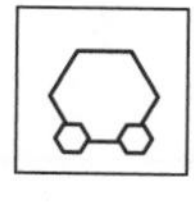
b

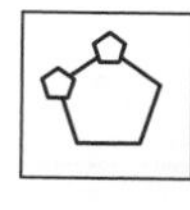
c

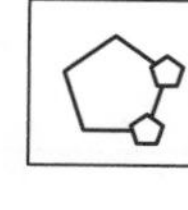
d

e

(____)

9.

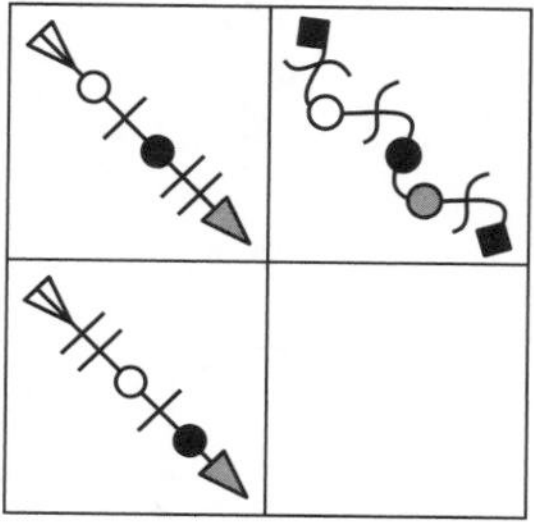

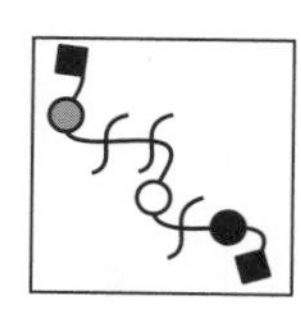
a

b

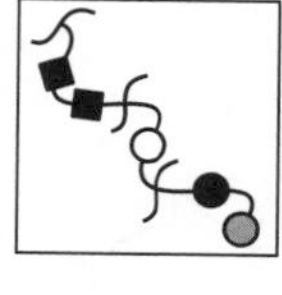
c

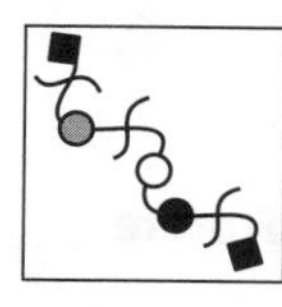
d

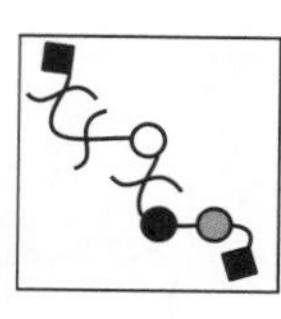
e

(____)

10.

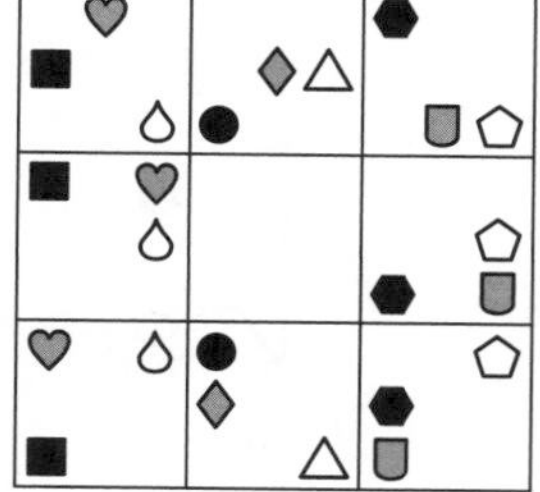

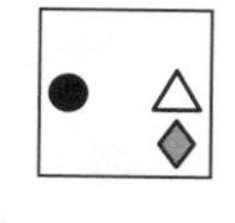
a

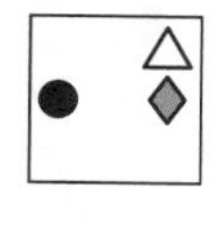
b

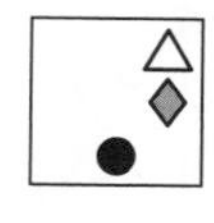
c

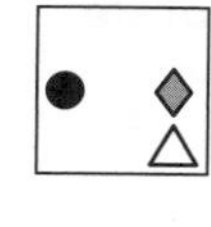
d

e

(____)

Rotation

You'll need to spot when shapes have been rotated and which direction they've been rotated in.

Warm Up

1. In each figure, the shape on the left has been rotated 90 degrees to become the shape on the right. Circle the correct **direction** of rotation for each figure.

a. 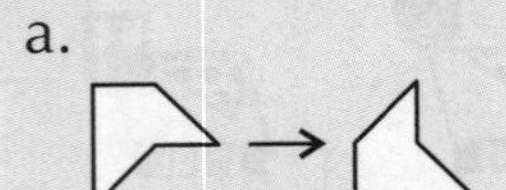

clockwise

anticlockwise

b.

clockwise

anticlockwise

c. 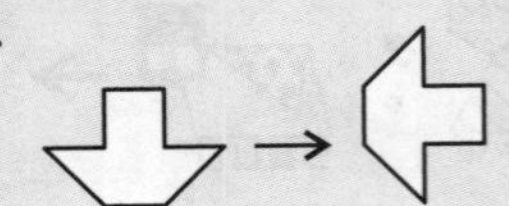

clockwise

anticlockwise

d. 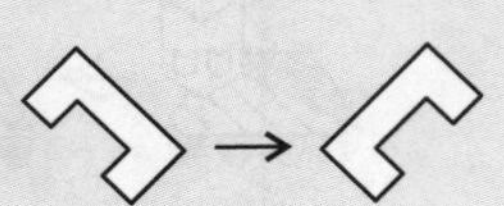

clockwise

anticlockwise

2. Circle all the figures that are **identical** apart from **rotation**.

Rotate the Figure

Work out which option would look like the figure on the left if it was rotated.

Example:

 Rotate 

 a

b

 c

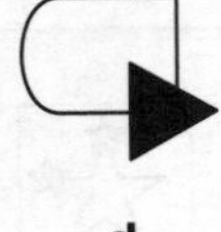 d

(a)

The figure has been rotated 90 degrees anticlockwise.

3.  Rotate 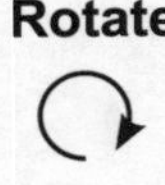

a

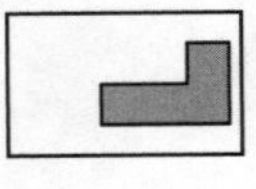 b

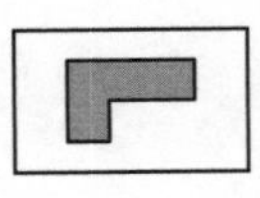 c

 d

(____)

4. 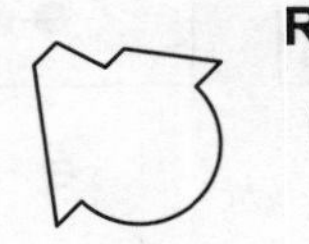 Rotate

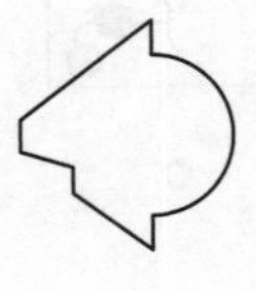 a

b

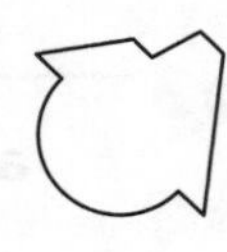 c

 d

(____)

5. 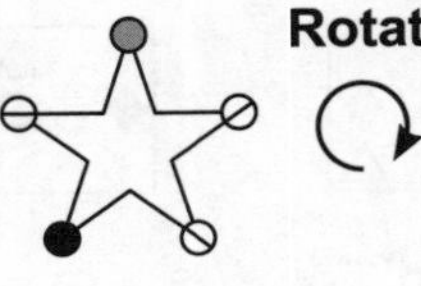 Rotate

a

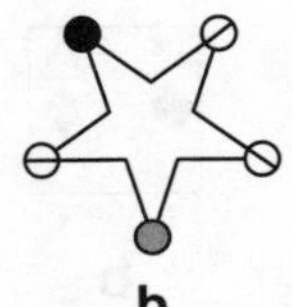 b

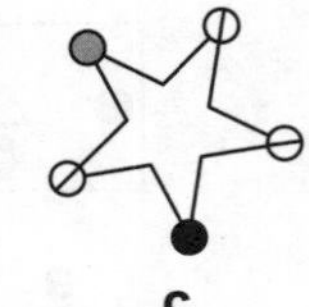 c

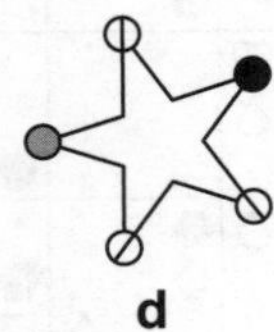 d

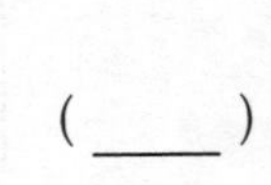

(____)

Reflection

Reflection and rotation can look very similar, so make sure you don't get them confused.

Warm Up

1. In each figure, is the right-hand shape a **reflection** (RE) or **rotation** (RO) of the left-hand shape?

a. 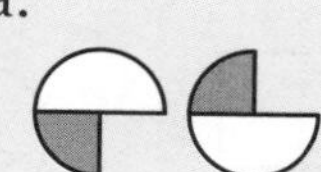 ______

b.  ______

c.  ______

d.  ______

e.  ______

f.  ______

2. Circle the part of each figure on the right that has been reflected **incorrectly**.

a. 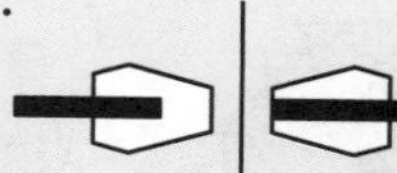

b. 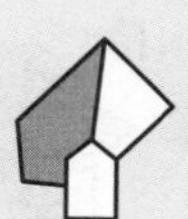

c. 

d. 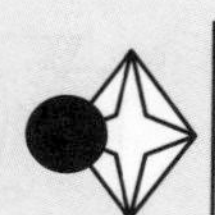 

Reflect the Figure

Work out which option would look like the figure on the left if it was reflected over the line.

Example:

Reflect

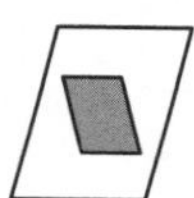

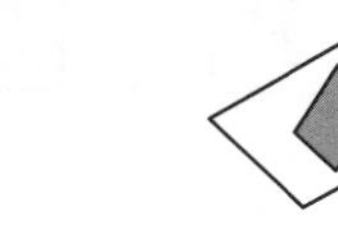 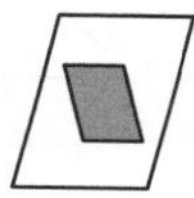 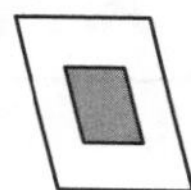 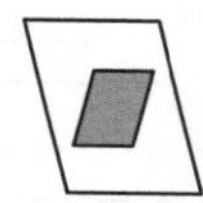

a b c d (d)

Option A is a rotation of the shape on the left. Option B has not been reflected. In option C, the grey parallelogram has not been reflected.

3. Reflect

a b c d (____)

4. Reflect

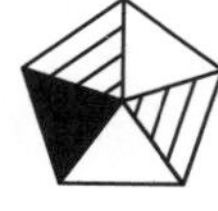

 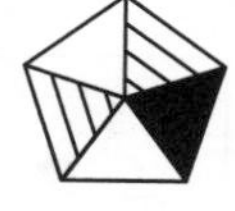 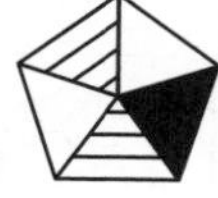 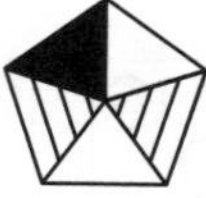

a b c d (____)

5. Reflect

 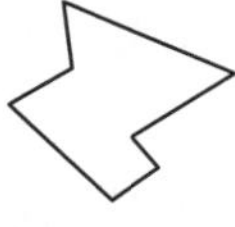 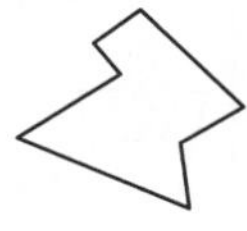 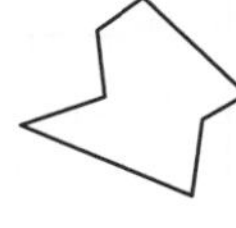 

a b c d (____)

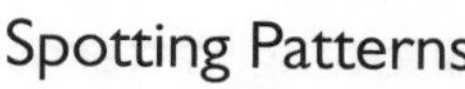

Layering

Layering is about the position of shapes in front of or behind other shapes.

Warm Up

1. Circle all the options that show what the shapes on the left could look like if they were **overlapping** each other.

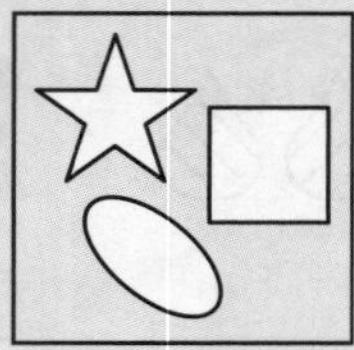

a.  b. 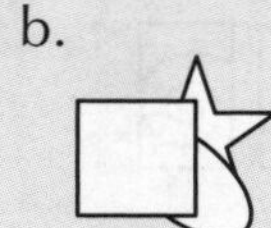 c.  d. 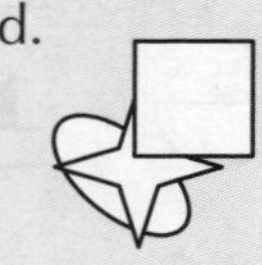 e. 

2. How many shapes are **in front of** the **square** in each figure?

a.  ______

b. 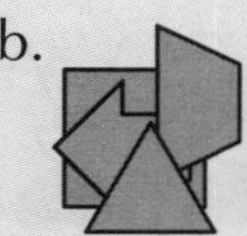 ______

c. 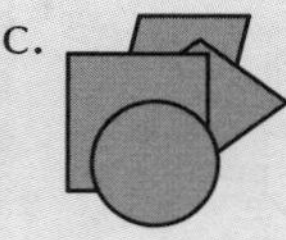 ______

d.  ______

e.  ______

f.  ______

3. Circle the black shape that is the **same** as the **inner shape** in these overlapping shapes. The black shape may have been rotated.

a. 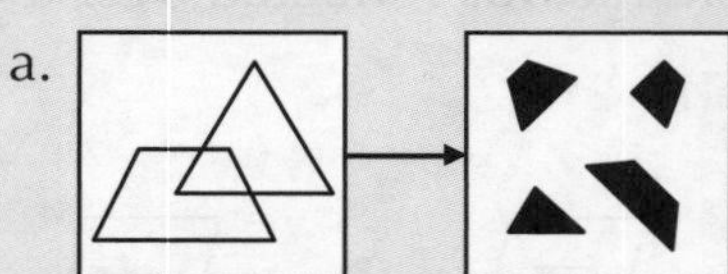

b. 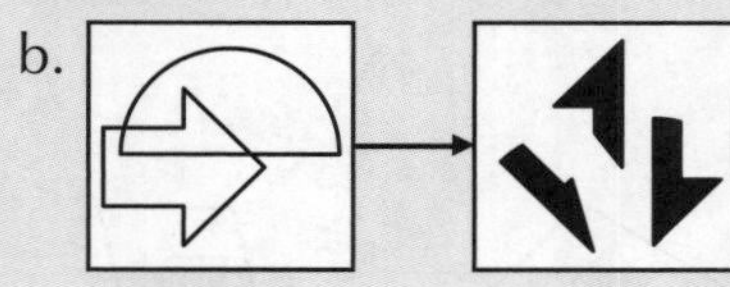

c. 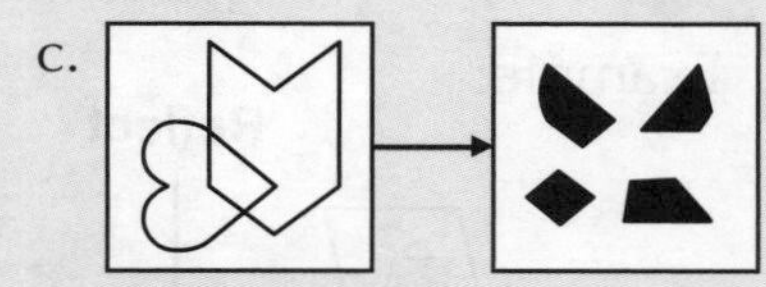

Horizontal Code

In the boxes on the left are shapes with code letters. The top letters have a different meaning from the bottom ones. Work out how the letters go with the shapes and then find the code for the new shape from the five codes on the right.

Example:

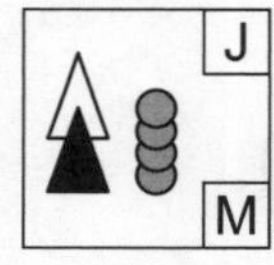 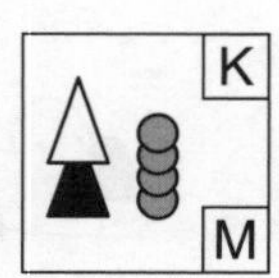 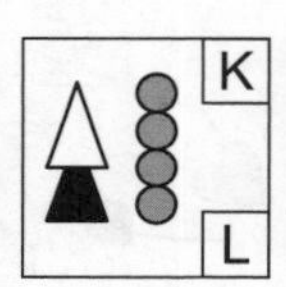  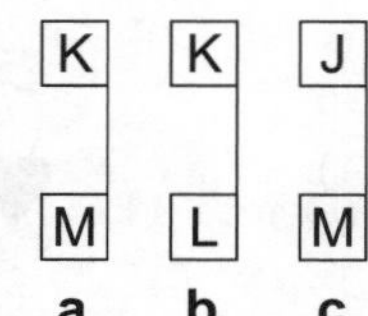 

There are also Vertical Code questions. They're solved in the same way as Horizontal Code questions, they just look different — see p.26-27.

(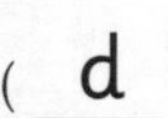)

J means the white triangle is behind the black triangle. L means the grey circles don't overlap.

4. 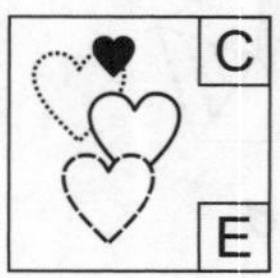  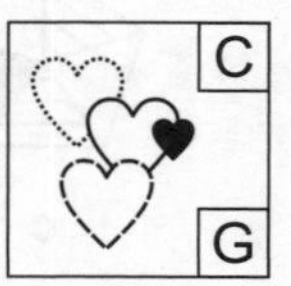  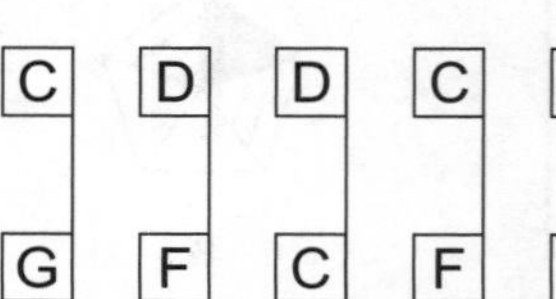

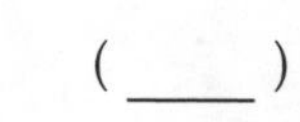

(____)

5.  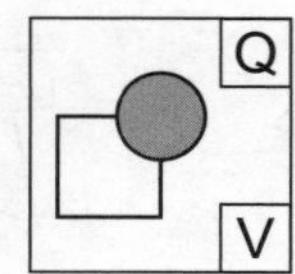 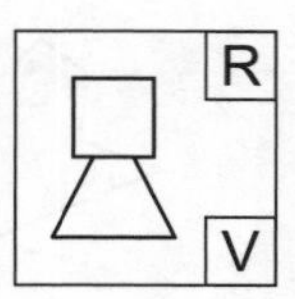 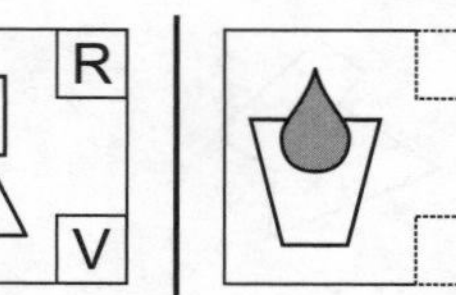 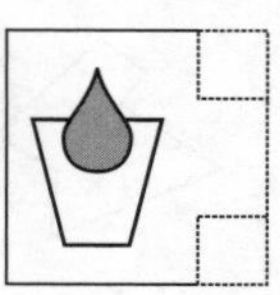 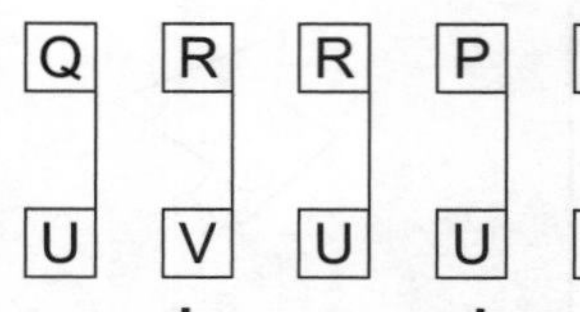

(____)

6.

M Z | N Y | O Z | M Y | ?

O	O	N	M	M
Y	Z	Z	Y	Z
a	b	c	d	e

(____)

7.

G W | H X | G V | H W | ?

G	H	G	I	J
V	W	X	X	X
a	b	c	d	e

(____)

Complete the Hexagonal Grid

Work out which of the options best fits in place of the missing hexagon in the grid.

Example:

a b c d (a)

Moving from hexagon to hexagon around the grid, the grey circles alternate between being at the front of the white hexagon and behind it.

8.

a b c d (____)

9.

a b c d (____)

10.

a b c d (____)

Rotating 3D Shapes

You might need to imagine what a 3D shape would look like if it was rotated.

Warm Up

1. Do each of the blocks below **appear in** the figure in the box, or not? Write 'Yes' or 'No' on the lines.

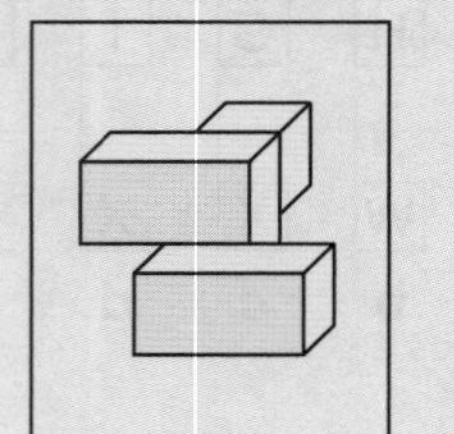

a. 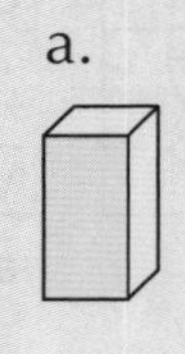 ________

b. 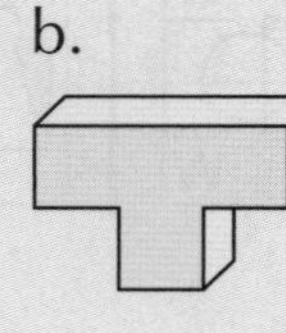 ________

c. 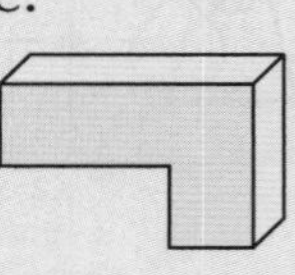 ________

d. 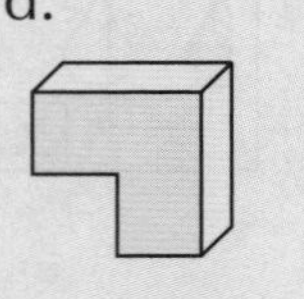 ________

e. 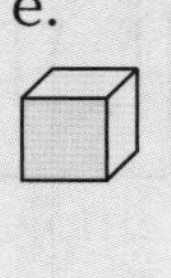 ________

2. Circle the options that show a **rotation** of the figure in the box.

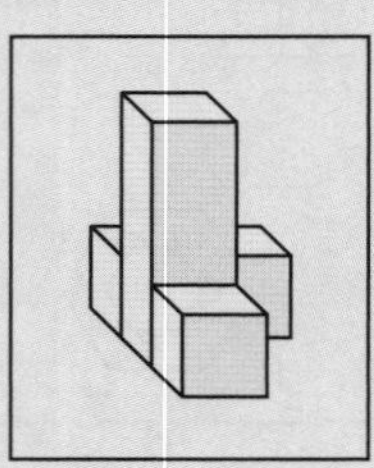

a. 

b. 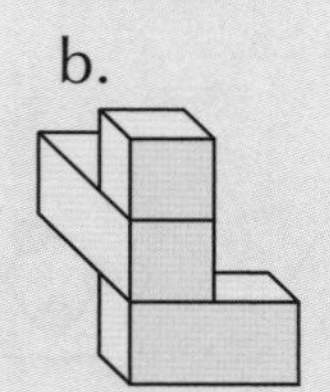

c. 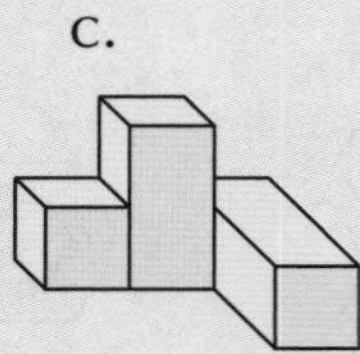

d. 

e. 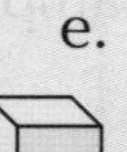 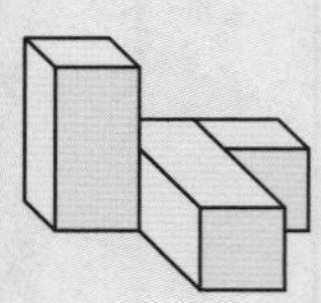

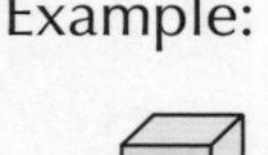

3D Building Blocks

Work out which set of blocks can be put together to make the 3D figure on the left.

Example:

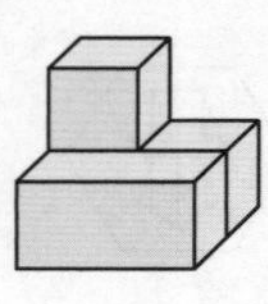

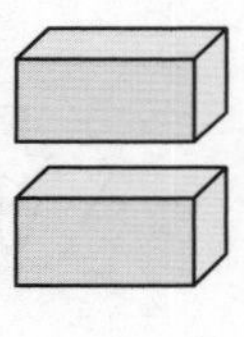

a

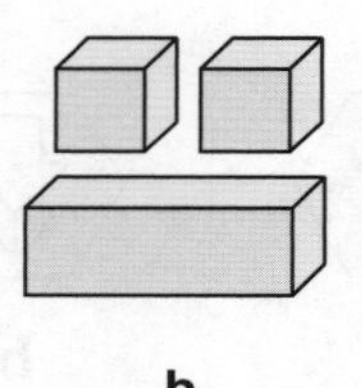

b

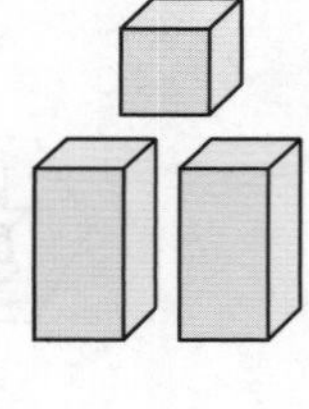

c

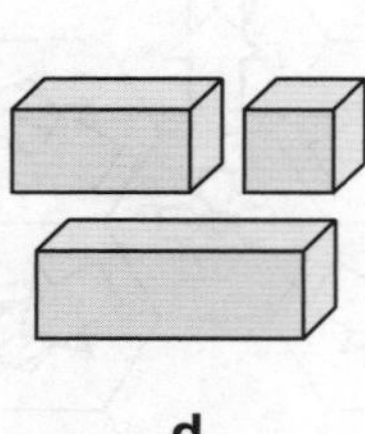

d

(C)

The bottom blocks rotate 90 degrees in the plane of the page and the cube moves on top of the back block.

3.

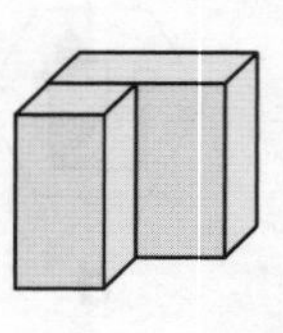

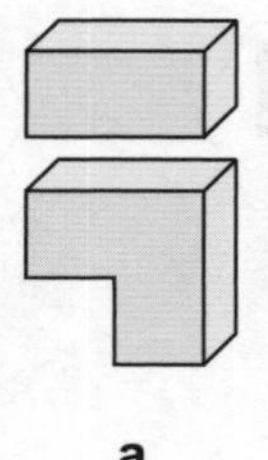

a

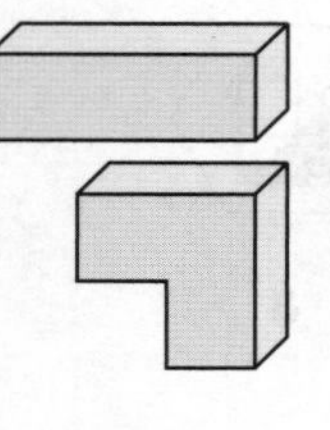

b

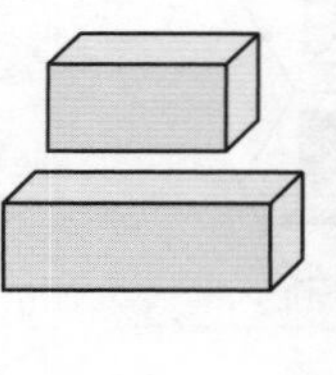

c

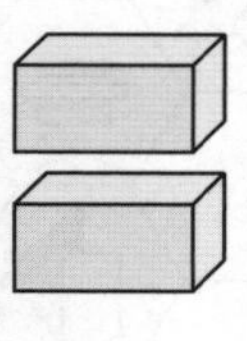

d

(____)

4.

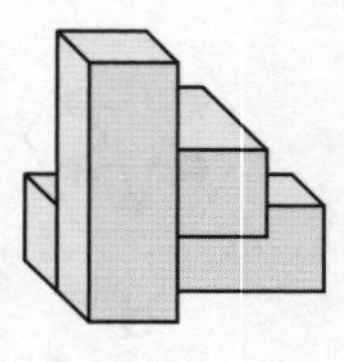

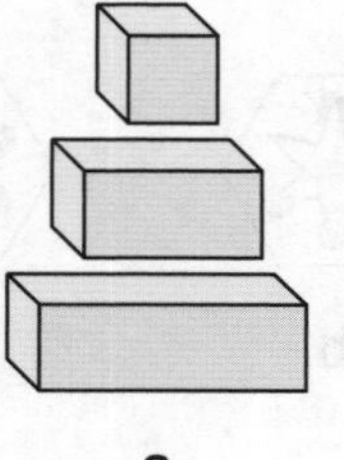

a

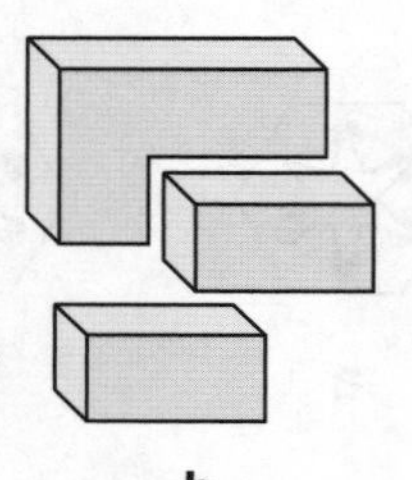

b

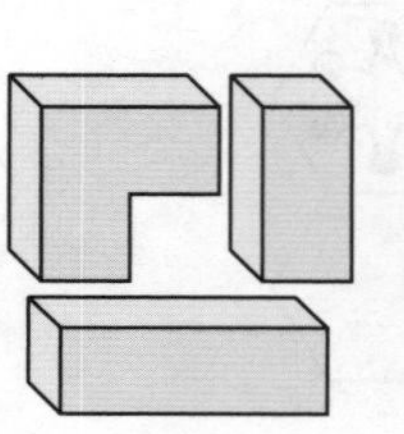

c

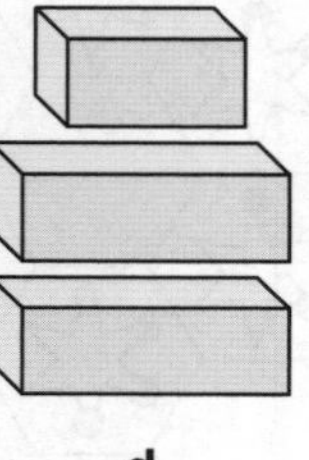

d

(____)

5.

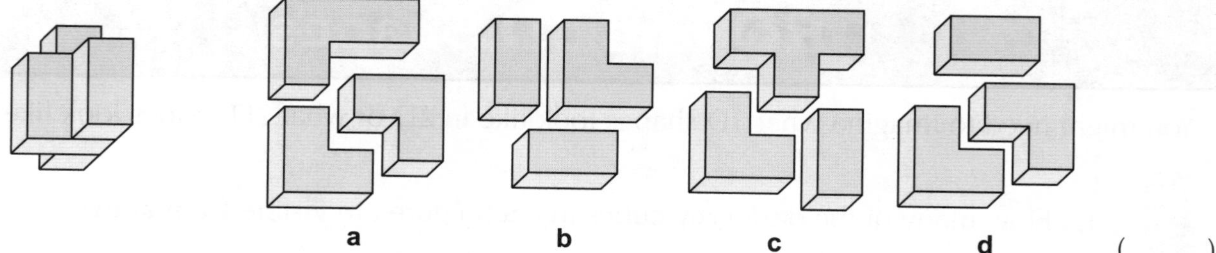

(____)

3D Rotation

Work out which 3D figure in the grey box has been rotated to make the new 3D figure.

Example:

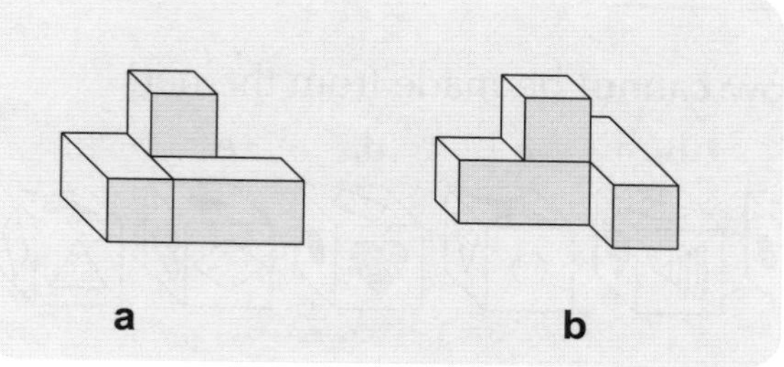

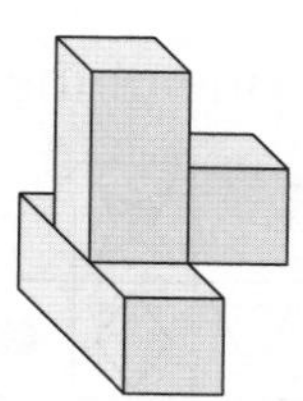

(b)

Figure B has been rotated 90 degrees clockwise in the plane of the page.

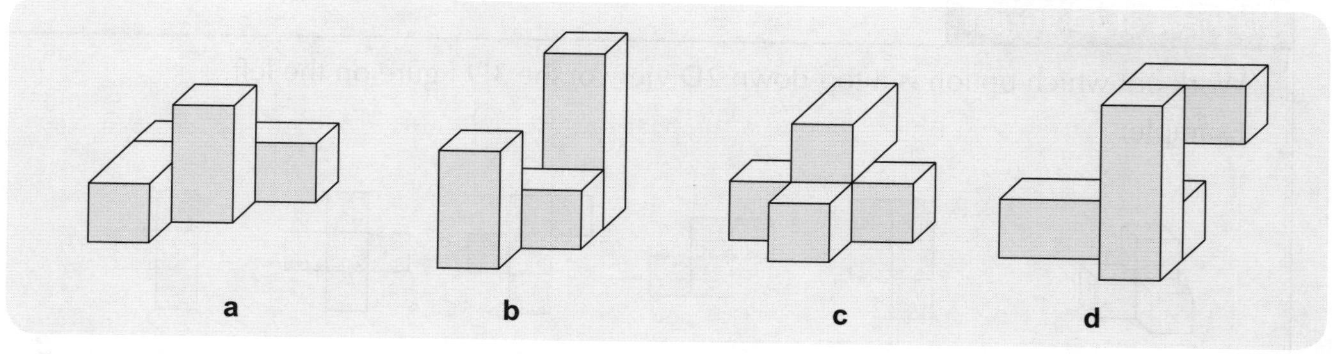

6.

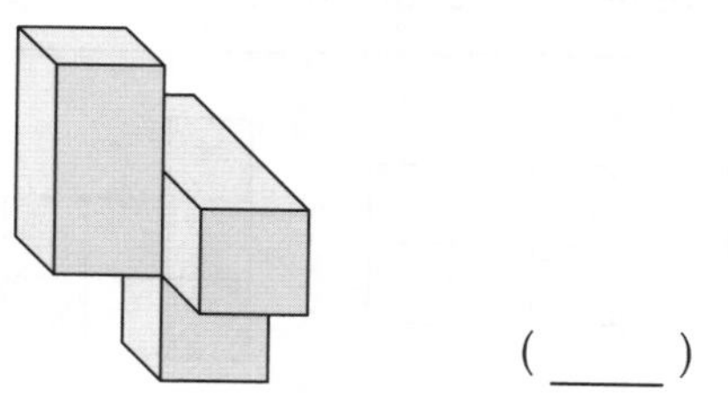

(____)

7.

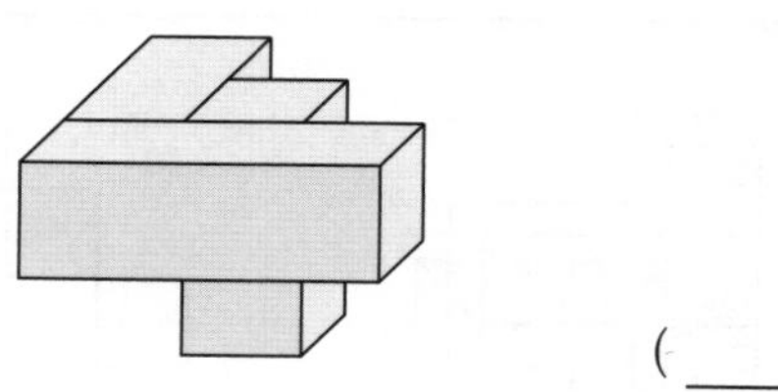

(____)

8.

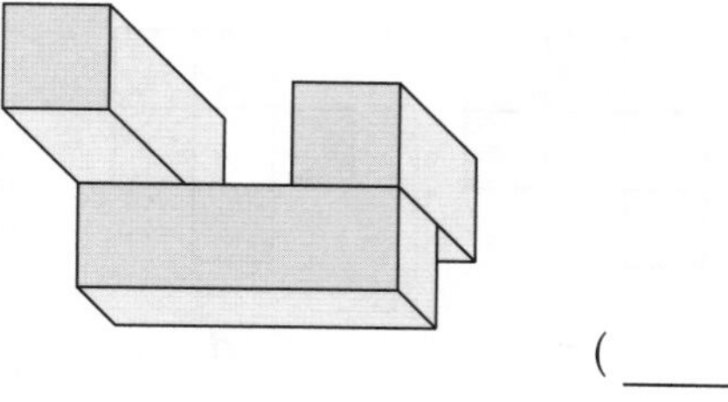

(____)

9.

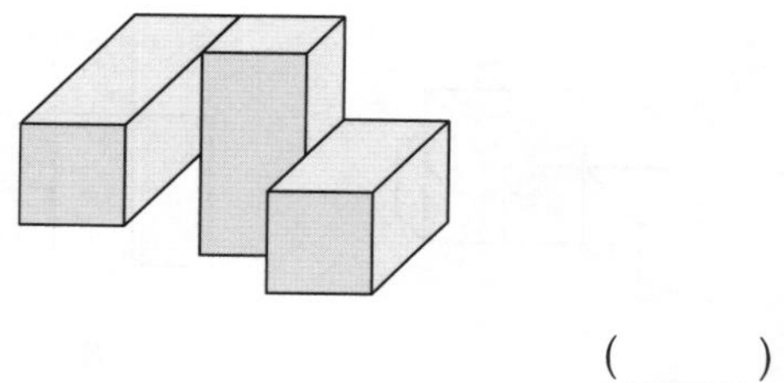

(____)

2D and 3D Shapes

You might need to imagine what 3D shapes look like in 2D or what 2D shapes look like in 3D.

Warm Up

1. How many of the **dark grey** cubes in each figure are visible **from above**?

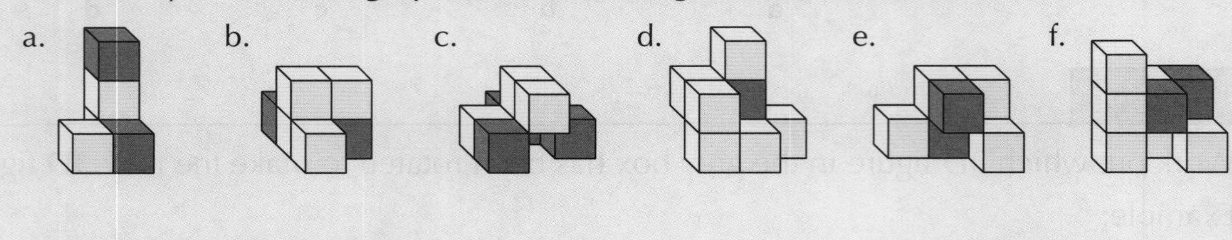

_____ _____ _____ _____ _____ _____

2. Which one of the cubes below **cannot** be made from the net?

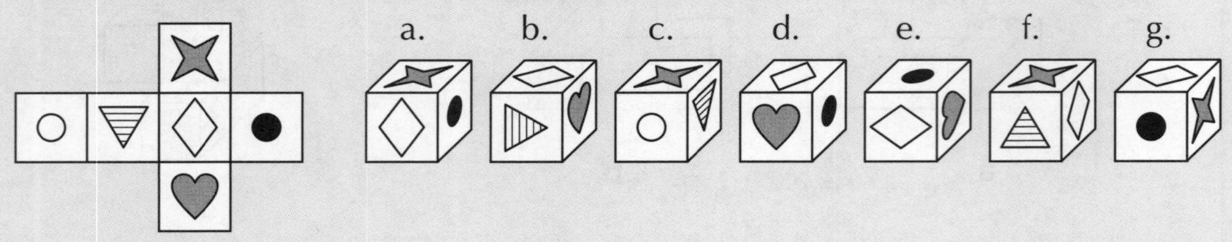

Option: _____

2D Views of 3D Shapes

Work out which option is a top-down 2D view of the 3D figure on the left.

Example:

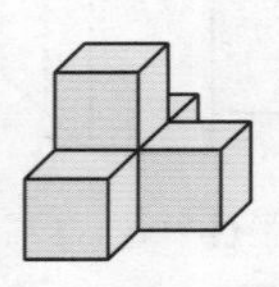

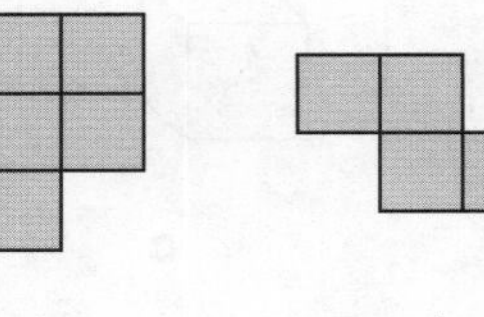

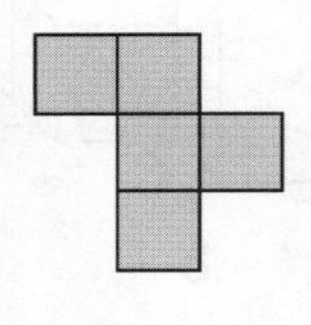

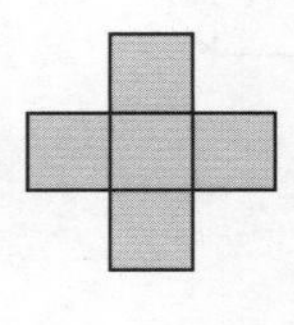

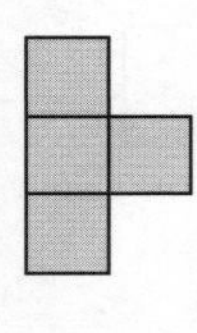

a b c d e (e)

There are four blocks visible from above, which rules out options A, C and D.
There are three rows of blocks visible from above, which rules out option B.

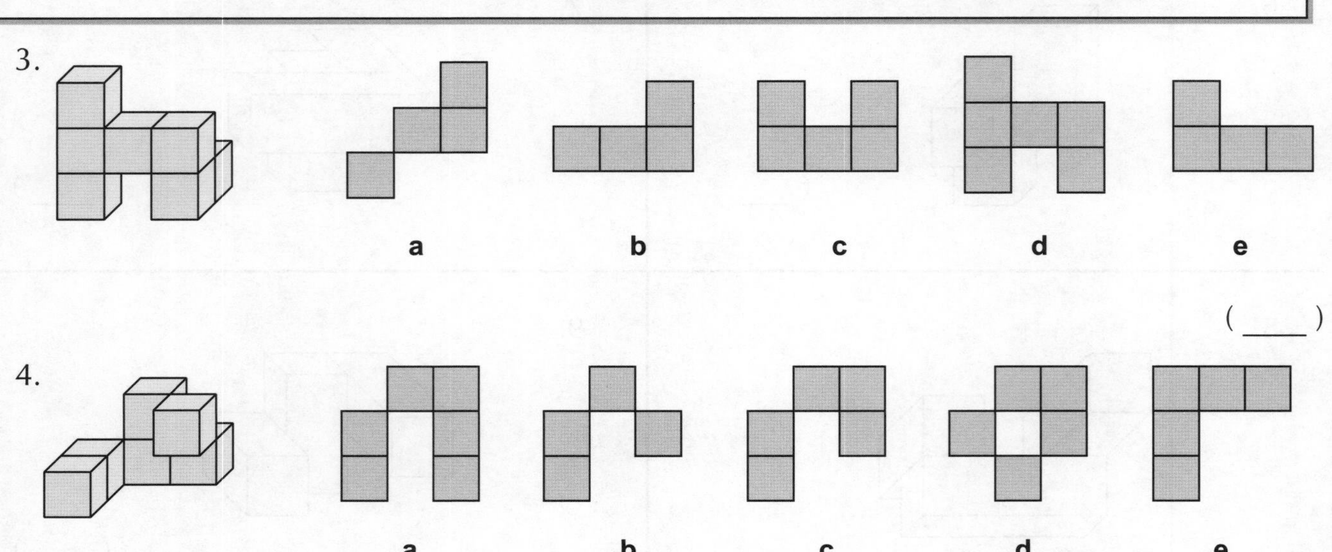

3. (_____)

4. (_____)

5.

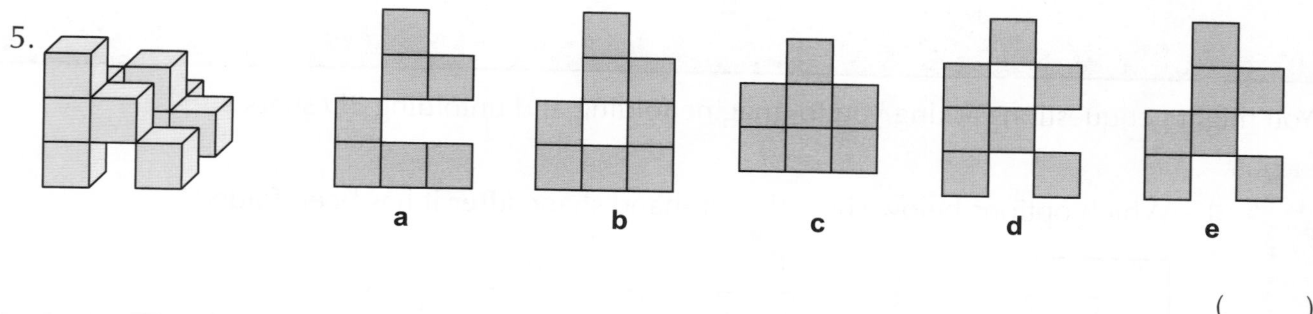

a b c d e

(____)

Cubes and Nets

Work out which of the four cubes can be made from the net.

Example:

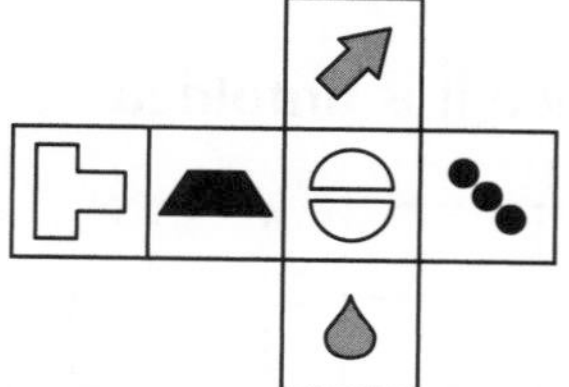

a

b

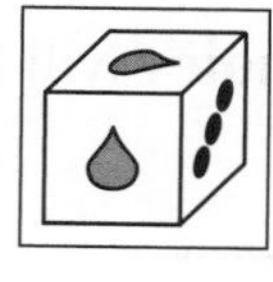

c

d

(b)

The black trapezium and the black circles must be on opposite sides, which rules out option A. There is only one grey teardrop, which rules out option C. There is no black pentagon, which rules out option D.

6.

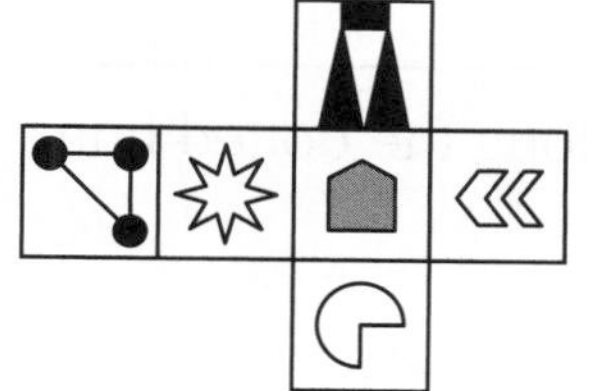

a b c d (____)

7.

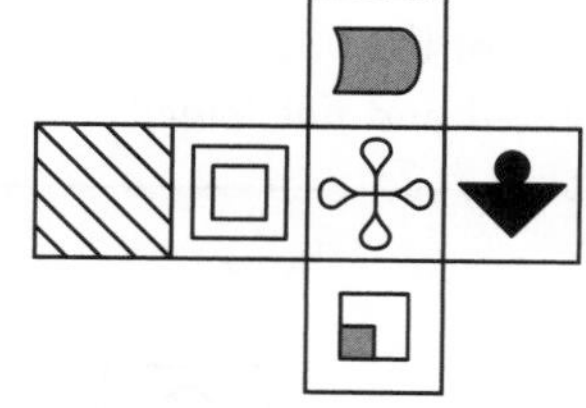

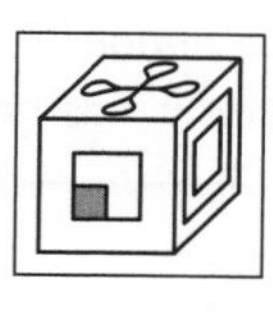

a b c

d (____)

8.

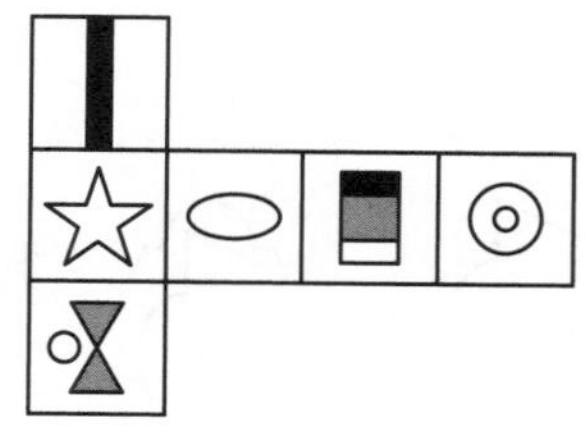

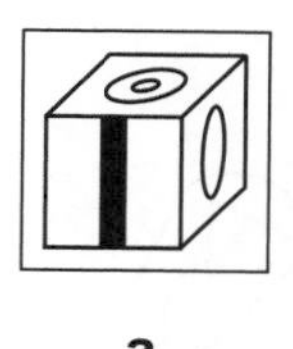

a

b

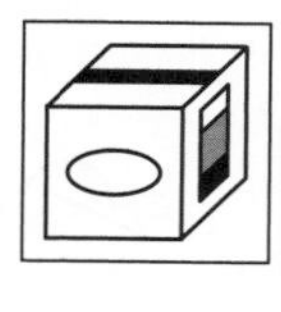

c

d (____)

Folding

You might get questions asking you to imagine folding and unfolding 2D shapes.

Warm Up

1. Which options below show the left-hand shape **after** it has been **folded**?

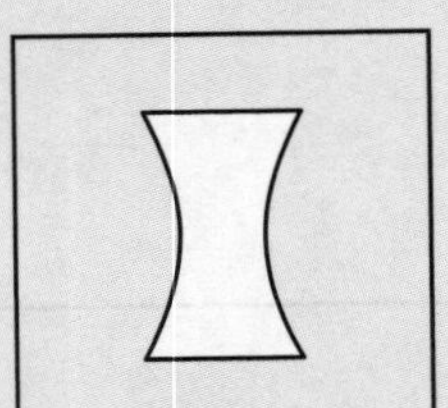

a. 
b. 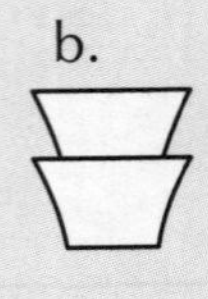
c. 
d. 
e. 
f. 
g. 

Options: ____________

2. How many **holes** will there be on each square of paper once it is **unfolded**?

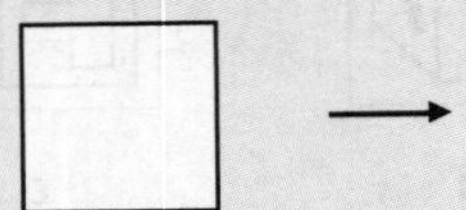

a. 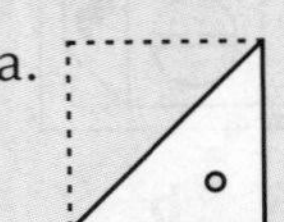 ____

b.  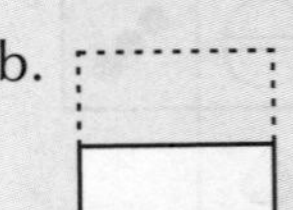 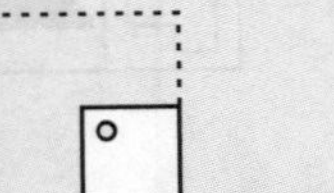 ____

c. 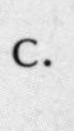 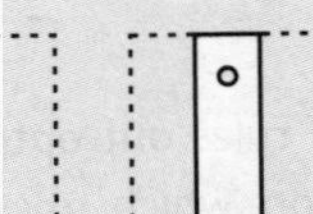 ____

d. 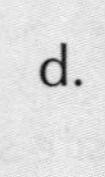 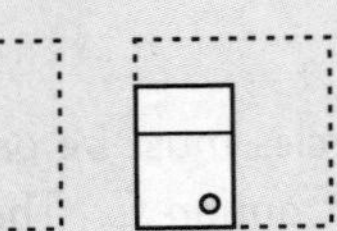 ____

e. 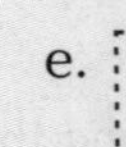 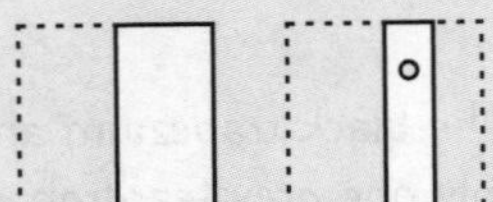 ____

Fold Along the Line

Work out which option shows the figure on the left when folded along the dotted line.

Example:

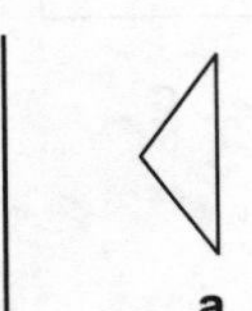 a

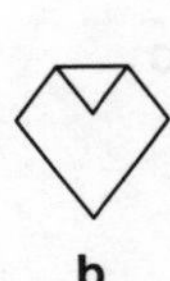 b

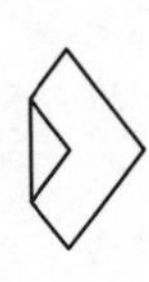 c

 d

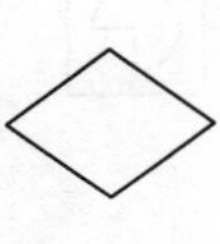 e

(C)

In options A and B, the fold line has moved. In option D, the part of the figure that has been folded is the wrong shape. Option E has been rotated and not folded.

3. 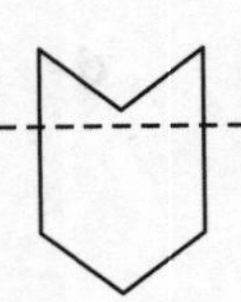

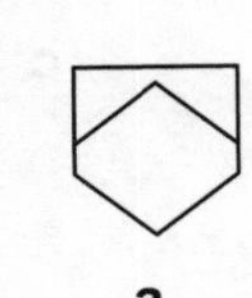 a

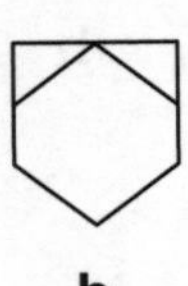 b

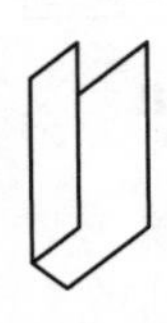 c

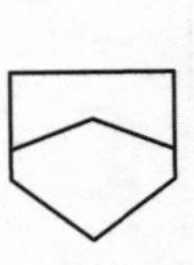 d

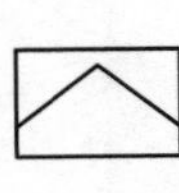 e

(____)

4. 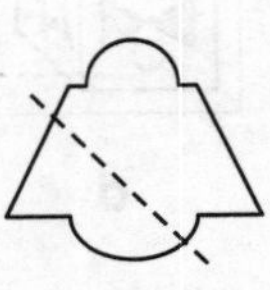

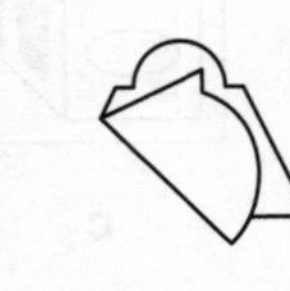 a

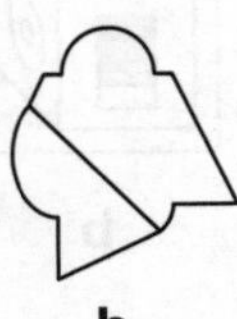 b

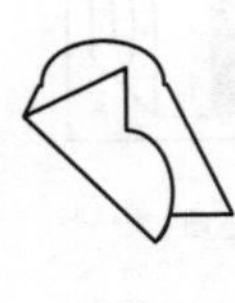 c

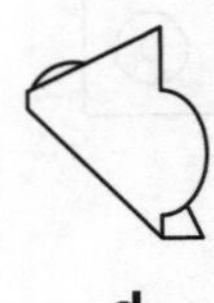 d

 e

(____)

5.

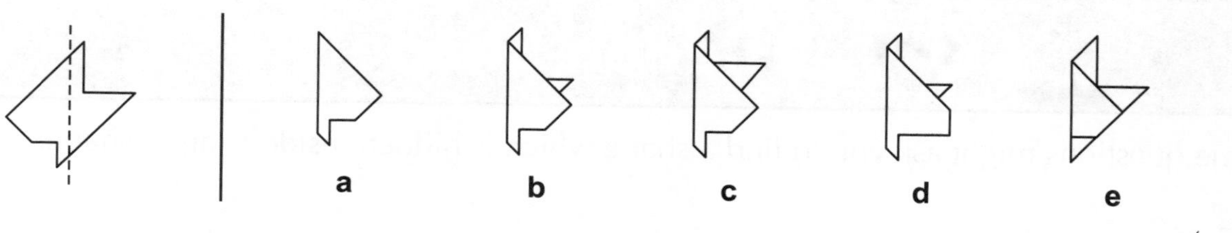

(____)

Fold and Punch

A square is folded and then a hole is punched, as shown on the left.
Work out which option shows the square when unfolded.

Example:

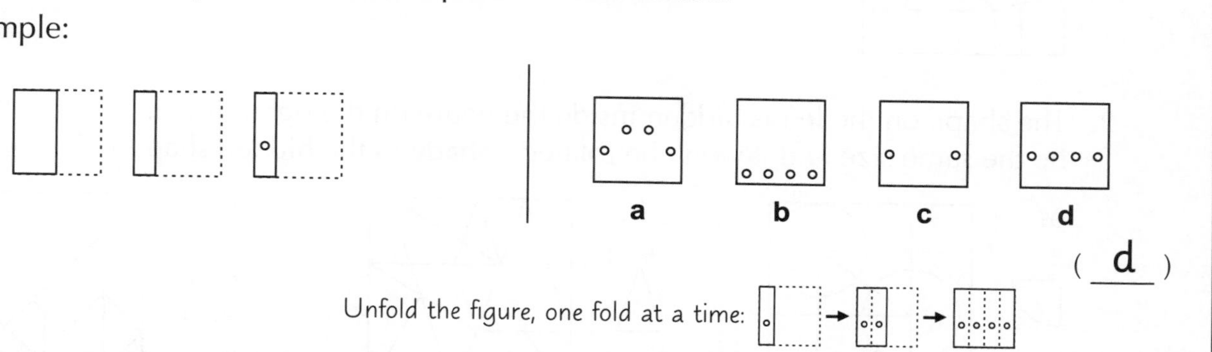

6.

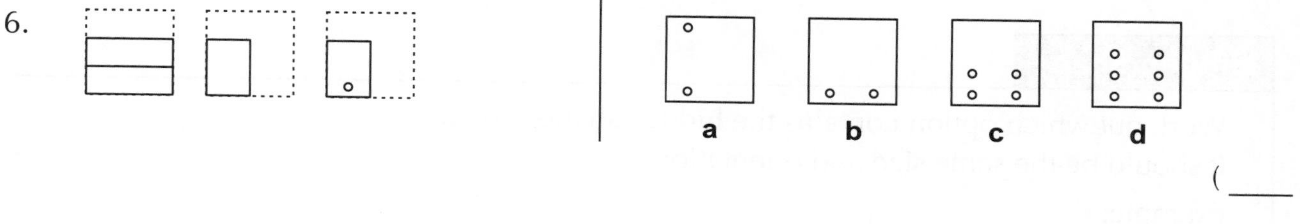

(____)

7.

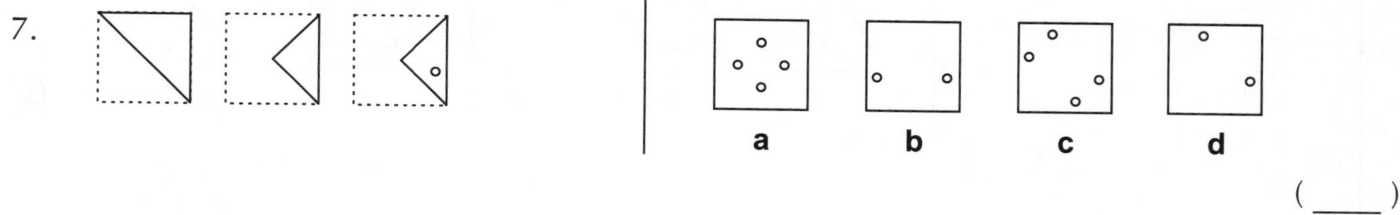

(____)

8.

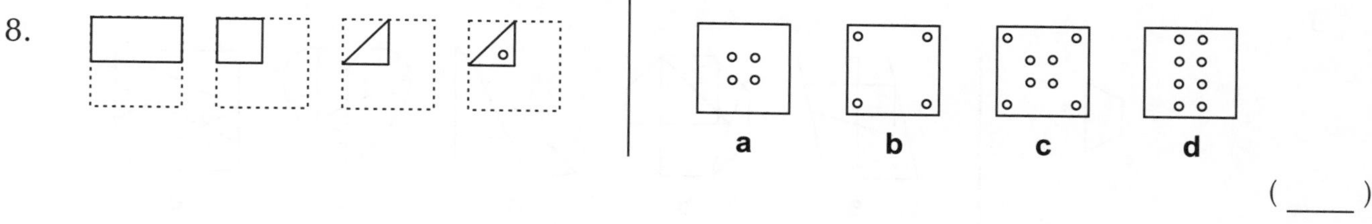

(____)

9.

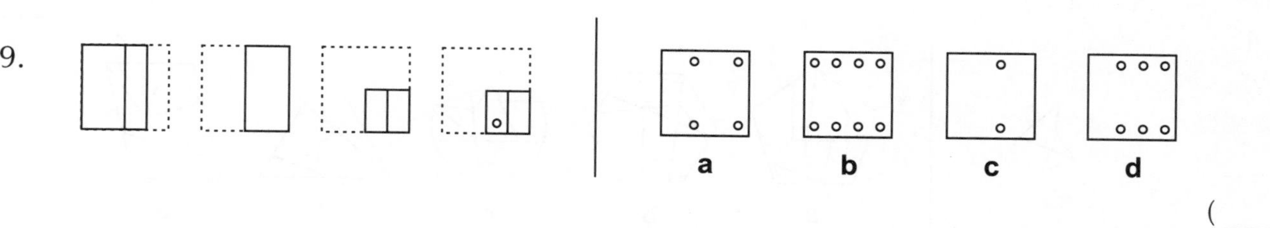

(____)

Hidden Shape

Some questions might ask you to find a shape which is hidden inside a larger shape.

Warm Up

1. Circle the shapes on the right that **appear in** the figure on the left.

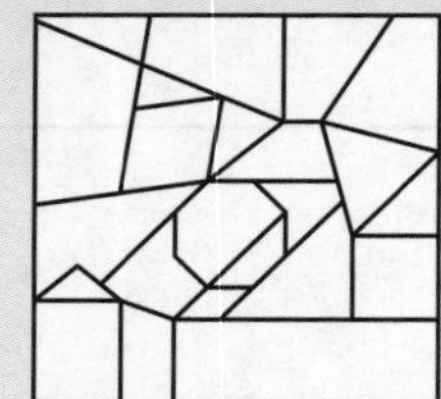

a.  b.  c.  d.  e. 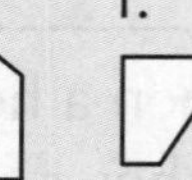 f.  g. 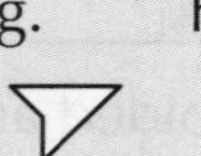 h.  i. 

2. The shape on the left is hidden inside the figure on the right. It will be the same size and it won't be rotated. **Shade in** the hidden shape.

a.  

b. 

c. 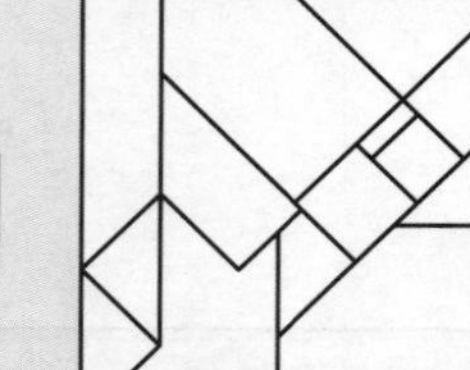

Hidden Shape

Work out which option contains the hidden shape shown.
It should be the same size and orientation.

Example:

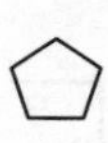

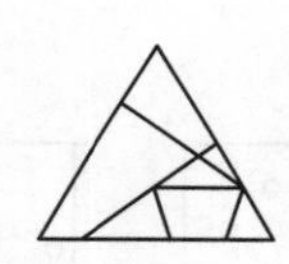 a 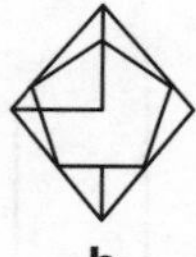 b 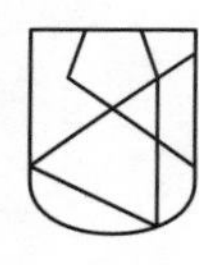 c 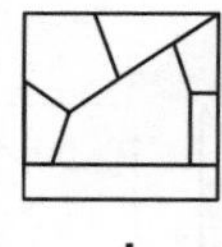 d  e

(a)

The hidden shape is here:

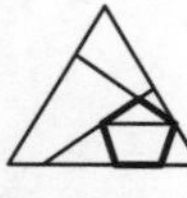

3.

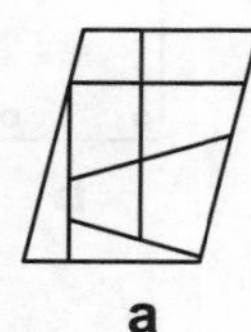 a 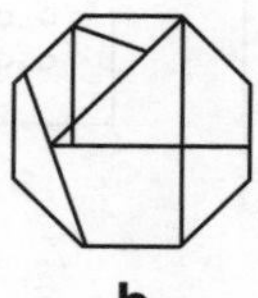 b 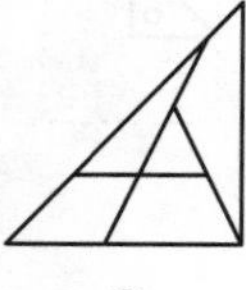 c  d 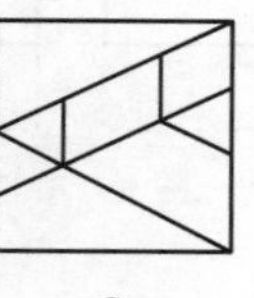 e

(____)

4.

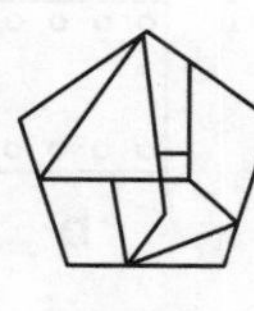 a 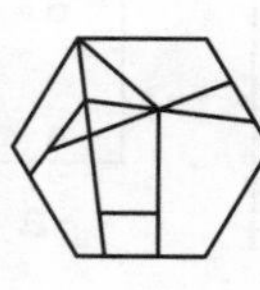 b 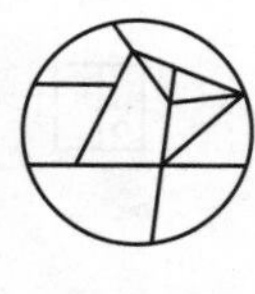 c 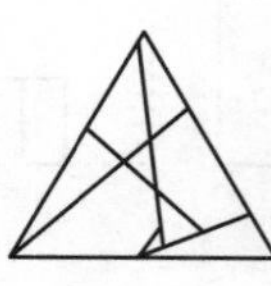 d 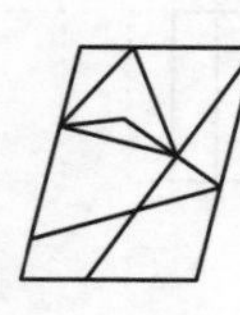 e

(____)

Connecting Shapes

You might get questions asking you to join a set of shapes together in your head.

Warm Up

1. The three shapes on the left are **joined** to make the figure on the right. This is done by connecting sides which have the **same letter**. Some of the shapes below are **missing** their letters. Which letter should go where each of the arrows is pointing?

a.

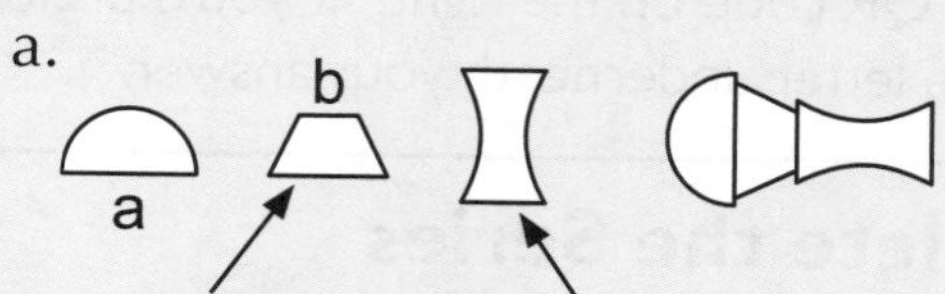

b.

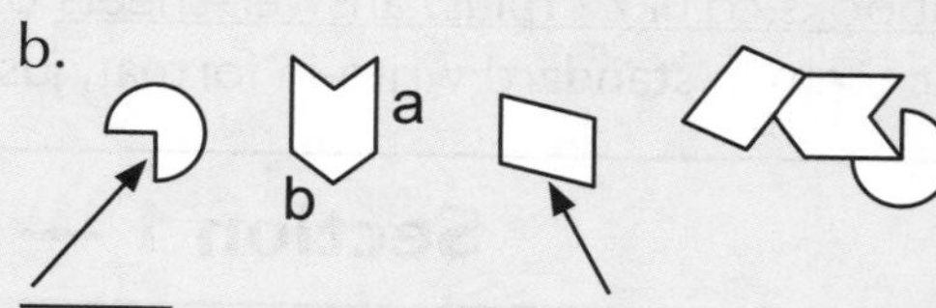

2. One of the shapes on the left needs to be joined to the figure in the box so that the sides with the same letter are connected. **Draw** the shapes in the right place in the box.

a.

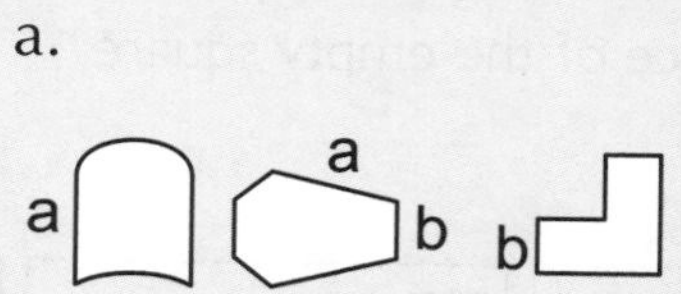

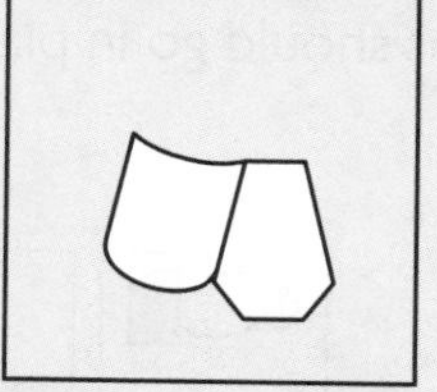

b.

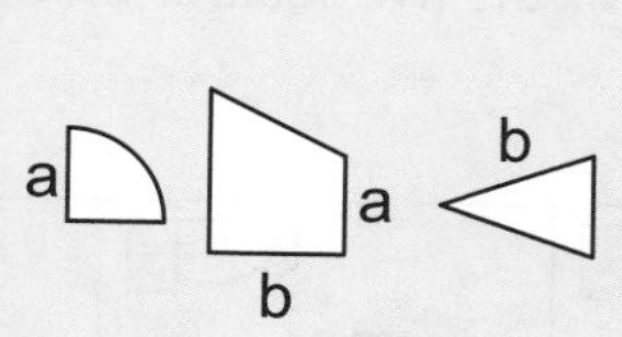

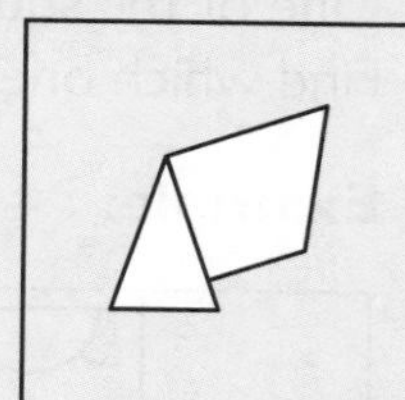

Connecting Shapes

Work out which option shows how the three shapes will look when they are joined by matching the sides with the same letter.

Example:

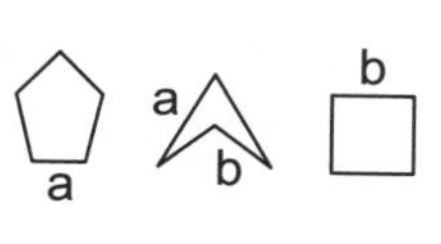

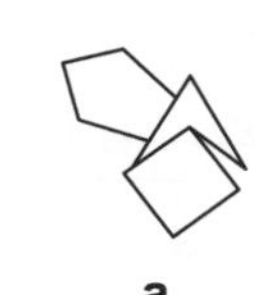
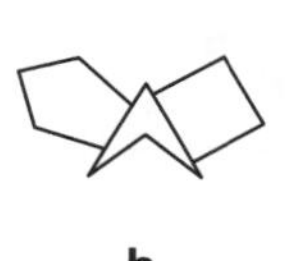
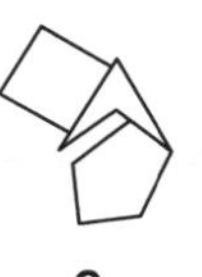
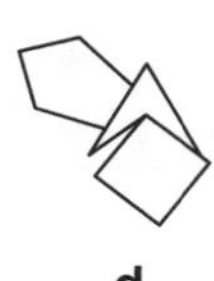

a b c d e

(d)

Options A and B are ruled out because the square is connected to the wrong side of the arrow. Option C is ruled out because the square and the pentagon are connected to the wrong sides of the arrow. Option E is ruled out because the wrong side of the pentagon is connected to the arrow.

3.

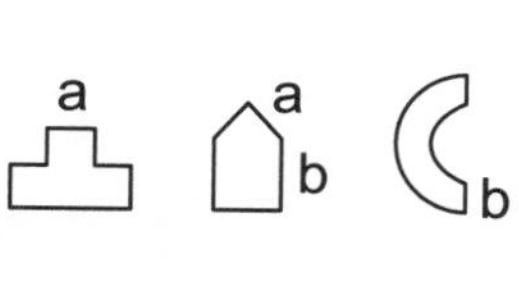

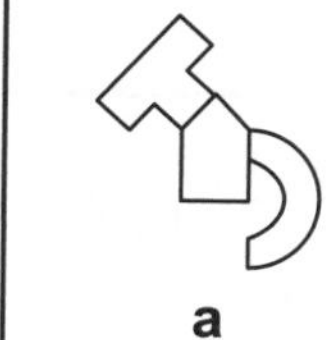

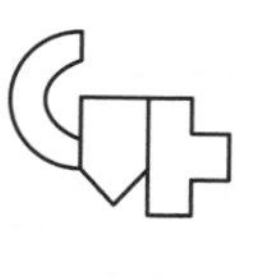

a b c d e

(____)

4.

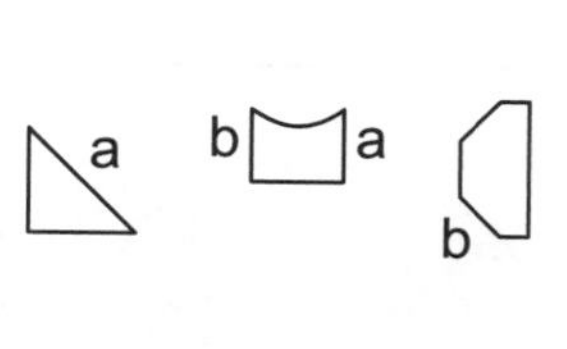

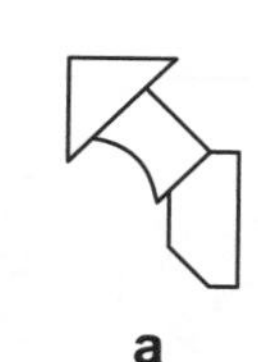
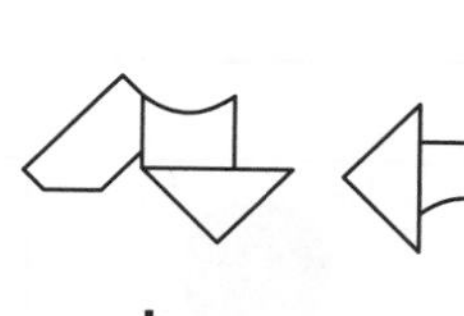
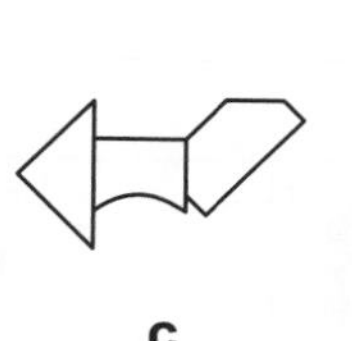
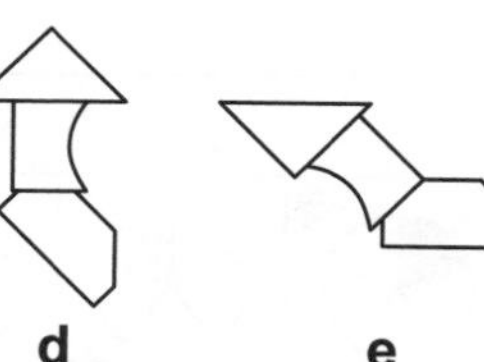

a b c d e

(____)

Assessment Test 1

This book contains eight assessment tests, which get harder as you work through them to help you improve your NVR skills.

Allow 30 minutes to do each test and work as quickly and as carefully as you can.
If you want to attempt each test more than once, you will need to print **multiple-choice answer sheets** for these questions from our website — go to cgpbooks.co.uk/11plus/answer-sheets or scan the QR code on the right. If you'd prefer to answer them in standard write-in format, just circle the letter underneath your answer.

Section 1 — Complete the Series

Each of these questions has five squares on the left that are arranged in order.
One of the squares is missing. One of the squares on the right should go in its place.
Find which one of the five squares on the right should go in place of the empty square.

Example:

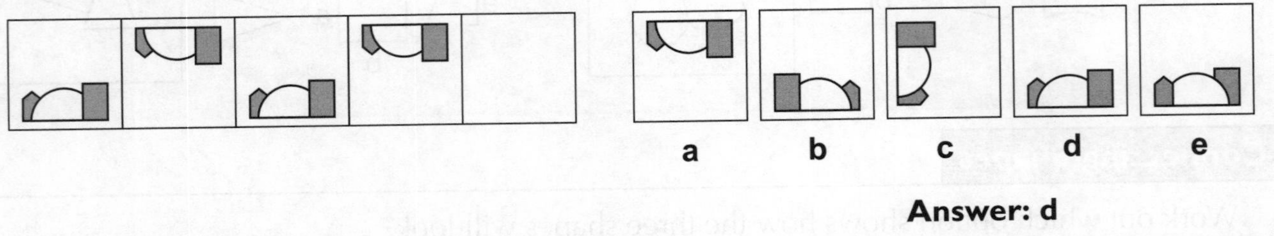

Answer: d

1

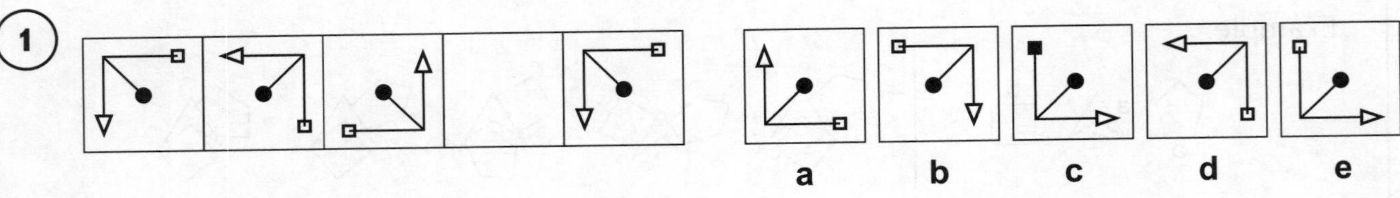

2

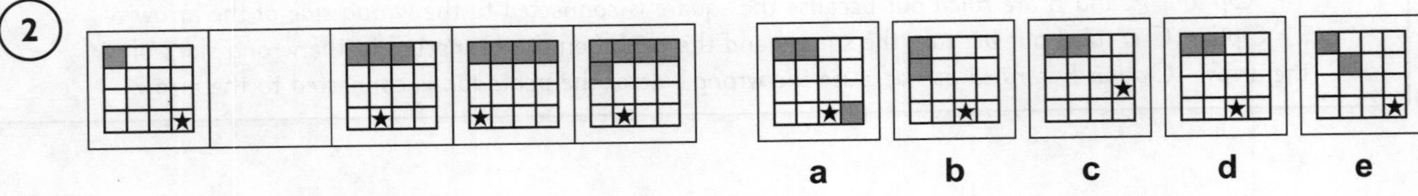

3

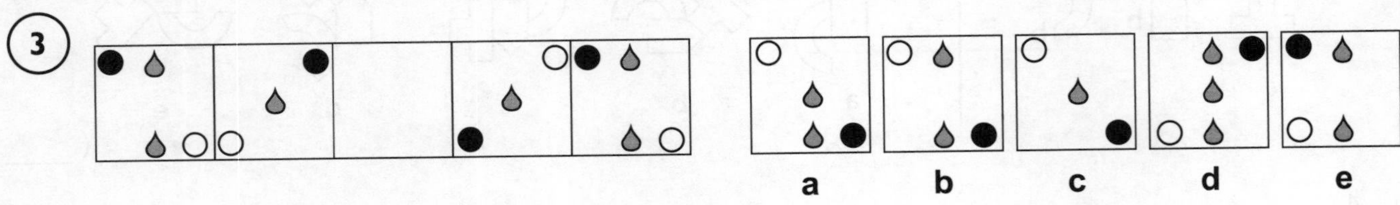

4

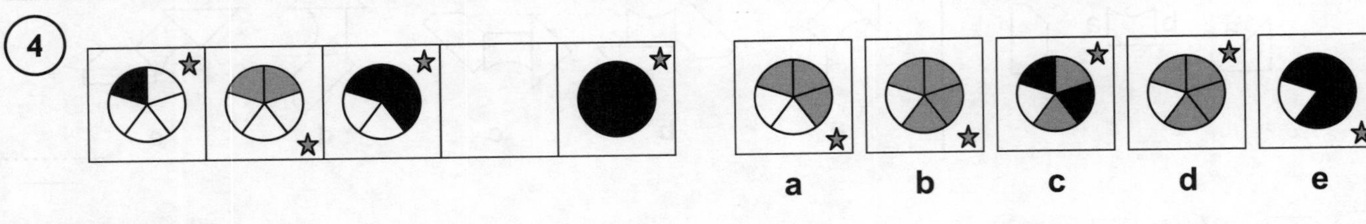

5

a b c d e

6

a b c d e

7

a b c d e

8

a b c d e

9

a b c d e

10

a b c d e

/ 10

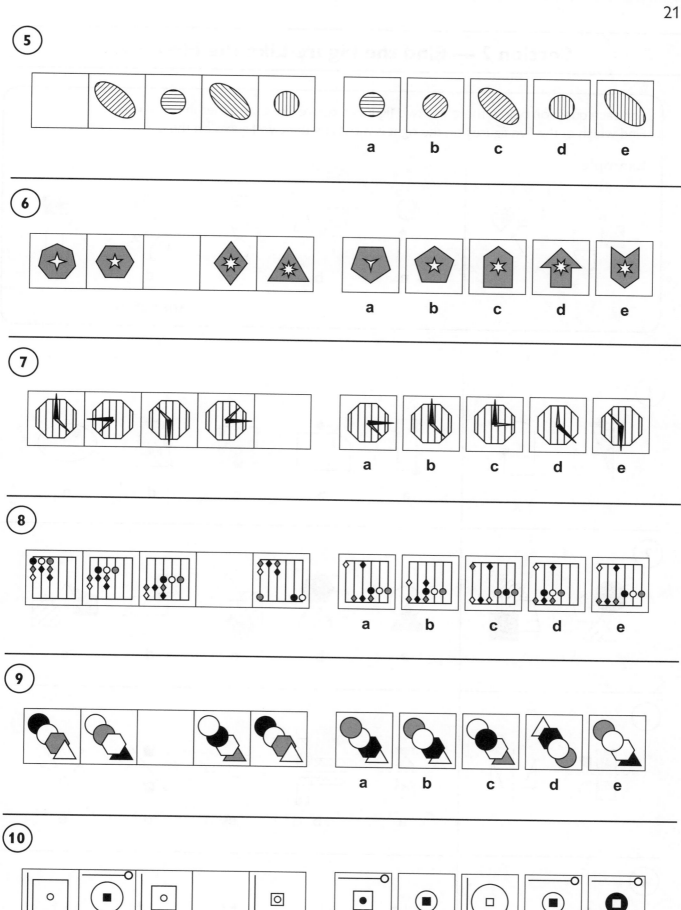

Carry on to the next question → →

Section 2 — Find the Figure Like the First Two

For each question below there are two figures that are like each other in some way.
Find which of the five figures on the right is most like the two figures on the left.

Example:

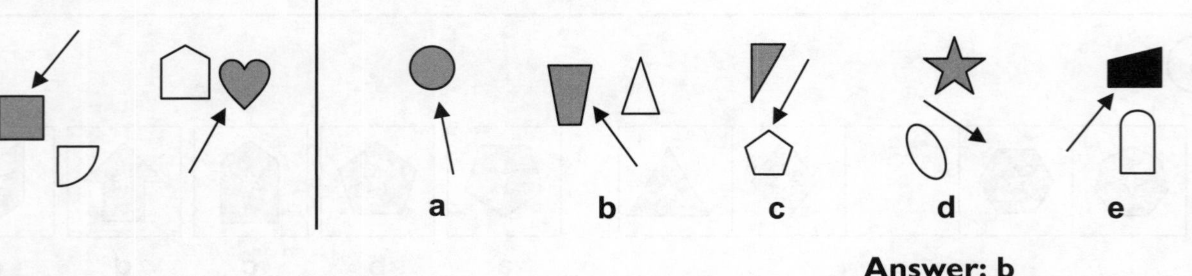

Answer: b

1

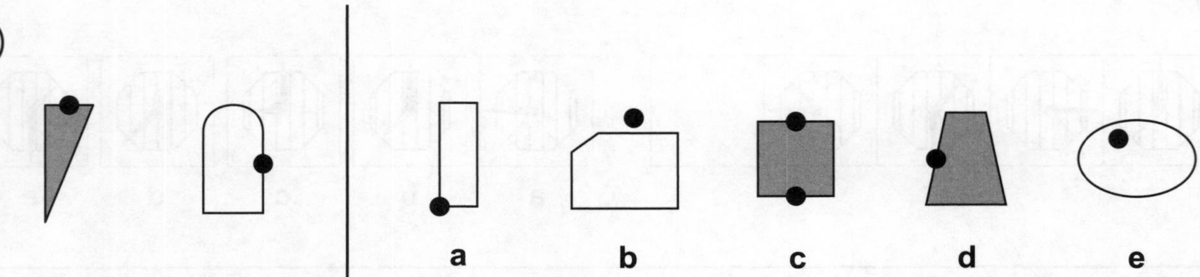

a b c d e

2

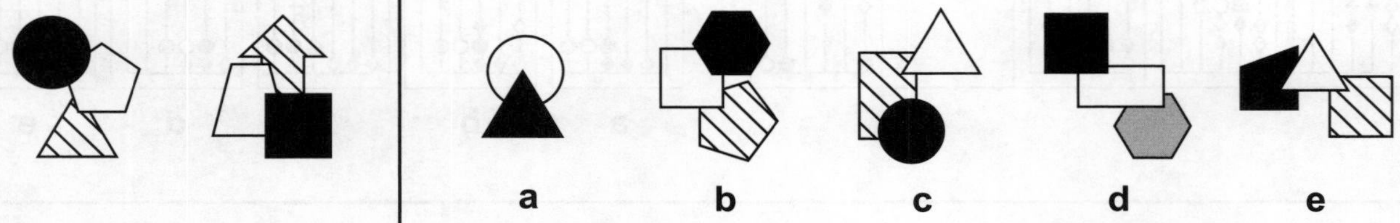

a b c d e

3

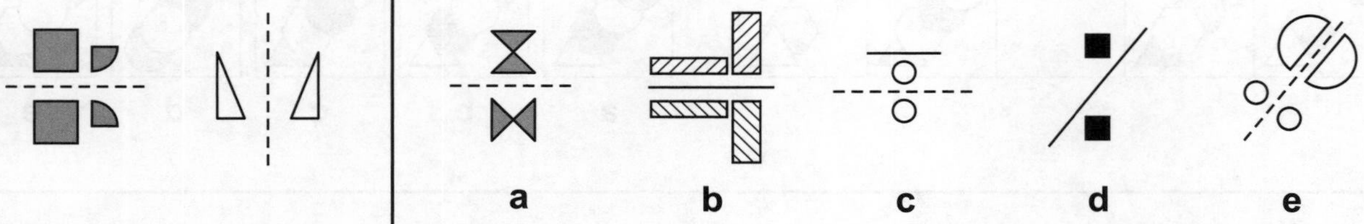

a b c d e

4

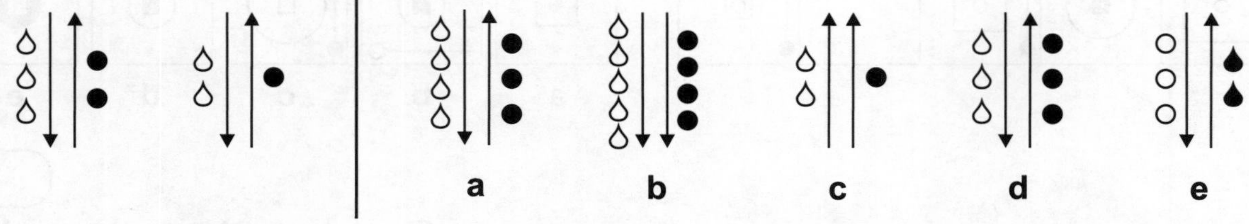

a b c d e

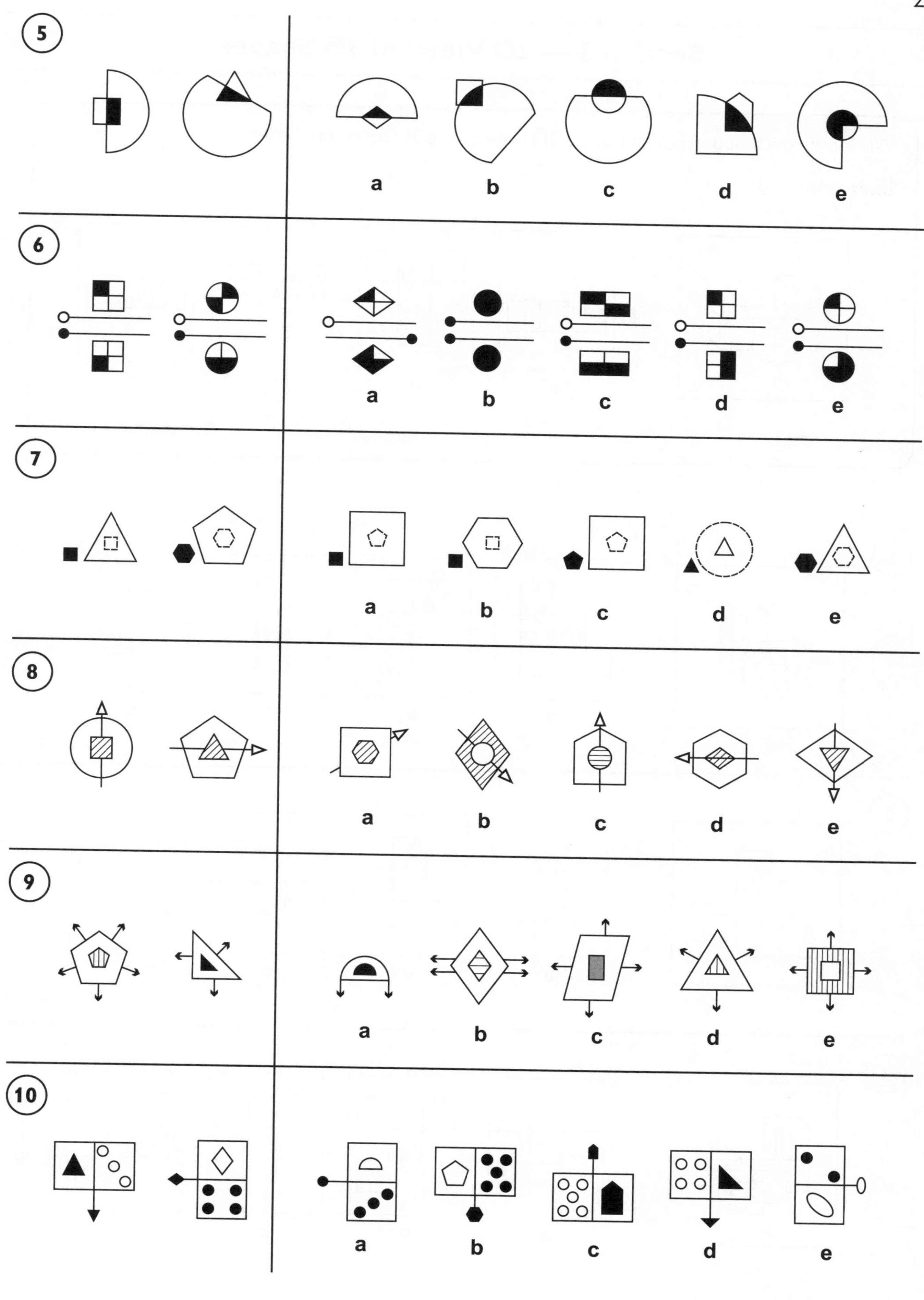

/ 10

Carry on to the next question → →

Section 3 — 2D Views of 3D Shapes

Work out which option is a top-down 2D view of the 3D figure on the left.

Example:

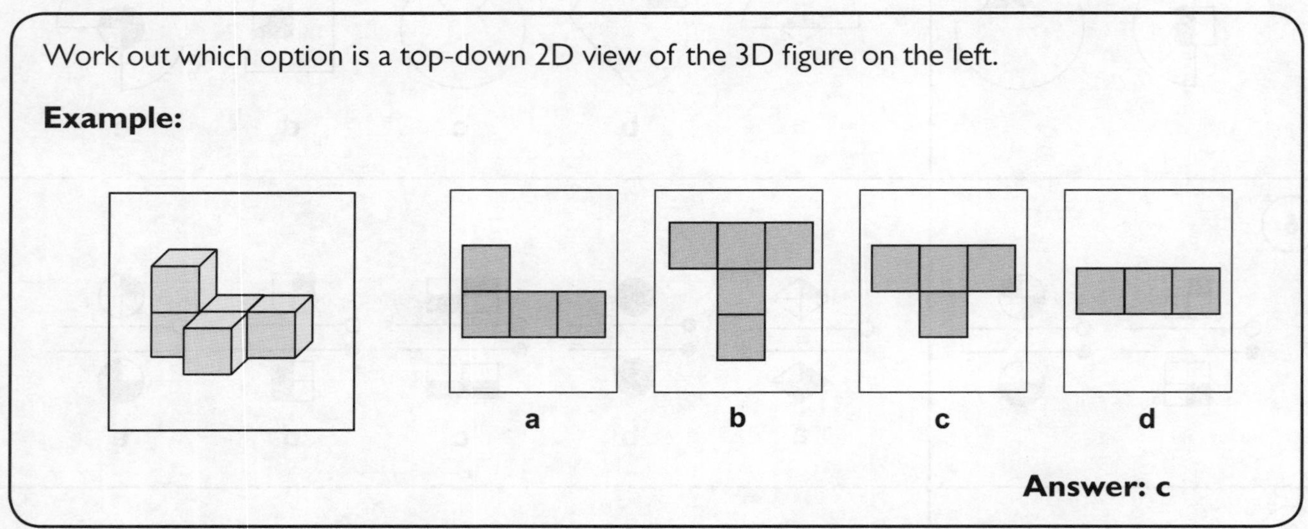

Answer: c

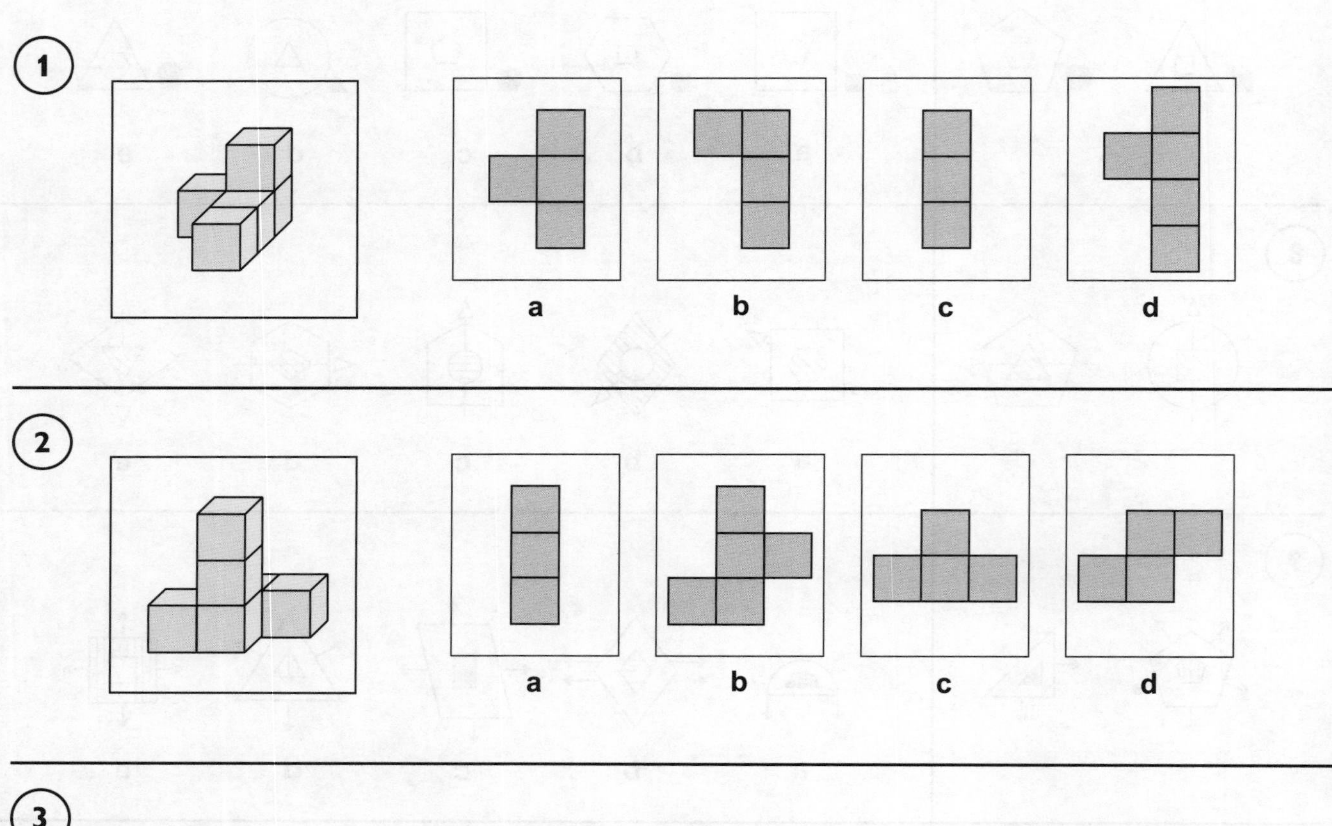

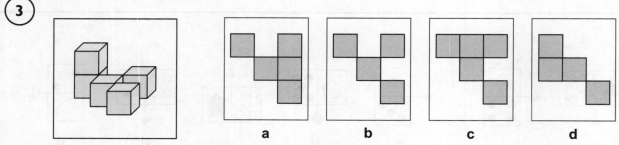

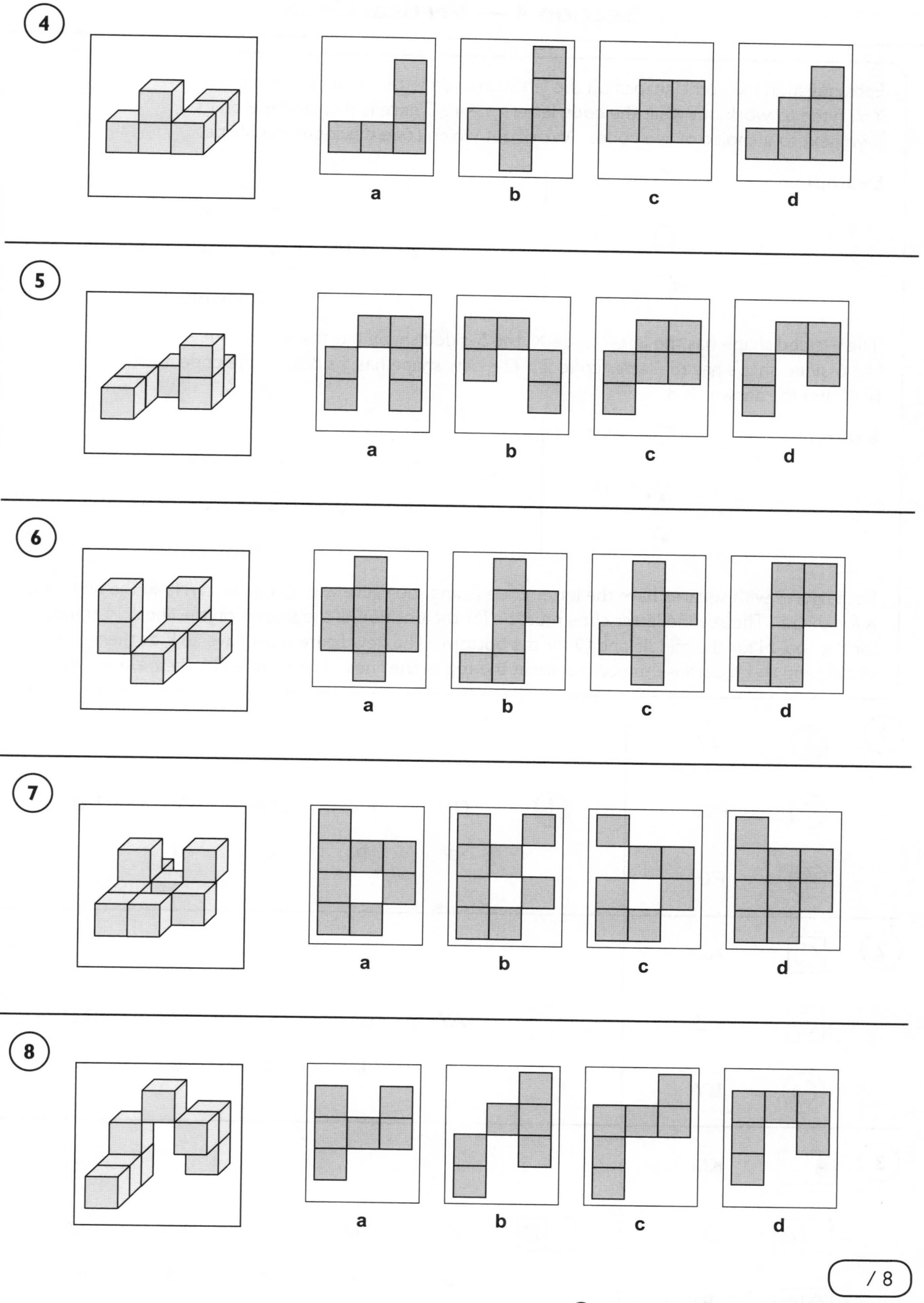

/ 8

Carry on to the next question → →

Section 4 — Vertical Code

Each question has some shapes on the left with code letters that describe them. You need to work out what the code letters mean. There is then a shape on its own next to a choice of five codes. Work out which code describes this shape.

Example:

 X

 Y

 Z

W	V	Z	Y	X
a	**b**	**c**	**d**	**e**

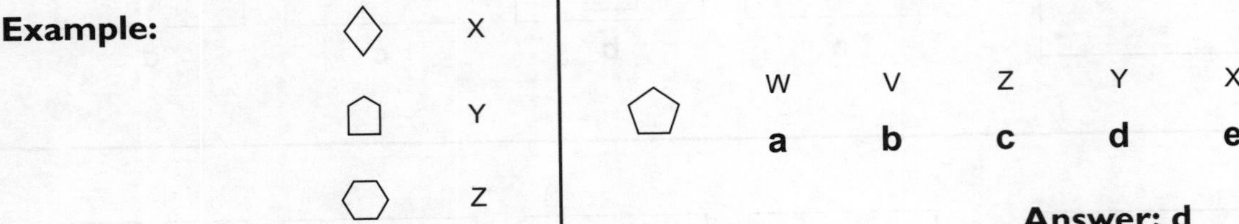

Answer: d

The 4-sided shape has the letter code X, the 5-sided shape has the letter code Y and the 6-sided shape has the letter code Z. The new shape has 5 sides, so the code must be Y and the answer is d.

Example:

 EM

 FO

 EN

FN	EO	FM	MN	FO
a	**b**	**c**	**d**	**e**

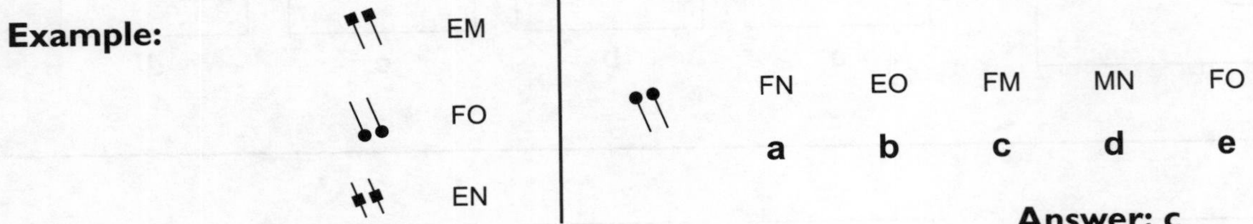

Answer: c

Both figures with squares have the letter code E, and the figure with circles has an F, so the first letter is for shape. The second letter code must be for the position of the shapes on the lines. M stands for the top, N for the middle and O for the bottom. The new figure must have an F, as there are circles, and an M, because the circles are at the top of the lines. The code is FM, so the answer is c.

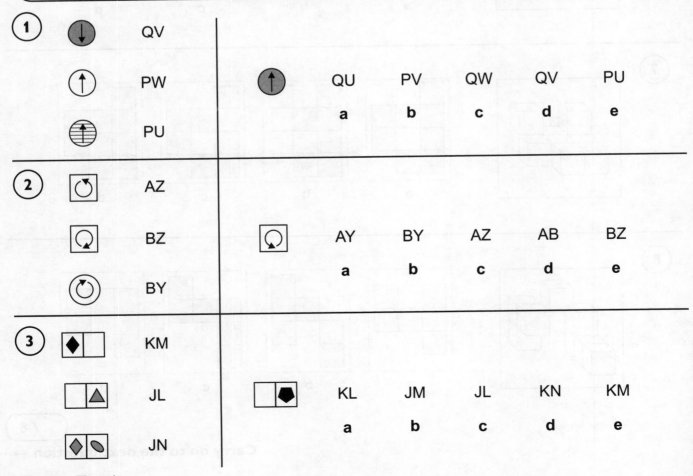

1

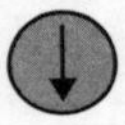

 QV

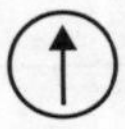

 PW

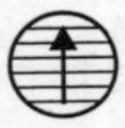

 PU

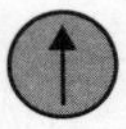

QU	PV	QW	QV	PU
a	**b**	**c**	**d**	**e**

2

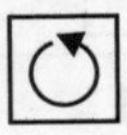

 AZ

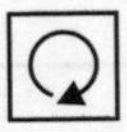

 BZ

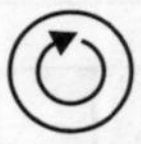

 BY

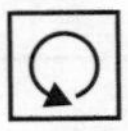

AY	BY	AZ	AB	BZ
a	**b**	**c**	**d**	**e**

3

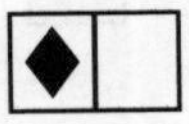

 KM

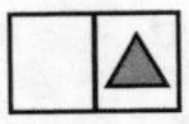

 JL

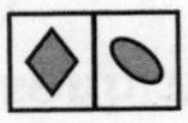

 JN

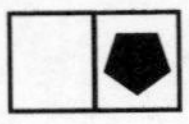

KL	JM	JL	KN	KM
a	**b**	**c**	**d**	**e**

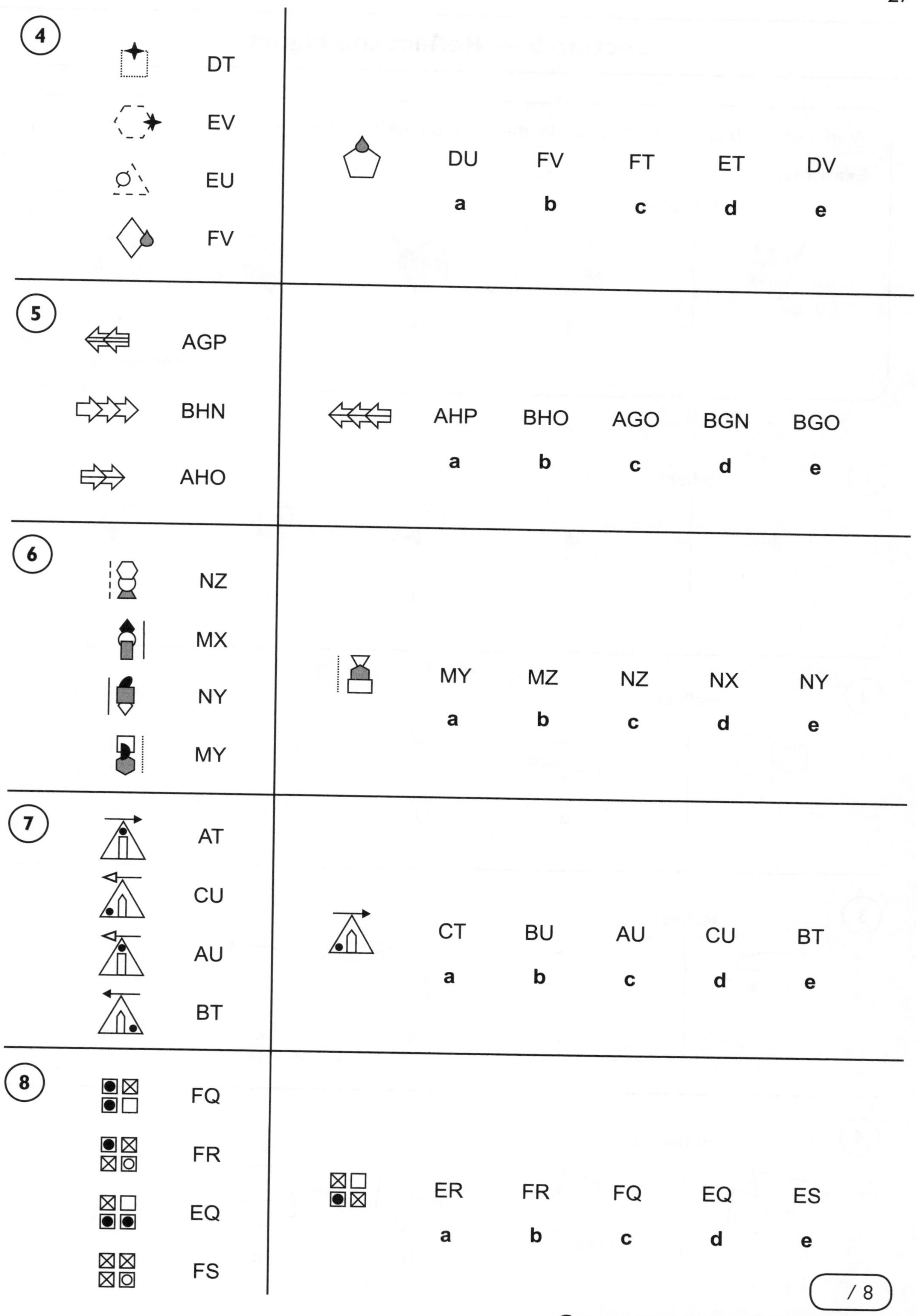

/ 8

Carry on to the next question → →

Section 5 — Reflect the Figure

Work out which option would look like the figure on the left if it was reflected over the line.

Example:

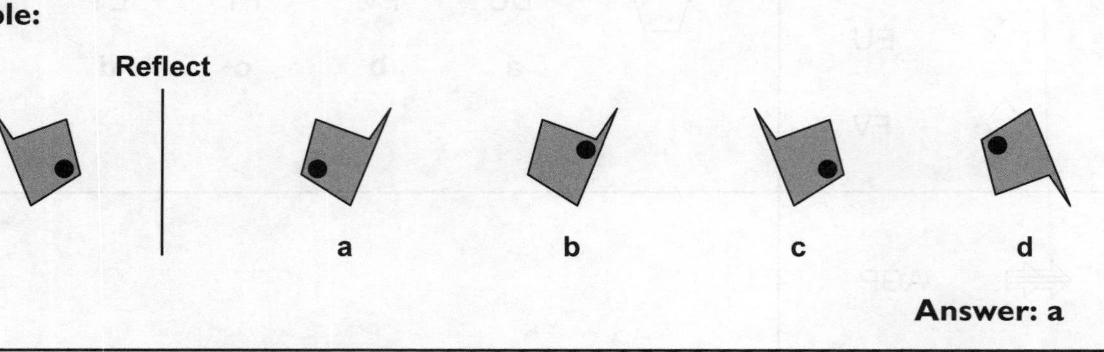

Answer: a

1 Reflect

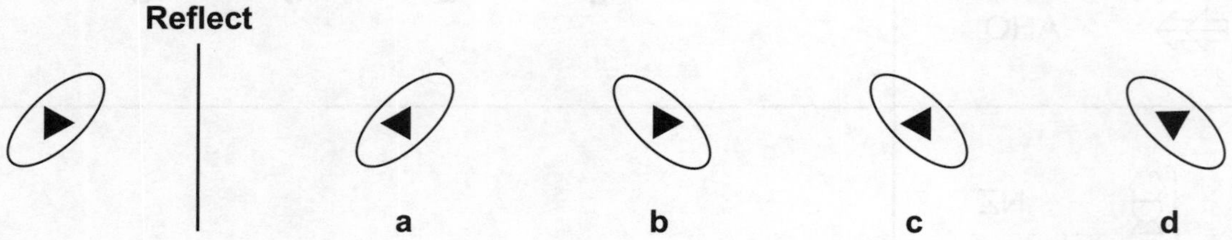

a b c d

2 Reflect

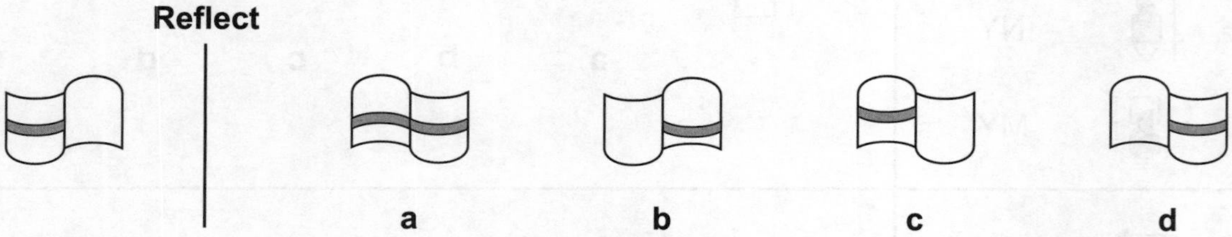

a b c d

3 Reflect

a b c d

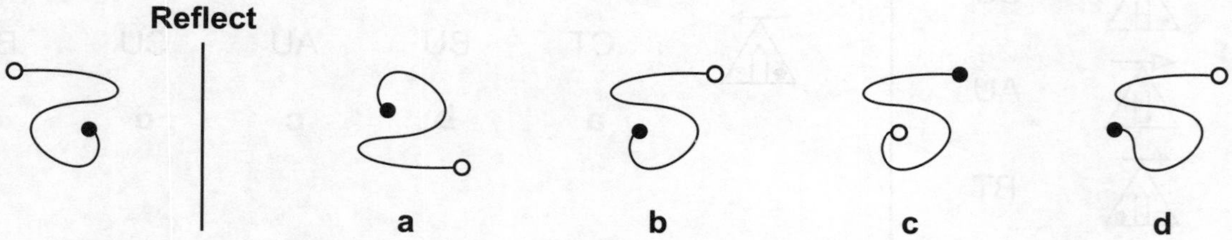

4

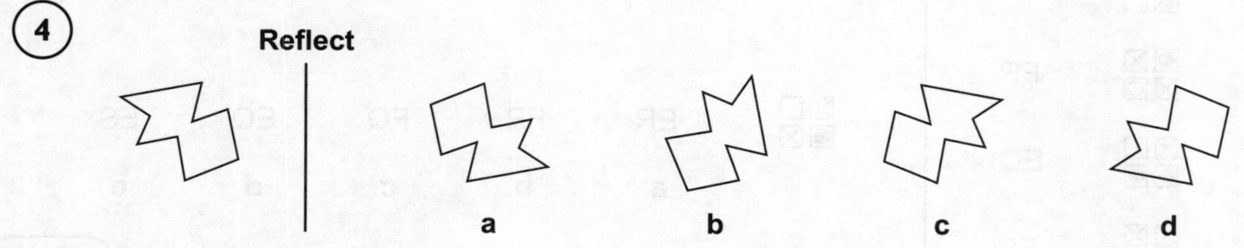

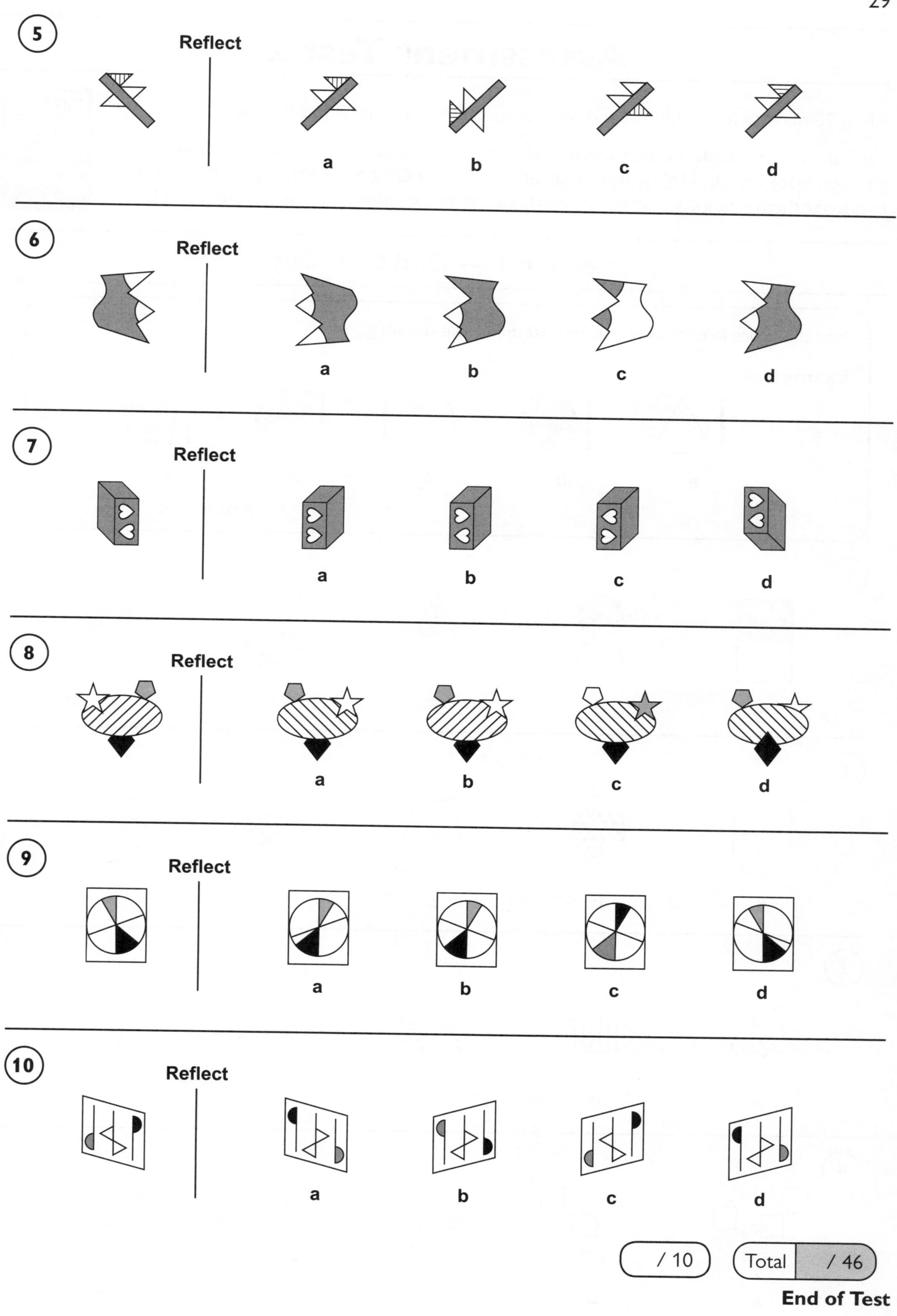
5
Reflect
a
b
c
d
6
Reflect
a
b
c
d
7
Reflect
a
b
c
d
8
Reflect
a
b
c
d
9
Reflect
a
b
c
d
10
Reflect
a
b
c
d
/ 10
Total / 46

End of Test

Assessment Test 2

Allow 30 minutes to do this test and work as quickly and as carefully as you can.

You can print **multiple-choice answer sheets** for these questions from our website — go to cgpbooks.co.uk/11plus/answer-sheets or scan the QR code on the right. If you'd prefer to answer them in standard write-in format, just circle the letter underneath your answer.

Section 1 — Odd One Out

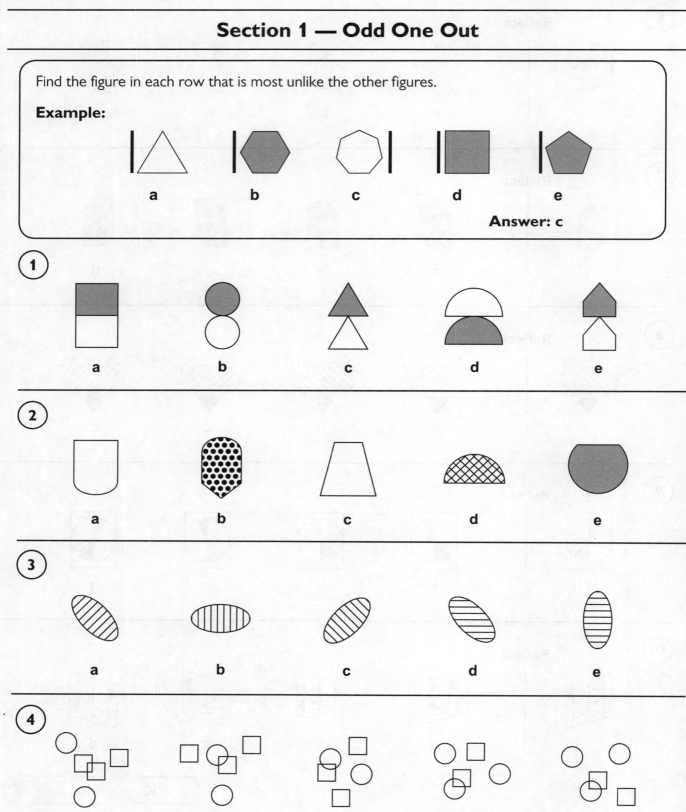

Find the figure in each row that is most unlike the other figures.

Example:

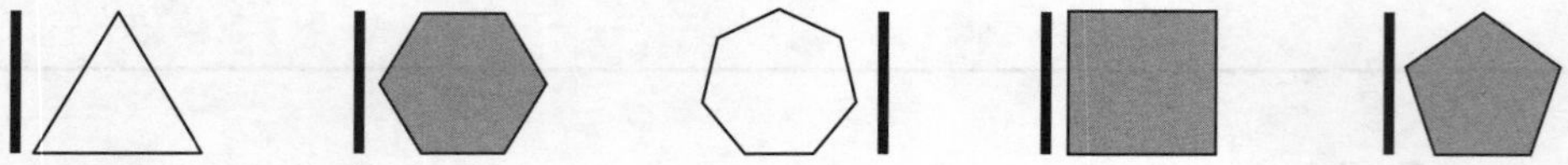

a b c d e

Answer: c

(1)

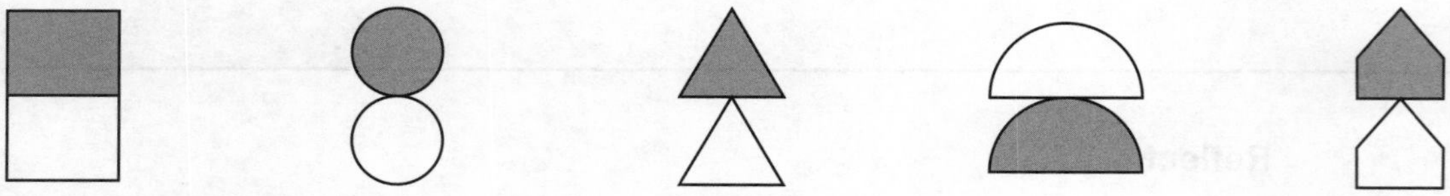

a b c d e

(2)

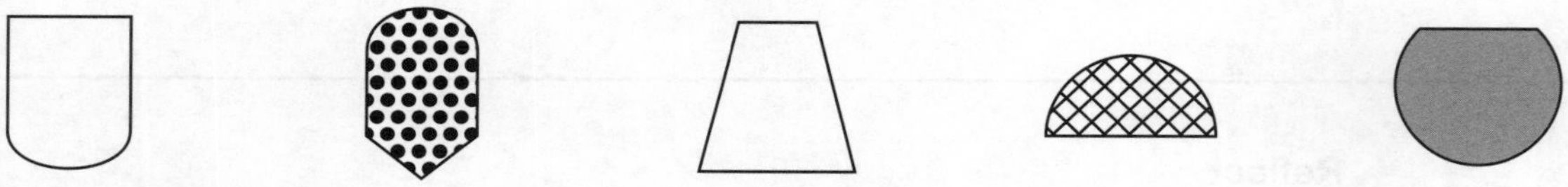

a b c d e

(3)

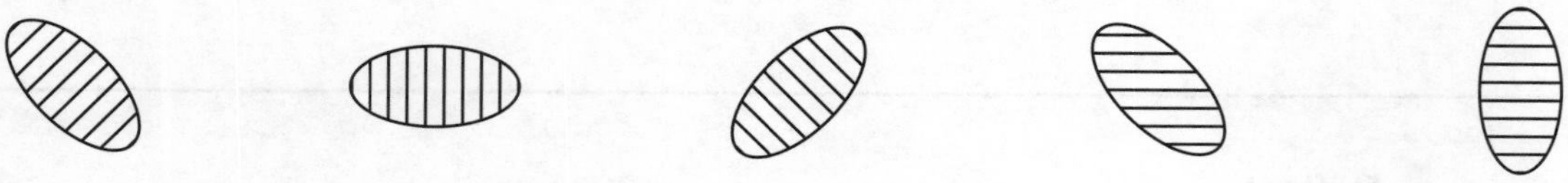

a b c d e

(4)

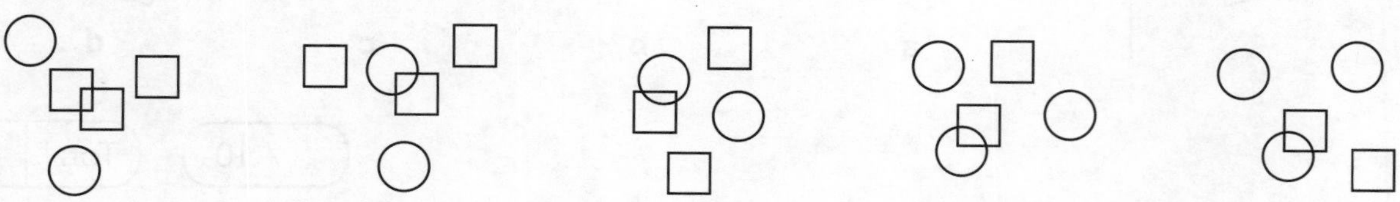

a b c d e

5

a b c d e

6

a b c d e

7

a b c d e

8

a b c d e

9

a b c d e

10

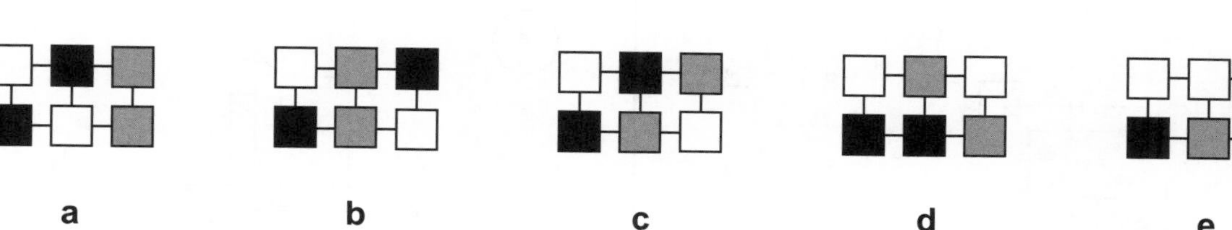

a b c d e

/ 10

Carry on to the next question →→

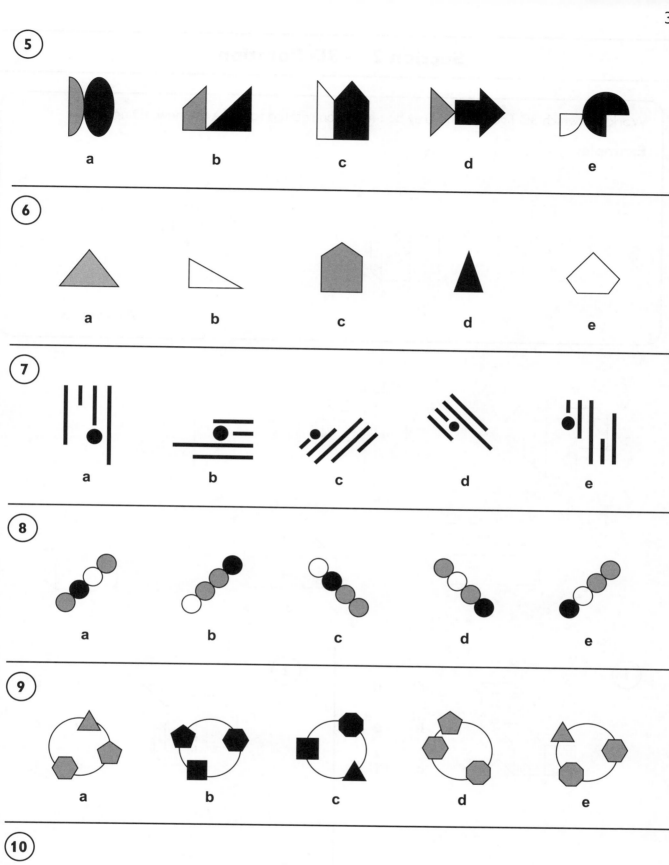

Section 2 — 3D Rotation

Work out which 3D figure in the grey box has been rotated to make the new 3D figure.

Example:

a b

a

b

Answer: a

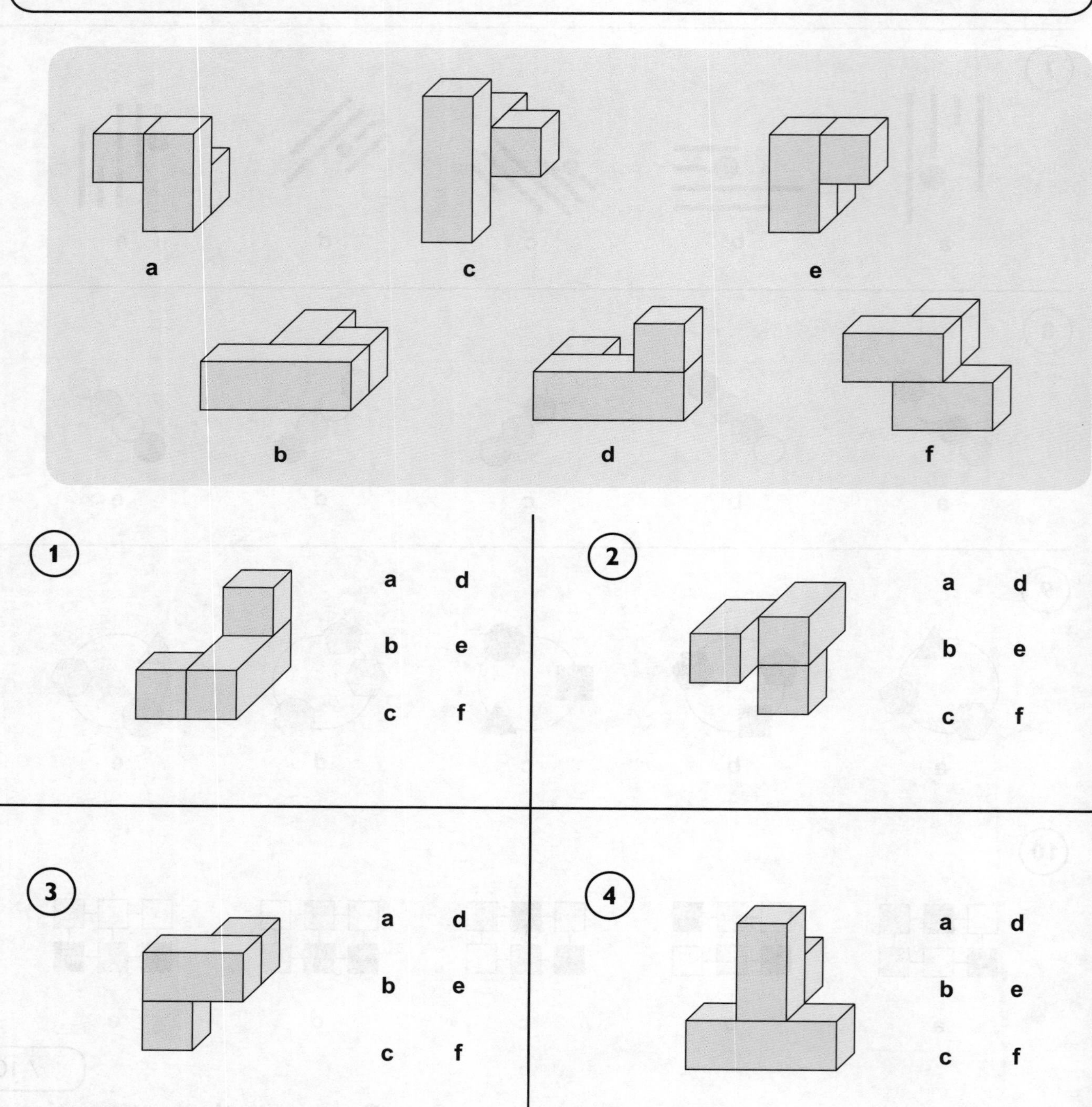

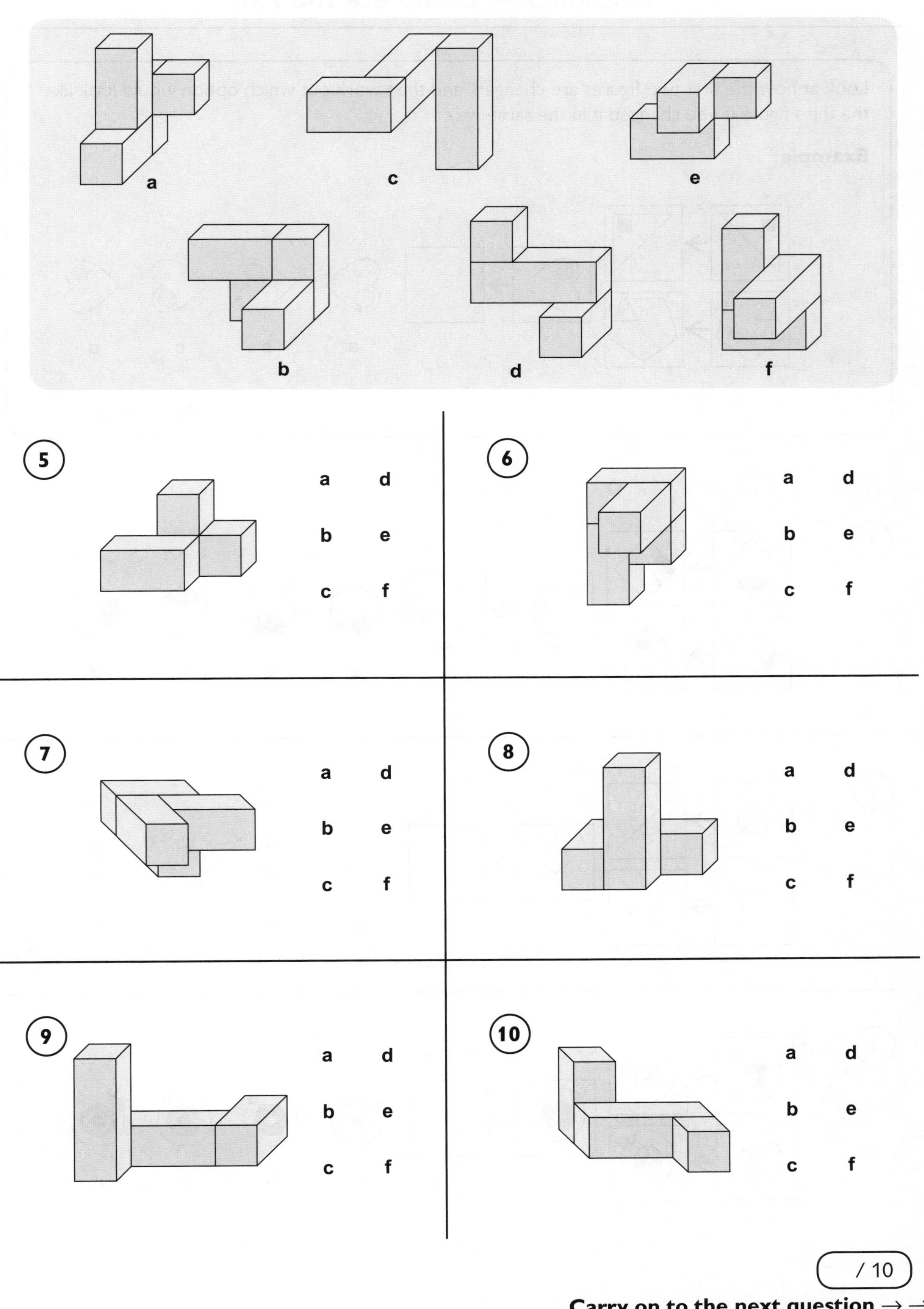

/ 10

Carry on to the next question → →

Section 3 — Complete the Pair

Look at how the first two figures are changed, and then work out which option would look like the third figure if you changed it in the same way.

Example:

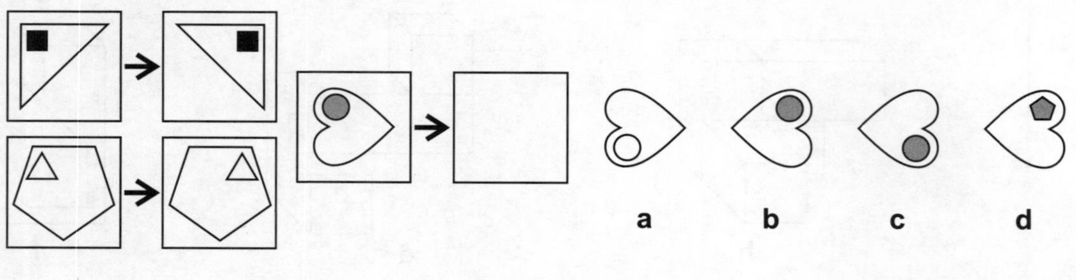

Answer: b

1

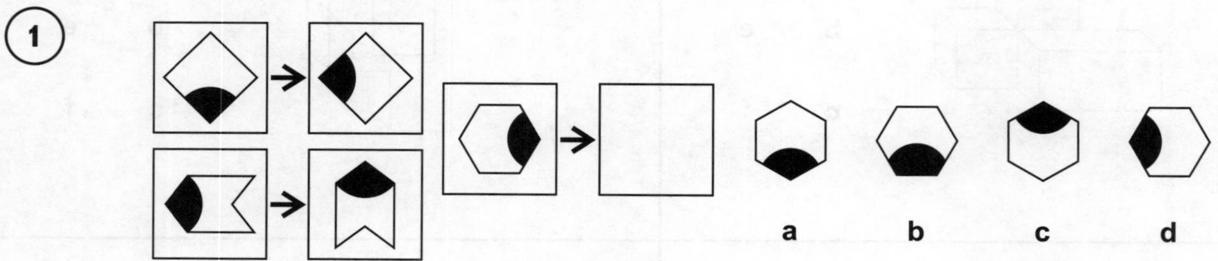

2

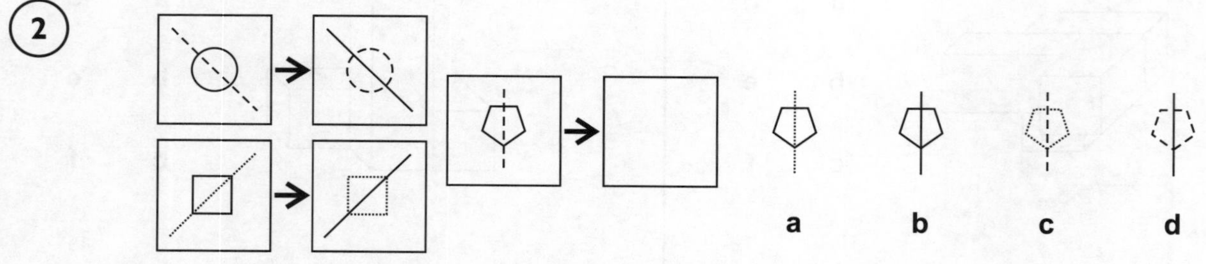

3

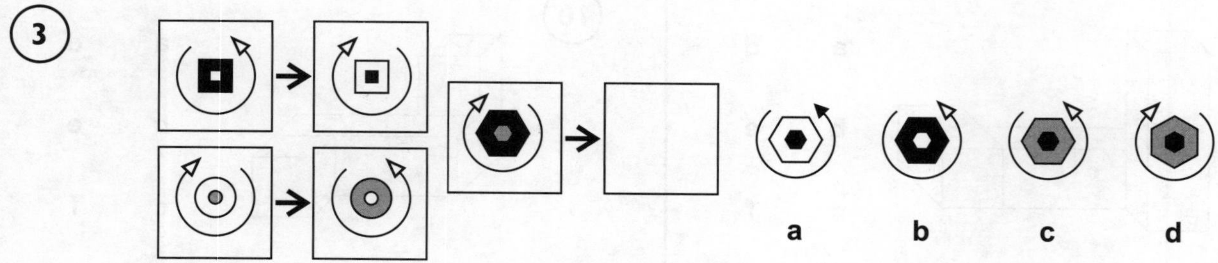

4

a b c d

5

a b c d

6

a b c d

7

a b c d

8

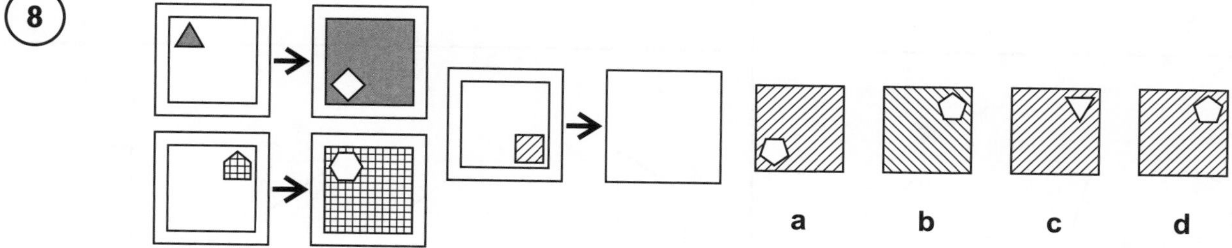

a b c d

/ 8

Carry on to the next question → →

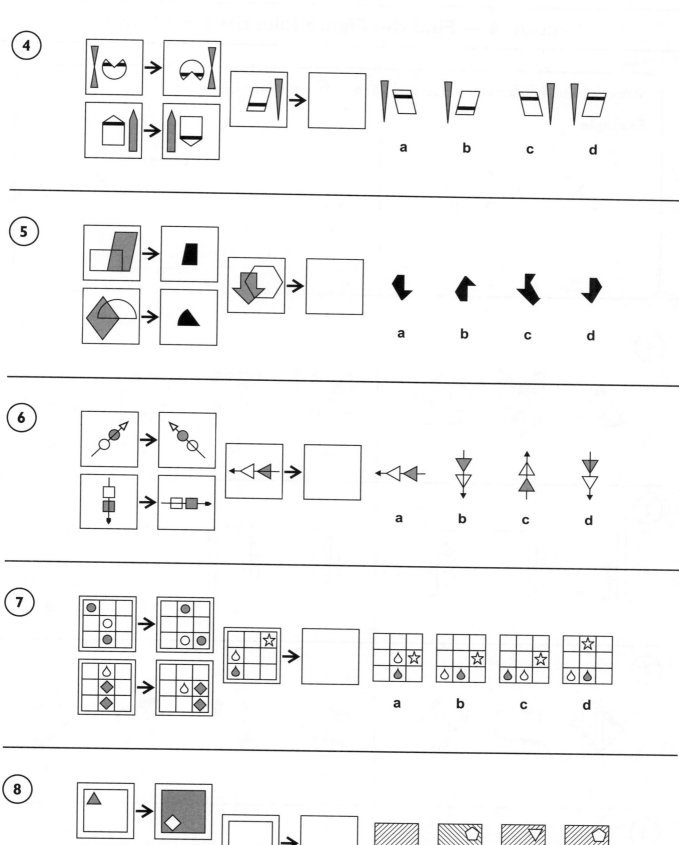

Section 4 — Find the Figure Like the First Three

Work out which option is the most like the three figures on the left.

Example:

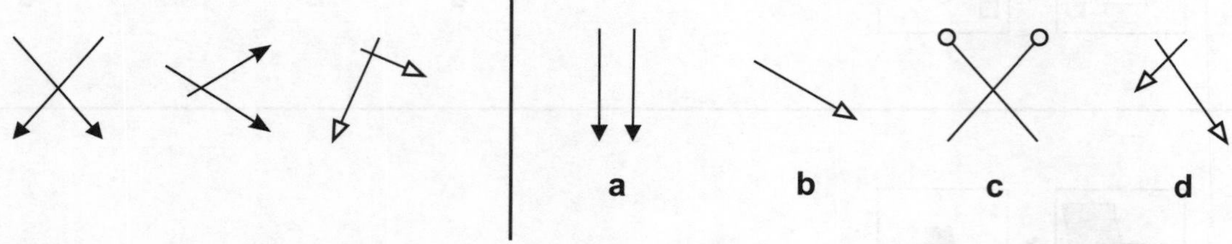

Answer: d

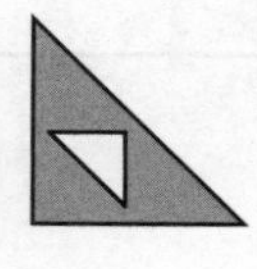
a

b
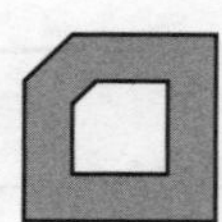
c
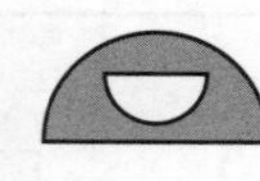
d

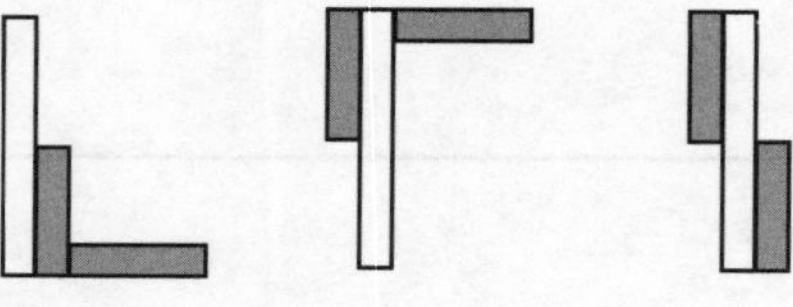

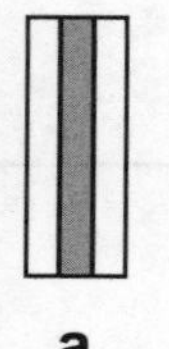
a
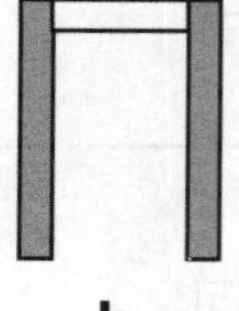
b
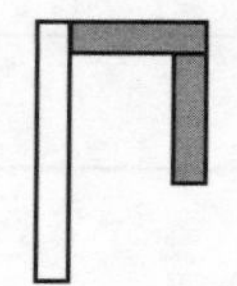
c
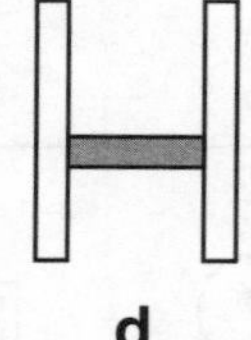
d

3

a

b

c

d

4

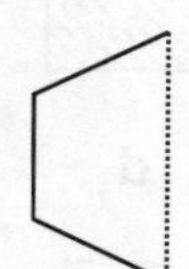

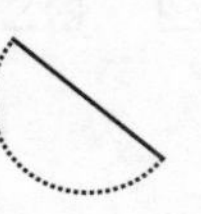

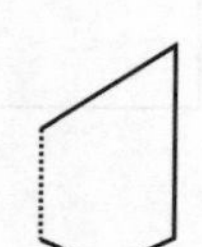
a
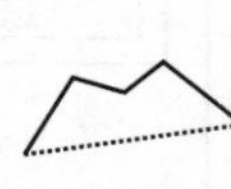
b
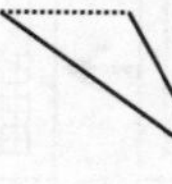
c
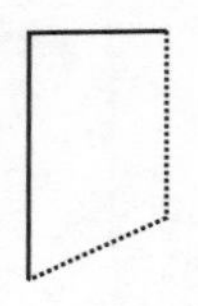
d

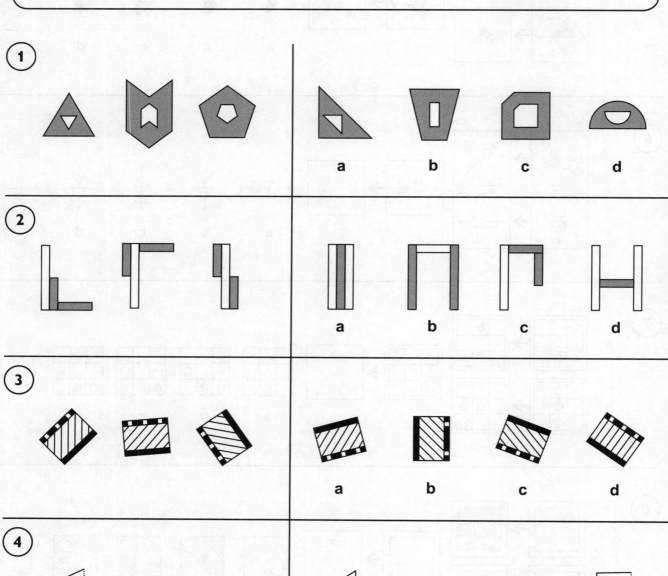

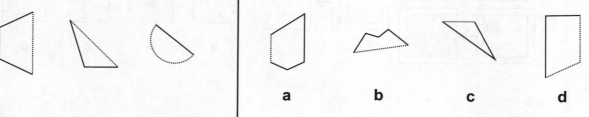

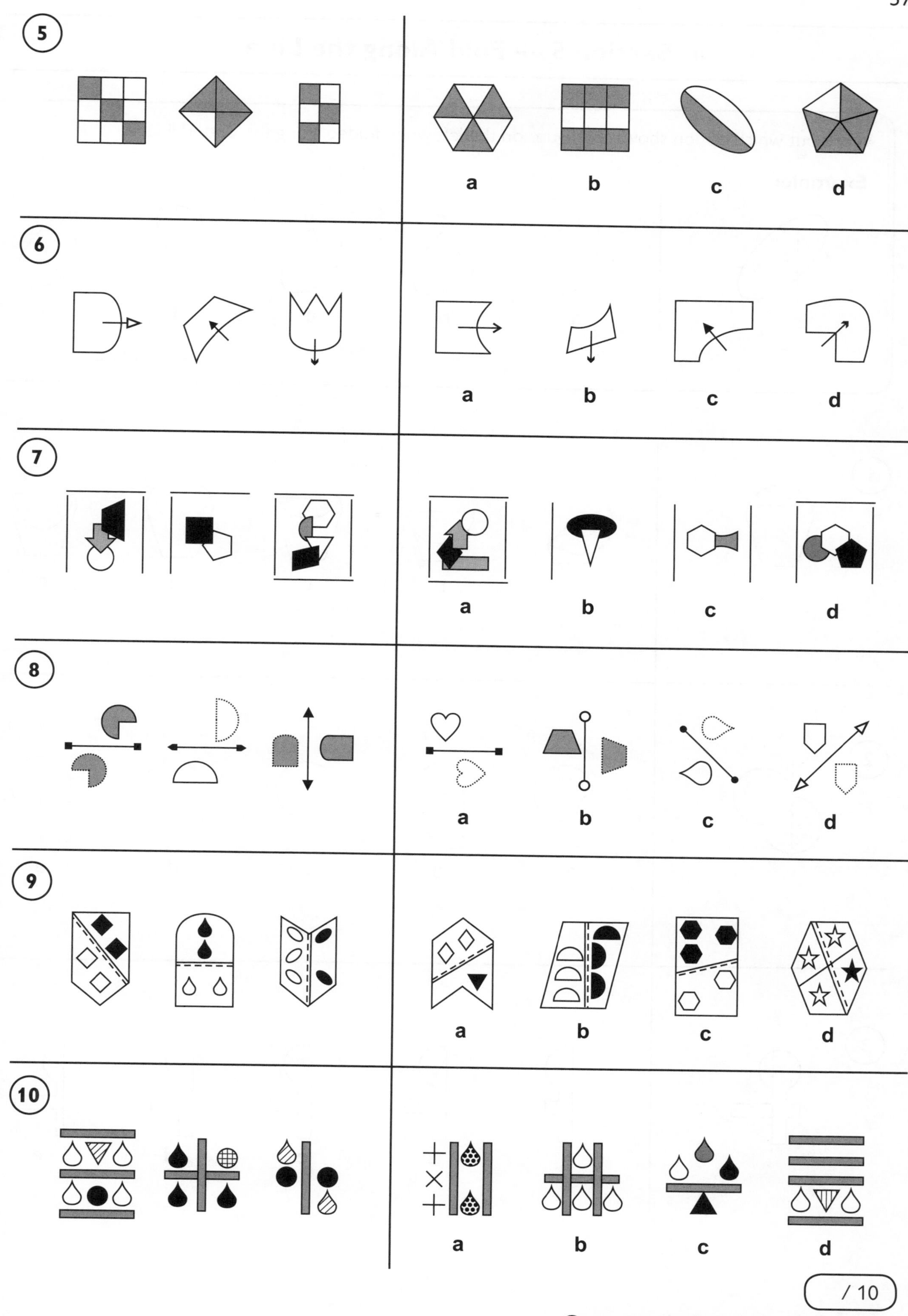

/ 10

Carry on to the next question → →

Section 5 — Fold Along the Line

Work out which option shows the figure on the left when folded along the dotted line.

Example:

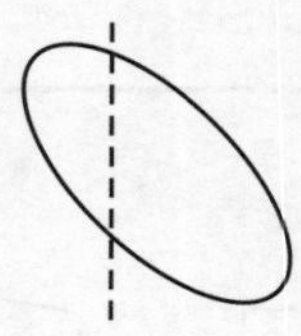

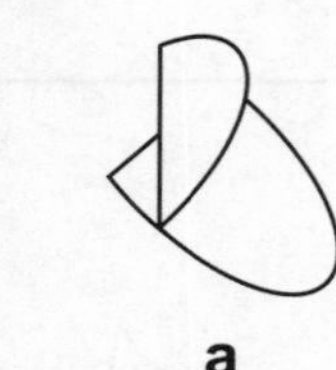
a

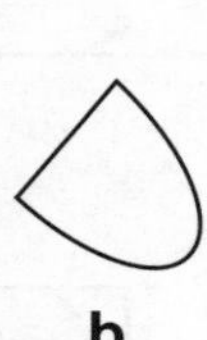
b

c

d

e

Answer: c

1

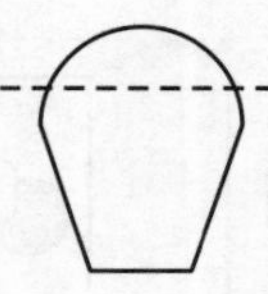

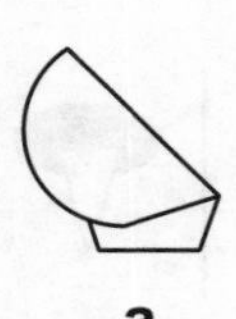
a

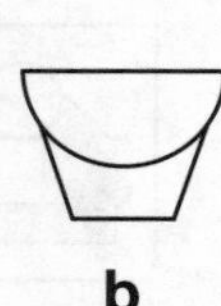
b

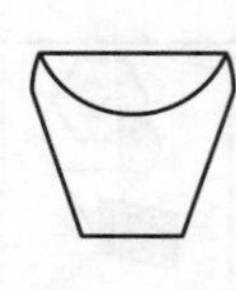
c

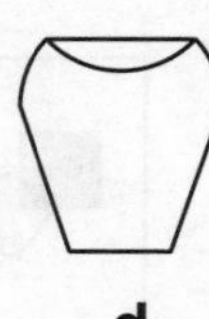
d

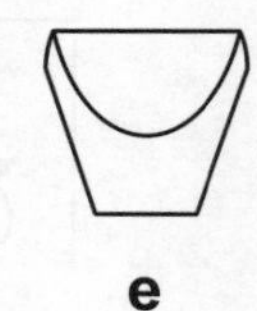
e

2

a

b

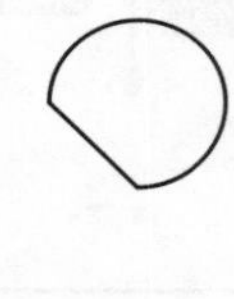
c

d

e

3

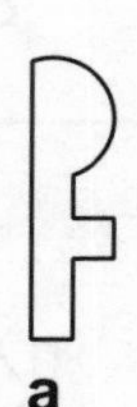
a

b

c

d

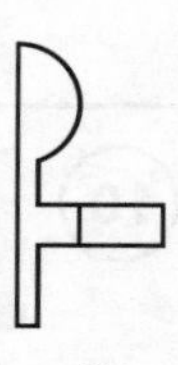
e

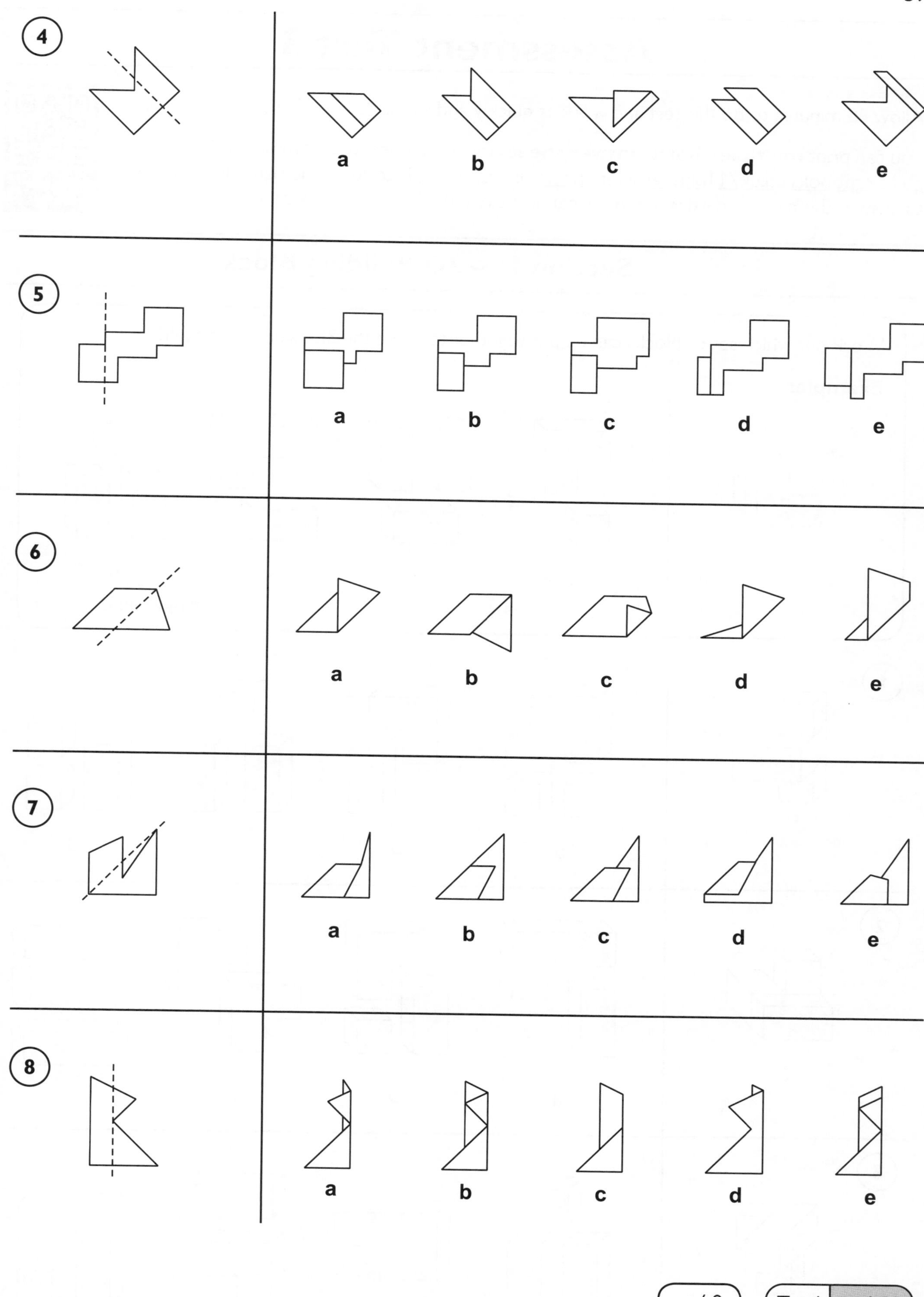

/ 8 Total / 46

End of Test

Assessment Test 3

Allow 30 minutes to do this test and work as quickly and as carefully as you can.

You can print **multiple-choice answer sheets** for these questions from our website — go to cgpbooks.co.uk/11plus/answer-sheets or scan the QR code on the right. If you'd prefer to answer them in standard write-in format, just circle the letter underneath your answer.

Section 1 — 3D Building Blocks

Work out which set of blocks can be put together to make the 3D figure on the left.

Example:

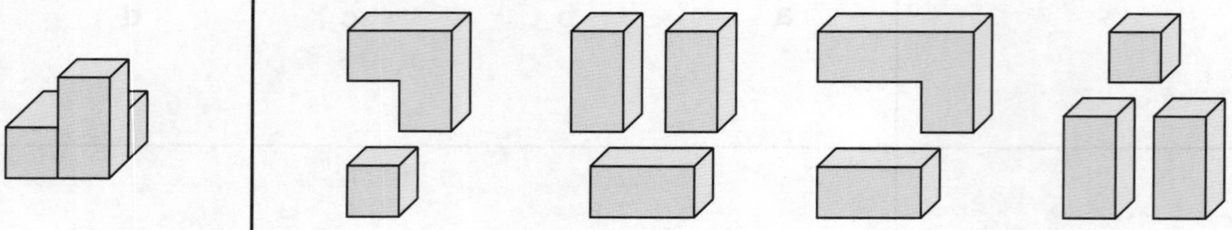

a b c d

Answer: d

1

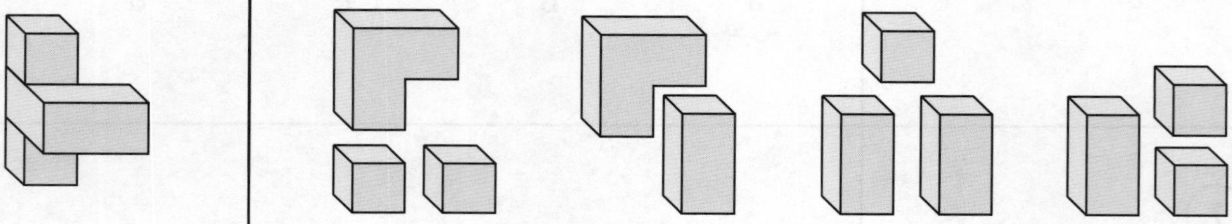

a b c d

2

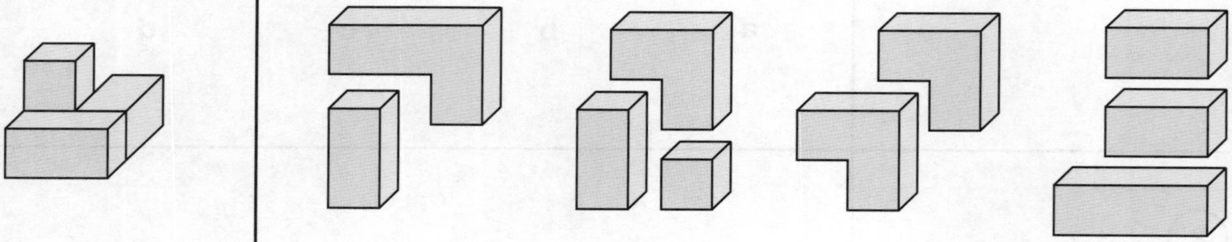

a b c d

3

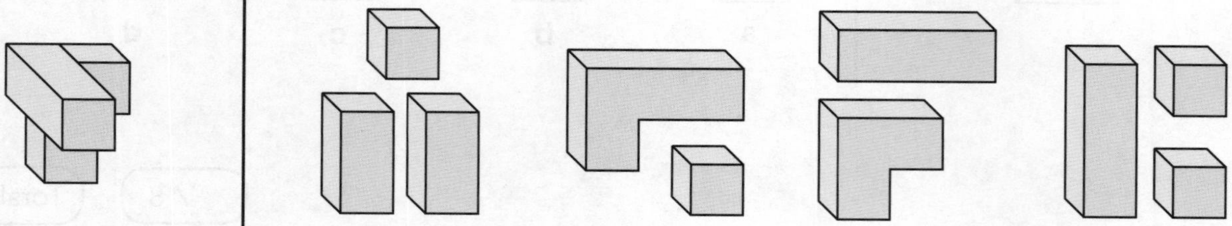

a b c d

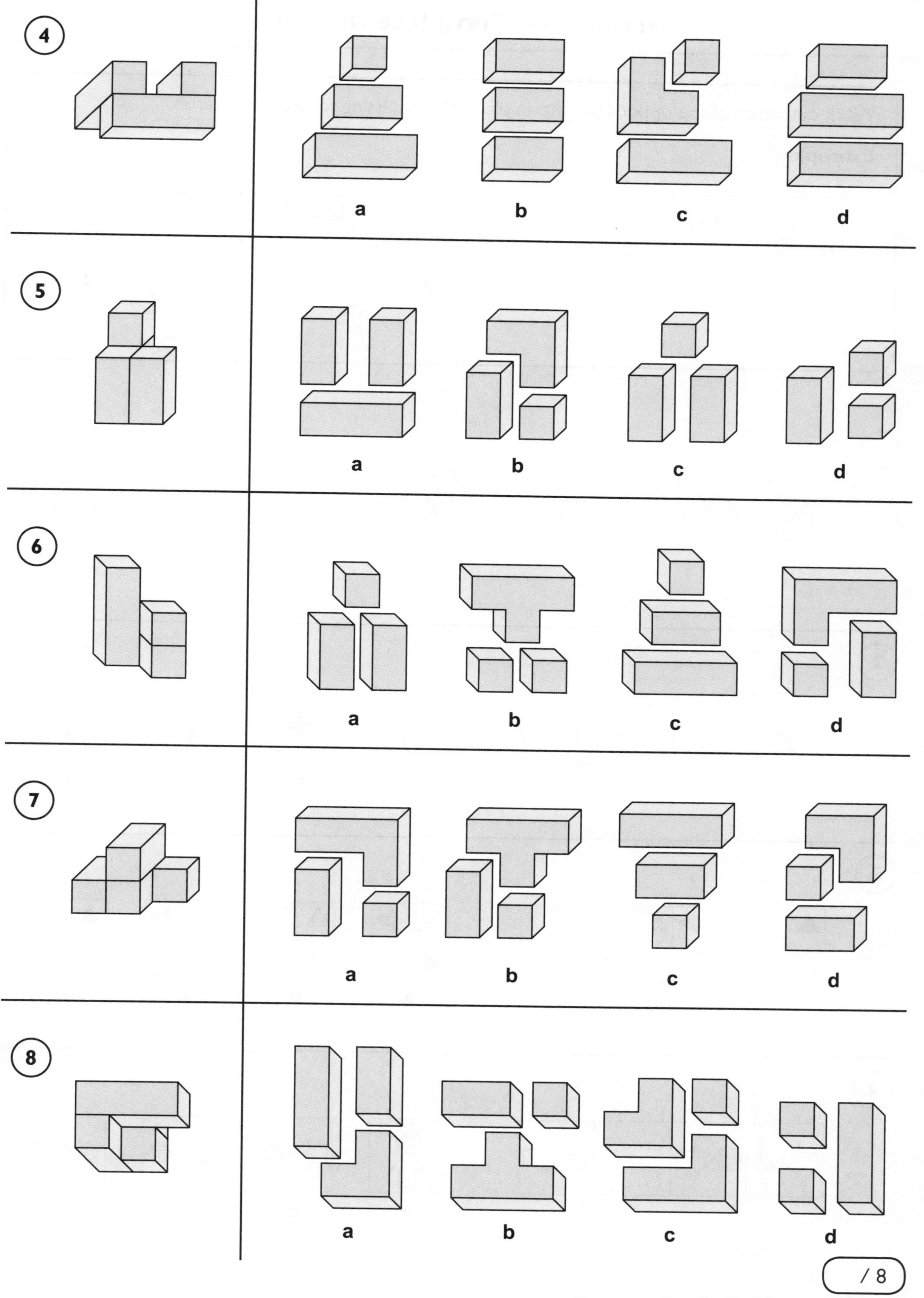

/ 8

Carry on to the next question → →

Section 2 — Complete the Series

Work out which of the options best fits in place of the missing square in the series.

Example:

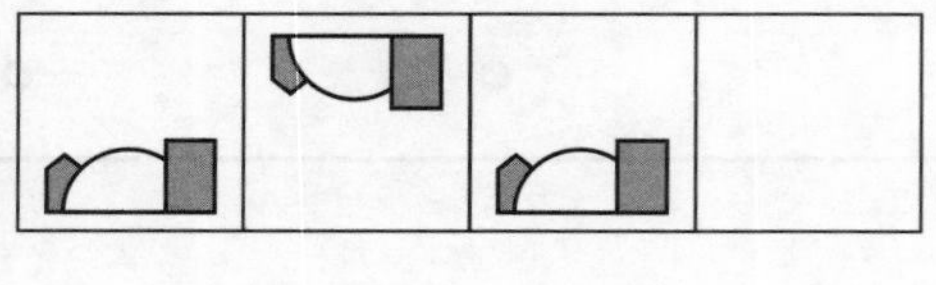

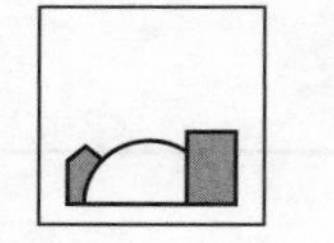
a

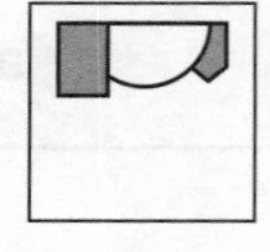
b

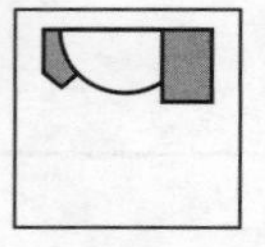
c

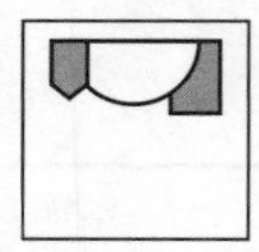
d

Answer: c

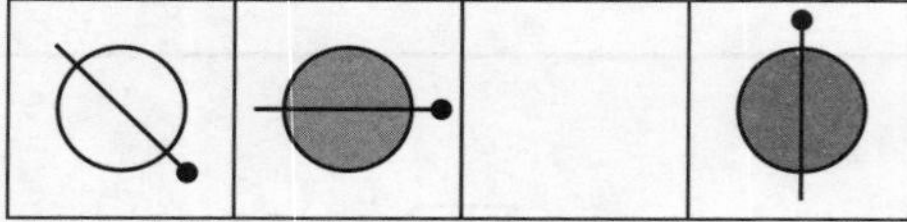

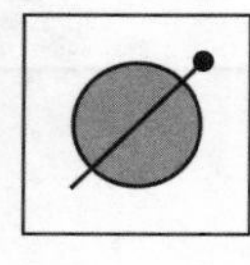
a

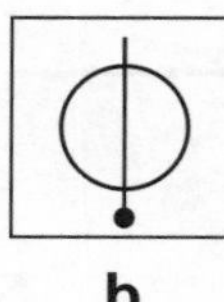
b

c

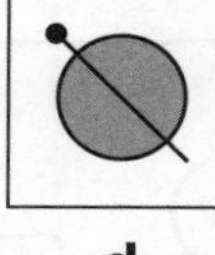
d

2

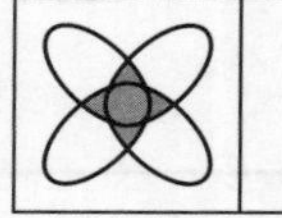

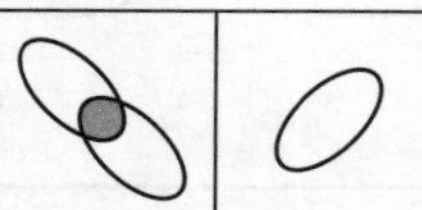

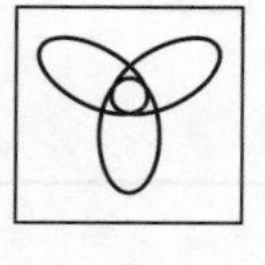
a

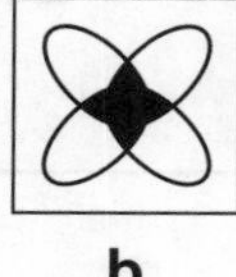
b

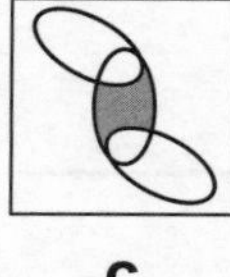
c

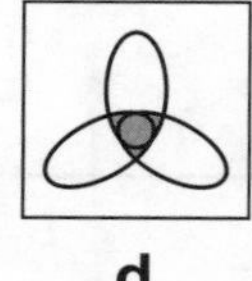
d

3

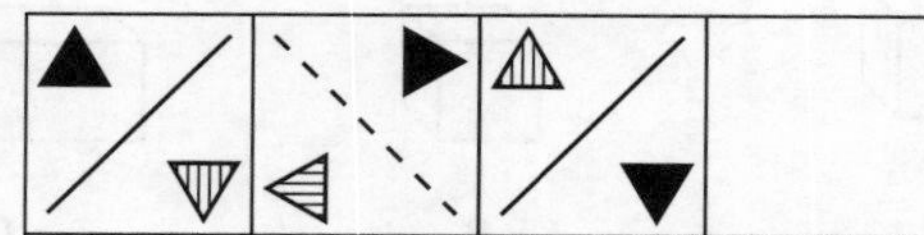

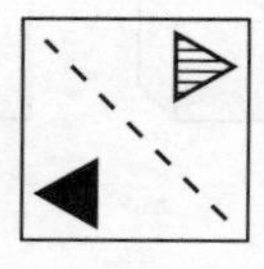
a

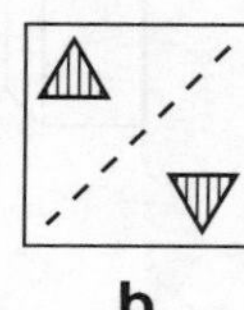
b

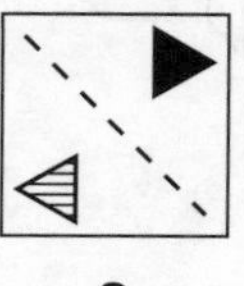
c

d

4

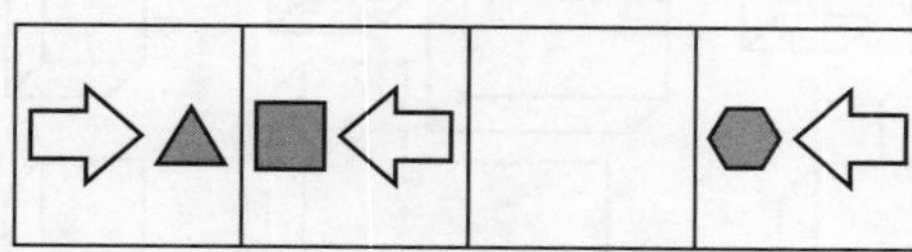

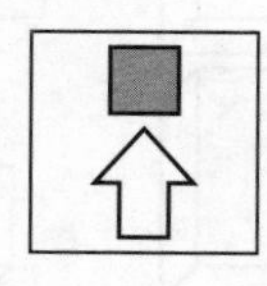
a

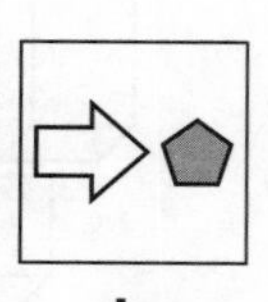
b

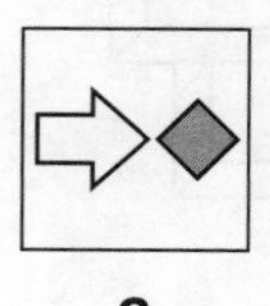
c

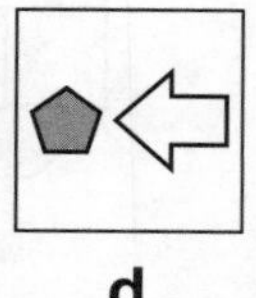
d

5

a b c d

6

a b c d

7

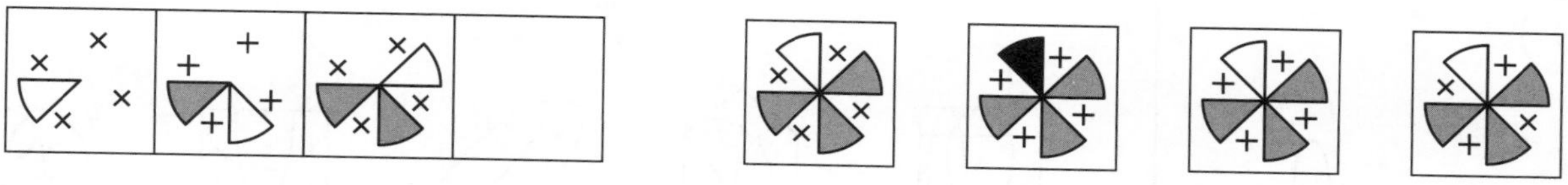

a b c d

8

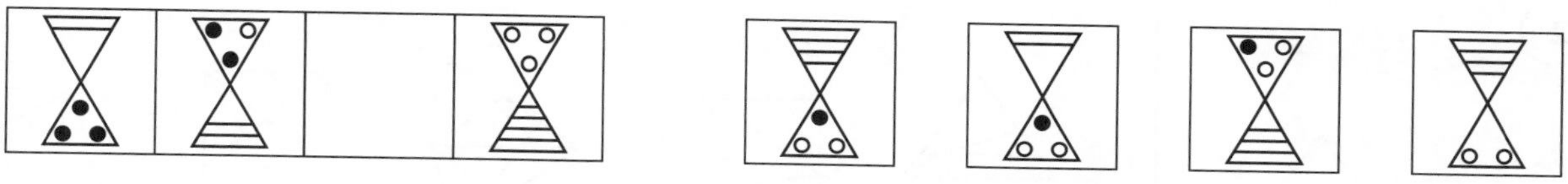

a b c d

9

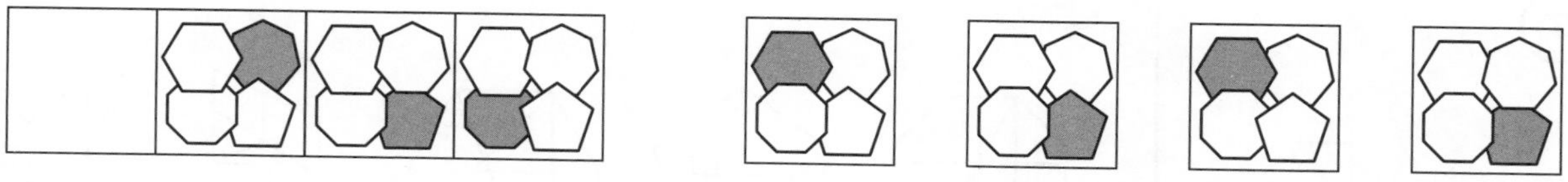

a b c d

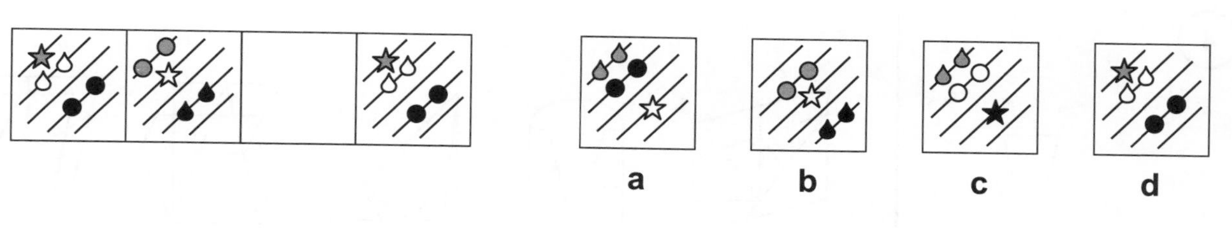

a b c d

/ 10

Carry on to the next question → →

Section 3 — Hidden Shape

Each of these questions has a single shape on the left.
This shape can be found in one of the five figures on the right.
The shape must be the same size and orientation.
Find which of the five figures contains the shape.

Example:

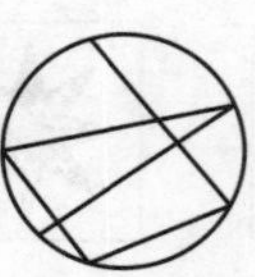  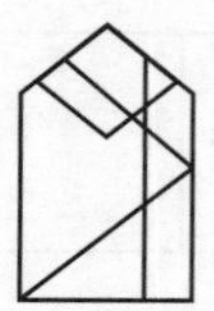 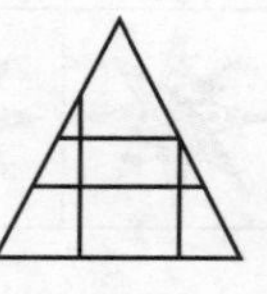 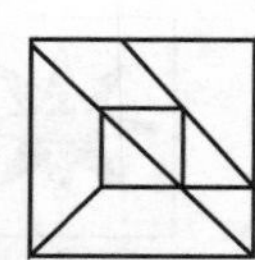

a **b** **c** **d** **e**

Answer: e

1

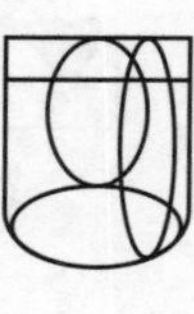  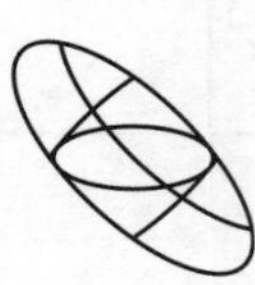 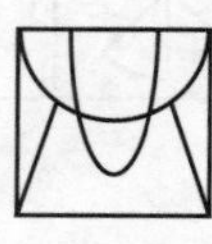 

a **b** **c** **d** **e**

2

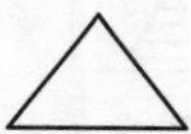

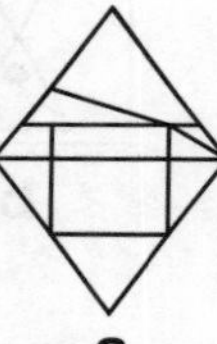 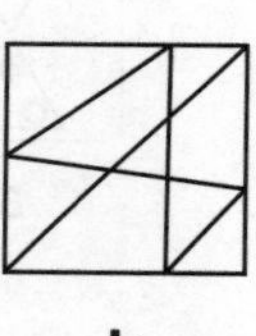 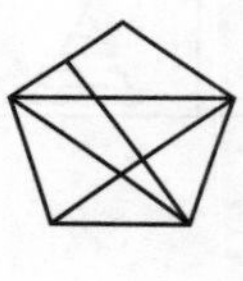 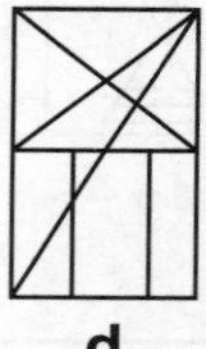 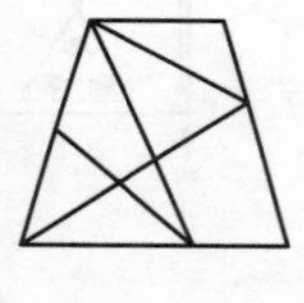

a **b** **c** **d** **e**

3

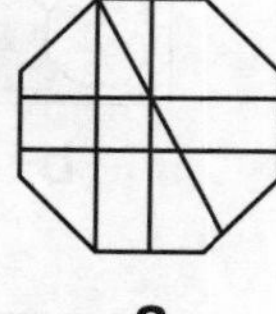 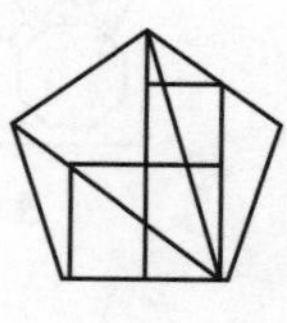 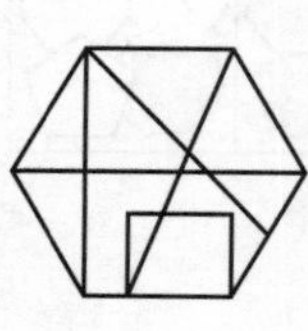 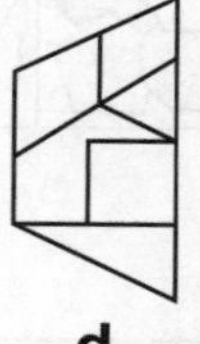 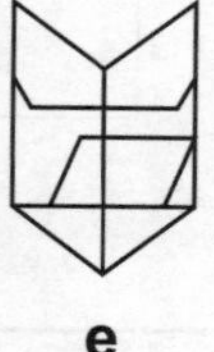

a **b** **c** **d** **e**

4

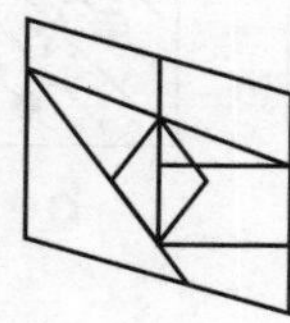  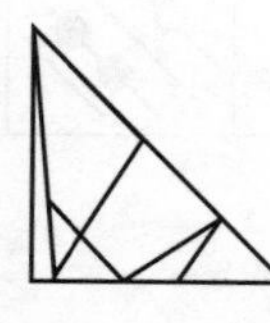 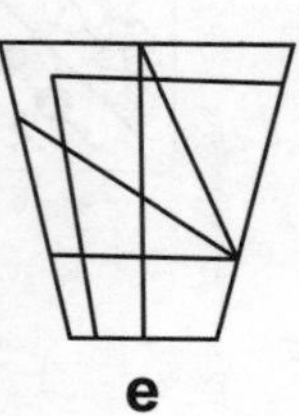

a **b** **c** **d** **e**

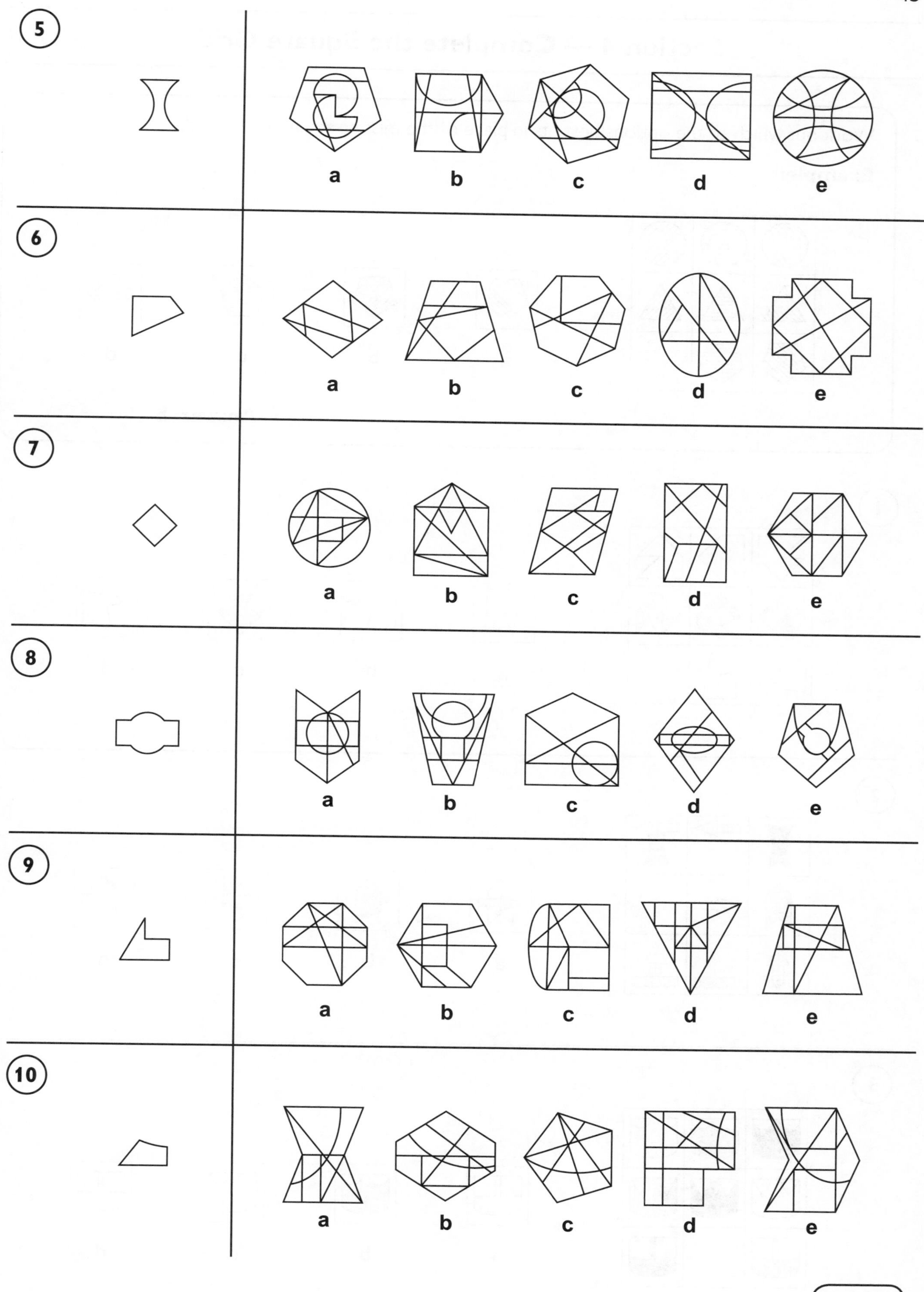

/ 10

Carry on to the next question →→

Section 4 — Complete the Square Grid

Work out which of the options best fits in place of the missing square in the grid.

Example:

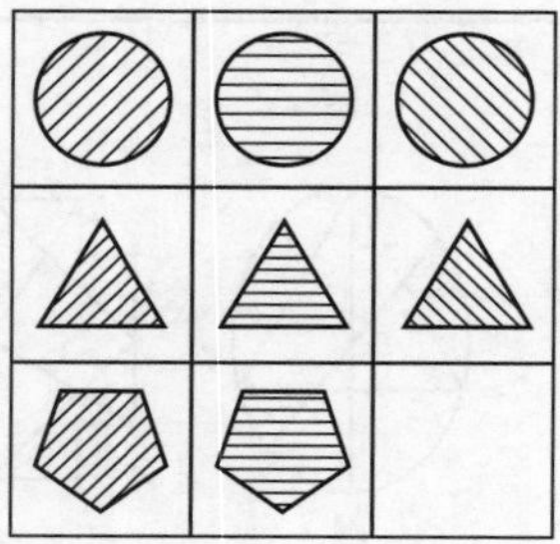

a **b** **c** **d**

Answer: b

1

a **b** **c** **d**

2

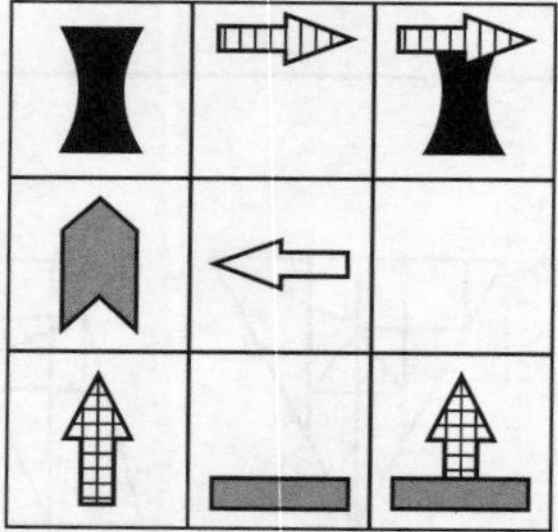

a **b** **c** **d**

3

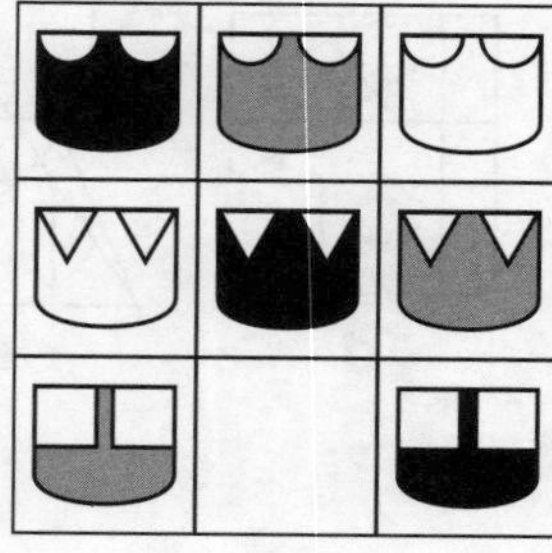

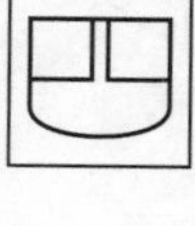

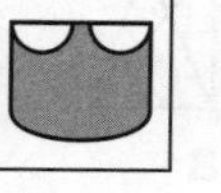

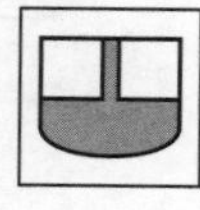

a **b** **c** **d**

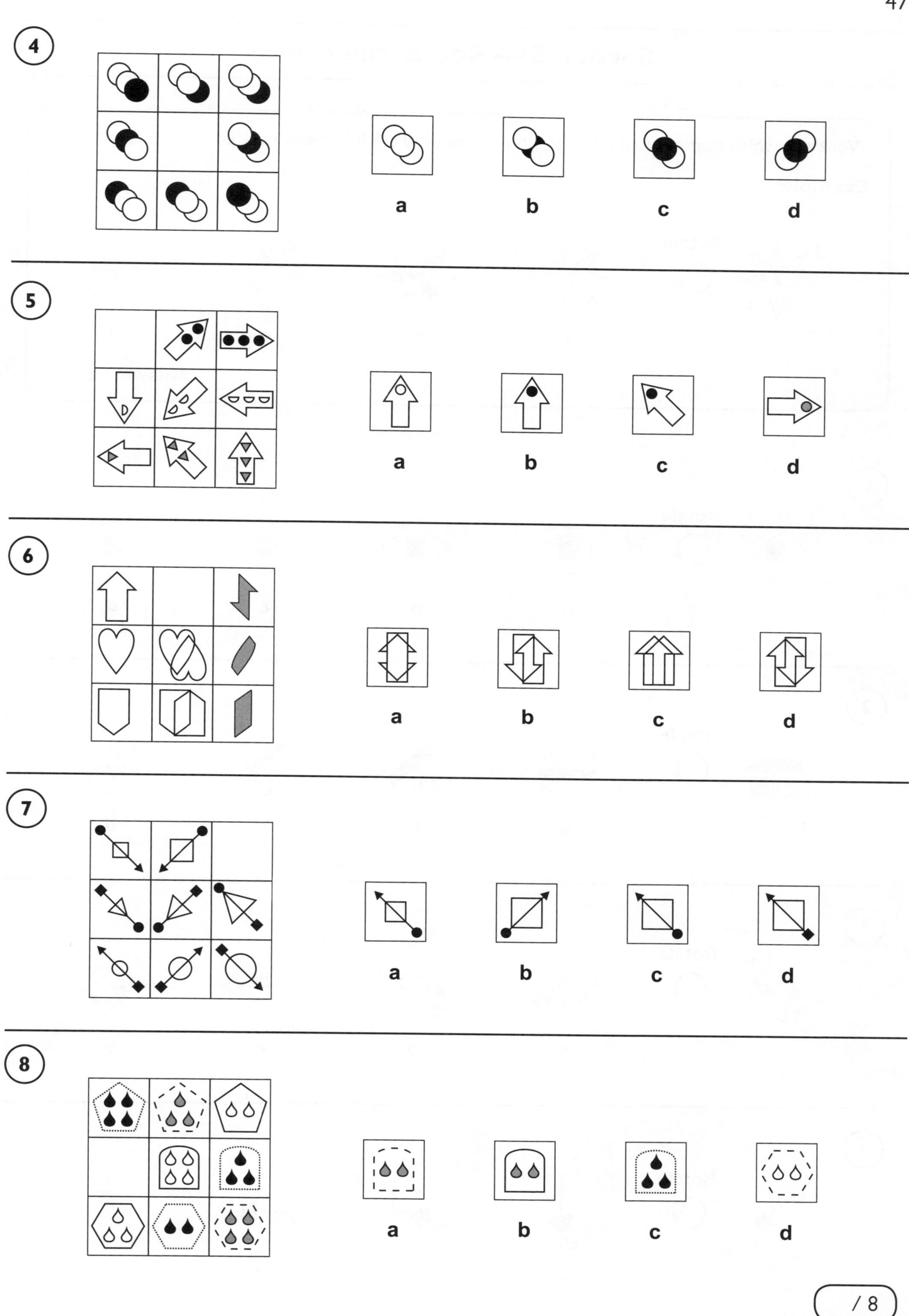

/ 8

Carry on to the next question → →

Section 5 — Rotate the Figure

Work out which option would look like the figure on the left if it was rotated.

Example:

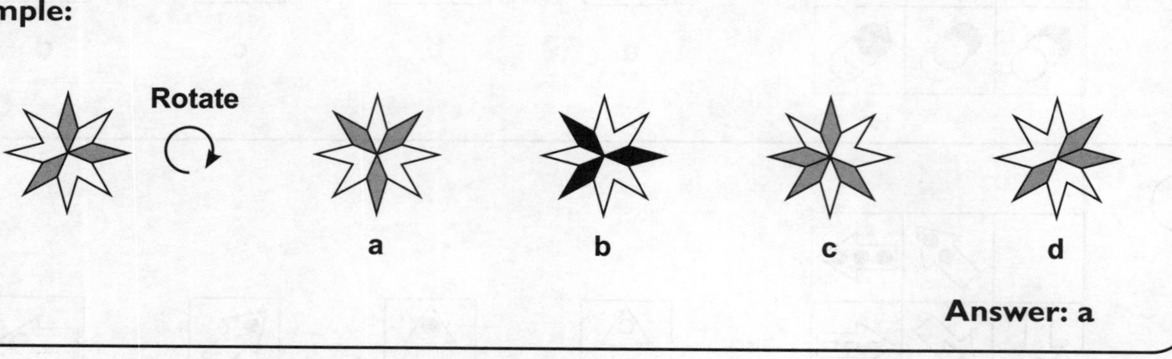

Answer: a

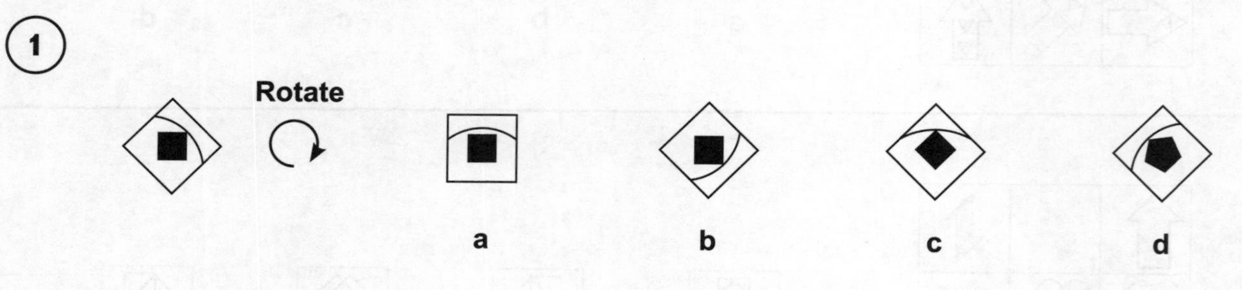

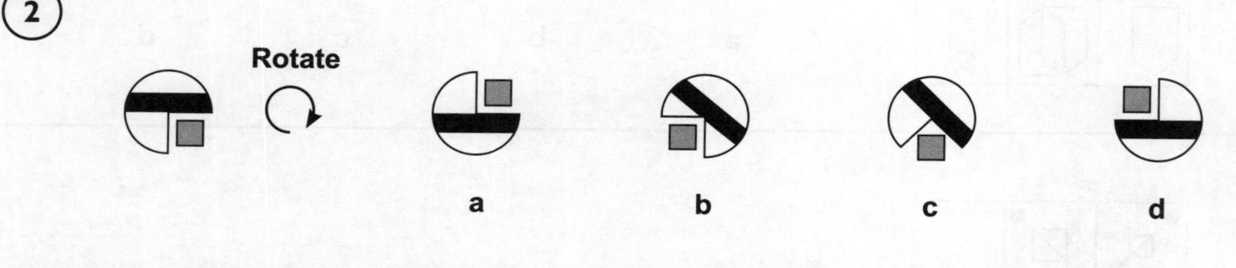

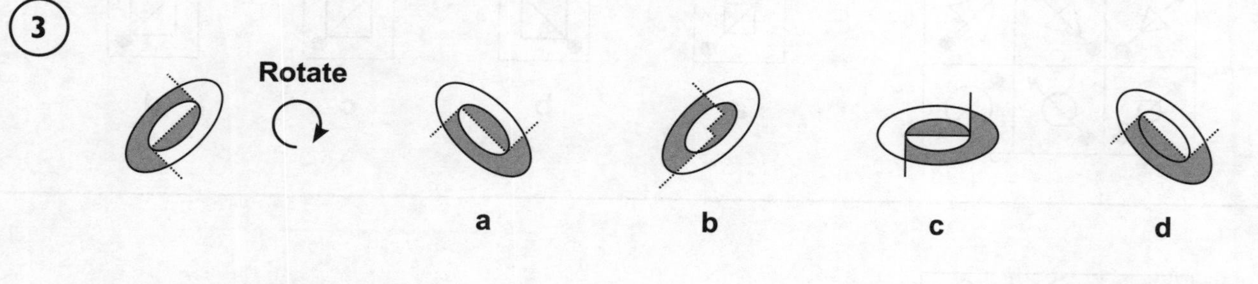

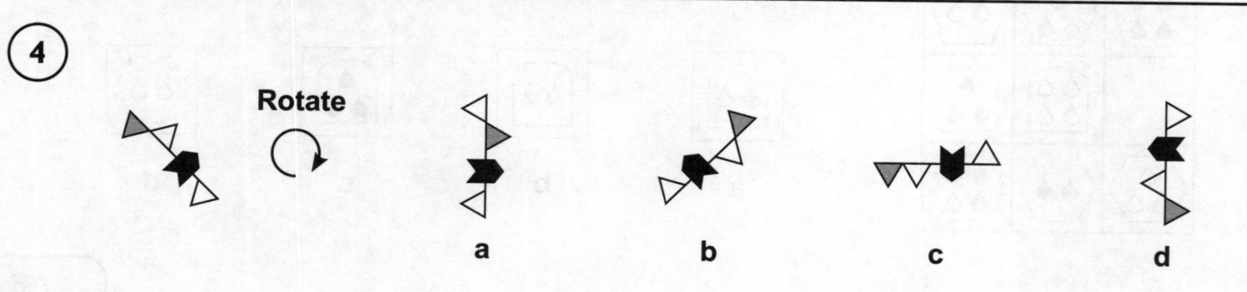

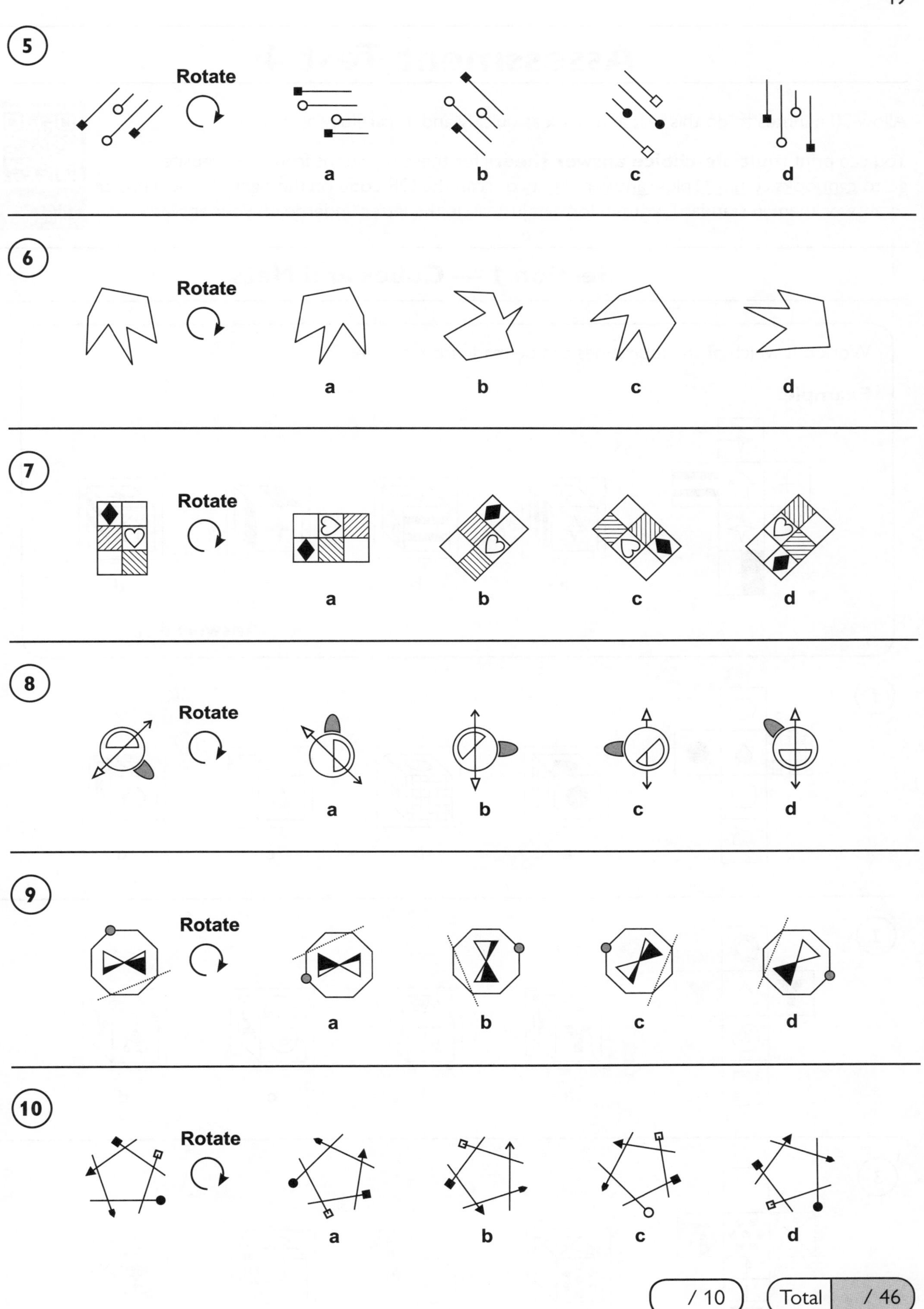

/ 10

Total / 46

End of Test

Assessment Test 4

Allow 30 minutes to do this test and work as quickly and as carefully as you can.

You can print **multiple-choice answer sheets** for these questions from our website — go to cgpbooks.co.uk/11plus/answer-sheets or scan the QR code on the right. If you'd prefer to answer them in standard write-in format, just circle the letter underneath your answer.

Section 1 — Cubes and Nets

Work out which of the four cubes can be made from the net.

Example:

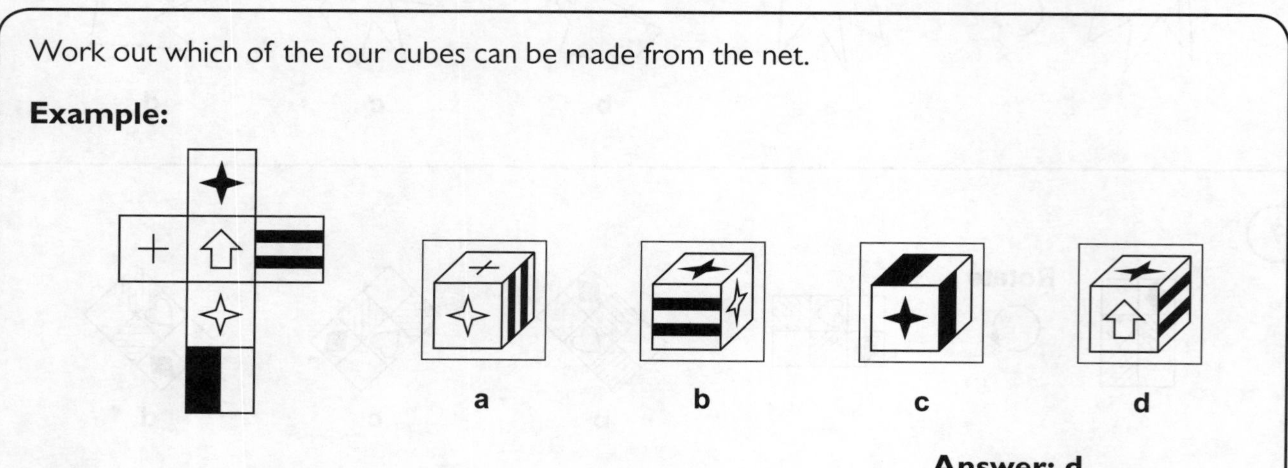

Answer: d

1

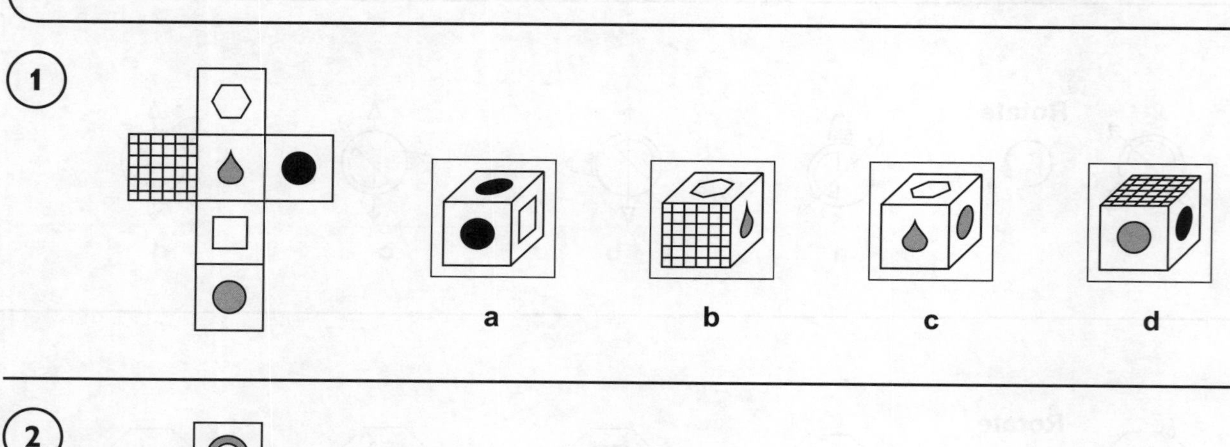

2

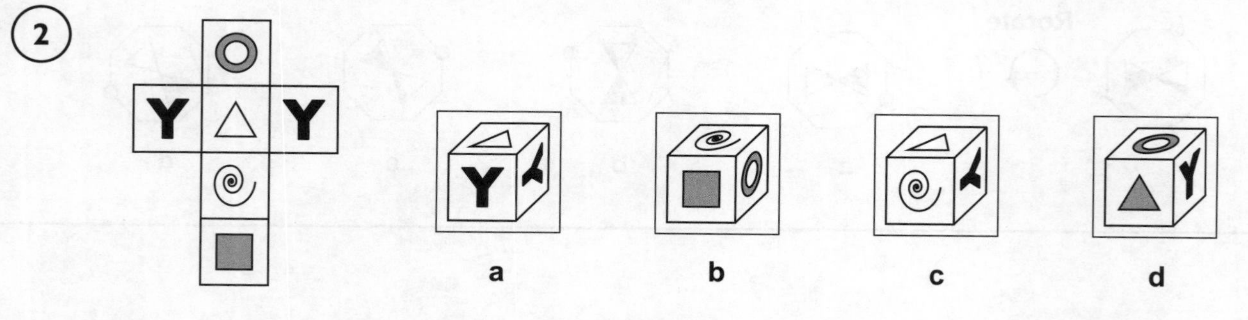

3

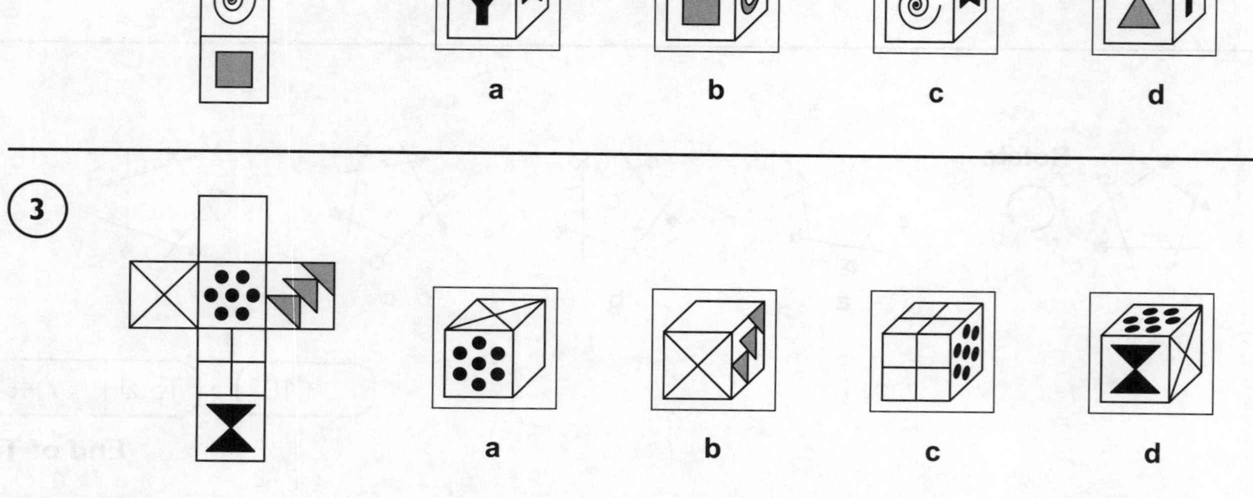

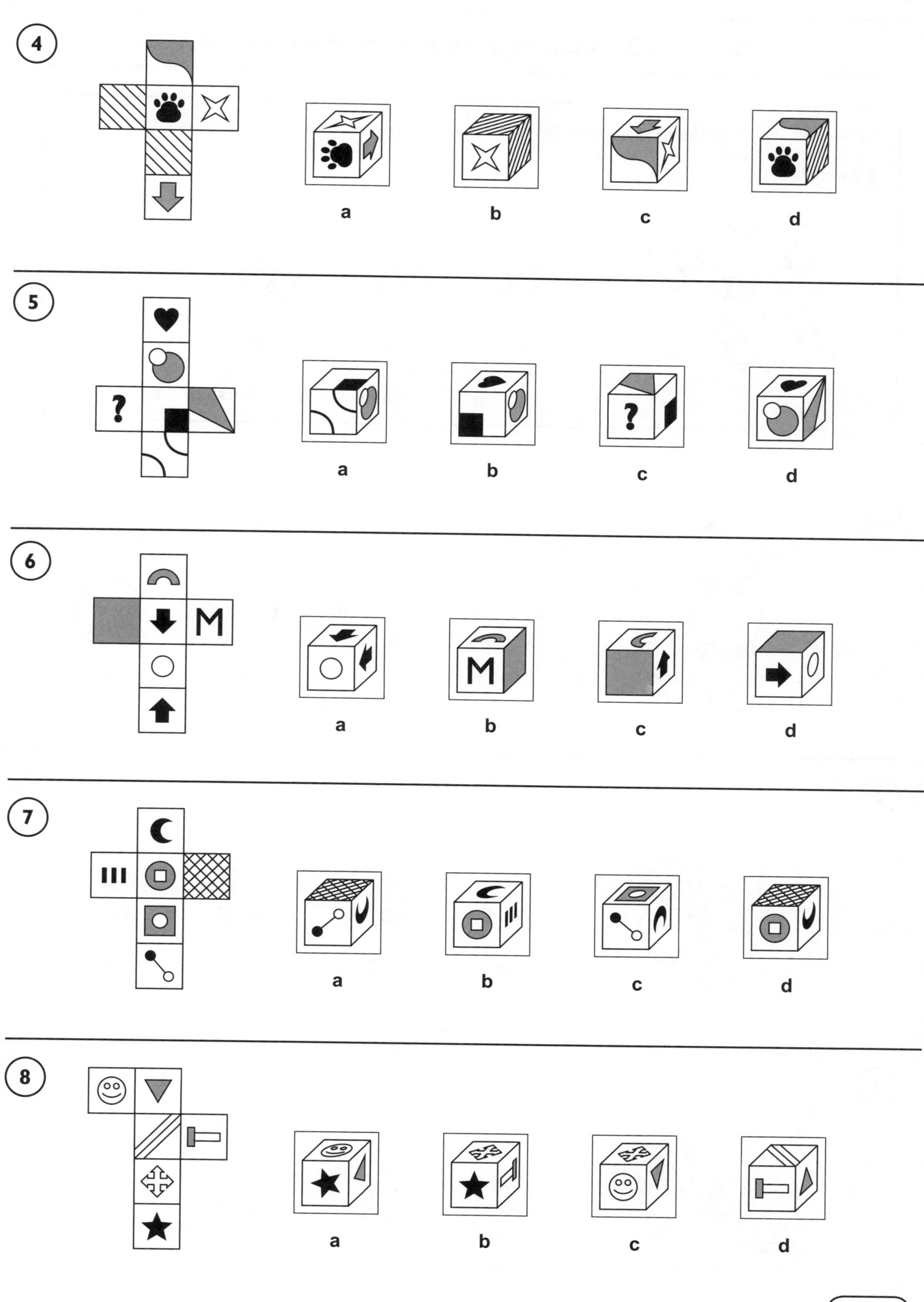

/ 8

Carry on to the next question → →

Section 2 — Complete the Hexagonal Grid

Work out which of the options best fits in place of the missing hexagon in the grid.

Example:

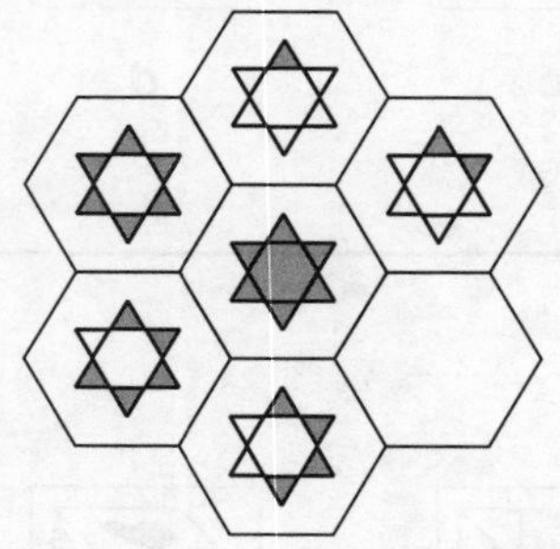

a

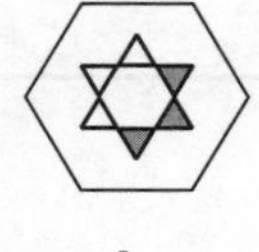

b

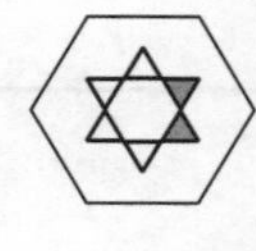

c

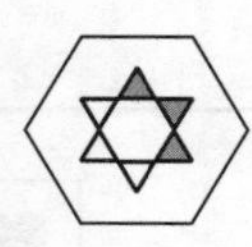

d

Answer: d

1

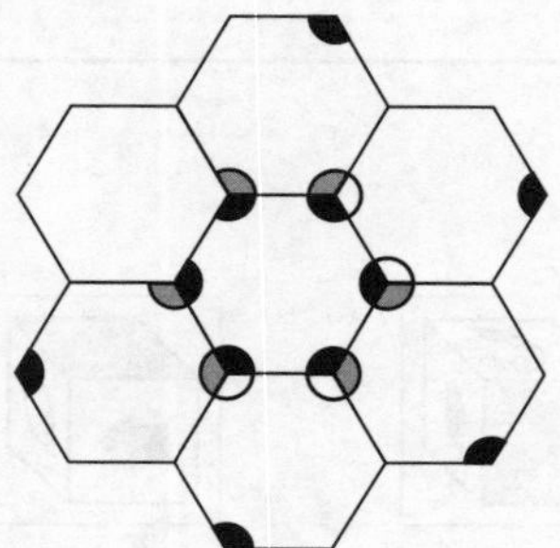

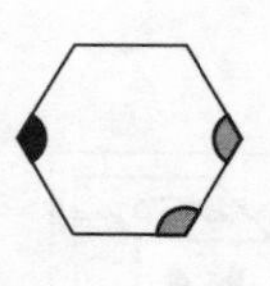

a

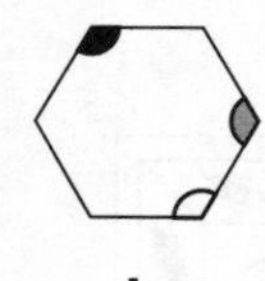

b

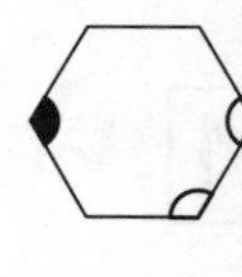

c

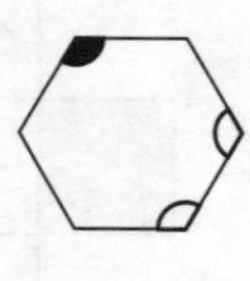

d

2

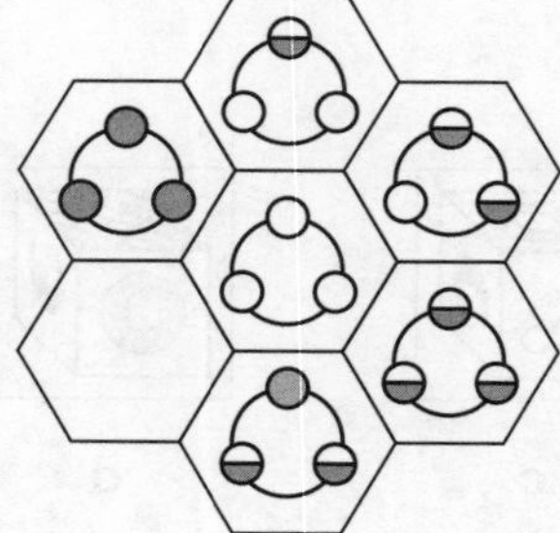

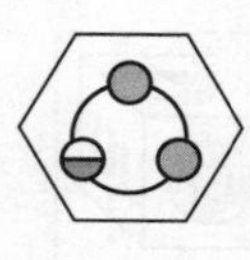

a

b

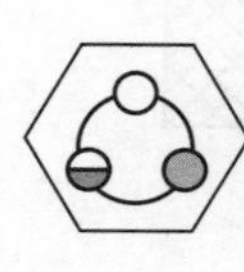

c

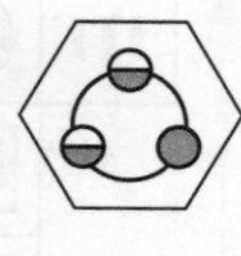

d

3

a

b

c

d

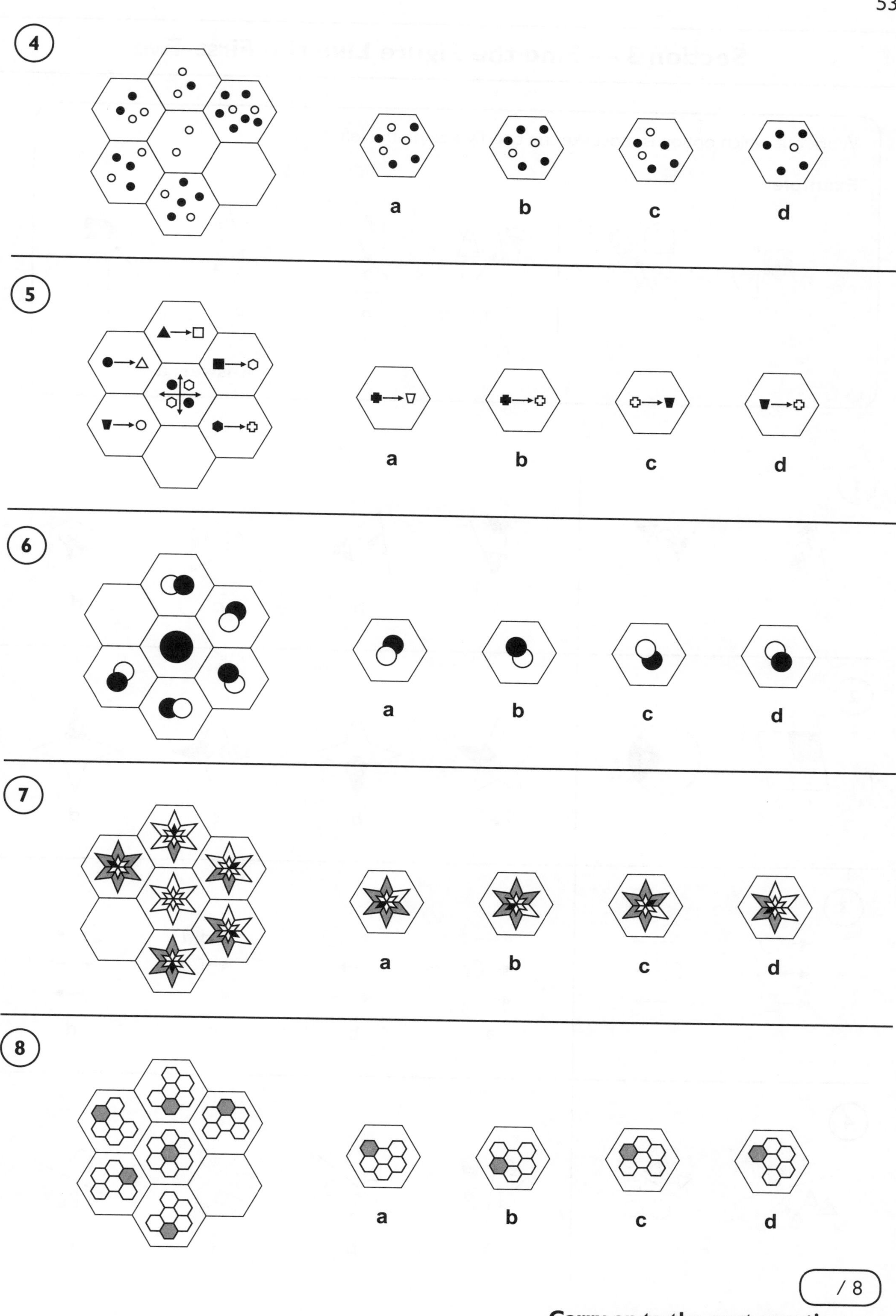

/ 8

Carry on to the next question → →

Section 3 — Find the Figure Like the First Two

Work out which option is most like the two figures on the left.

Example:

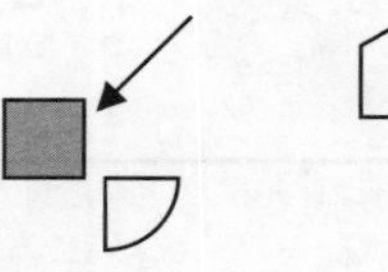
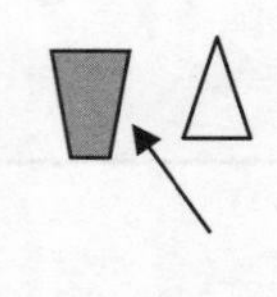
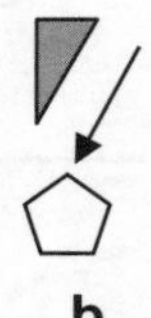

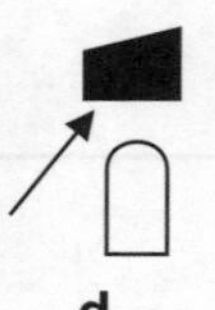

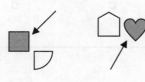

a b c d

Answer: a

(1)

a b c d

(2)

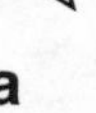

a b c d

(3)

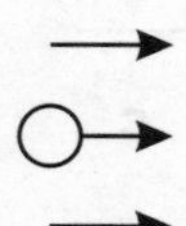
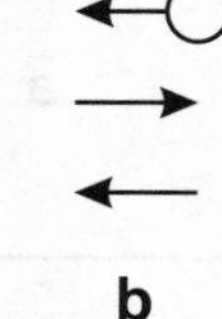
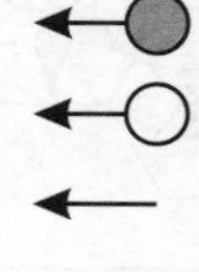
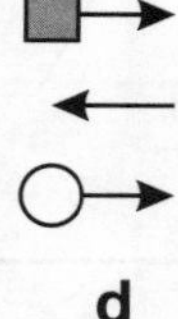

a b c d

(4)

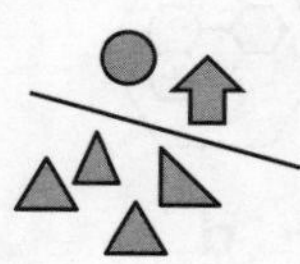
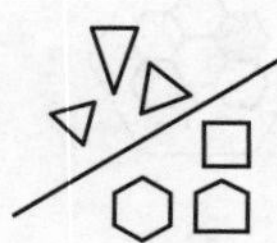
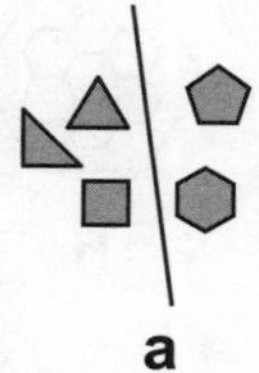
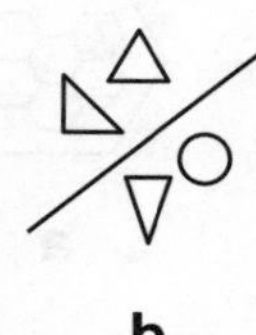
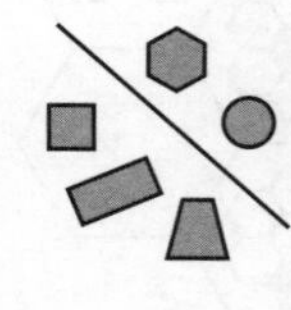
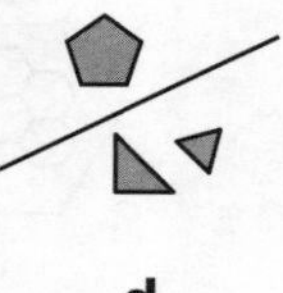

a b c d

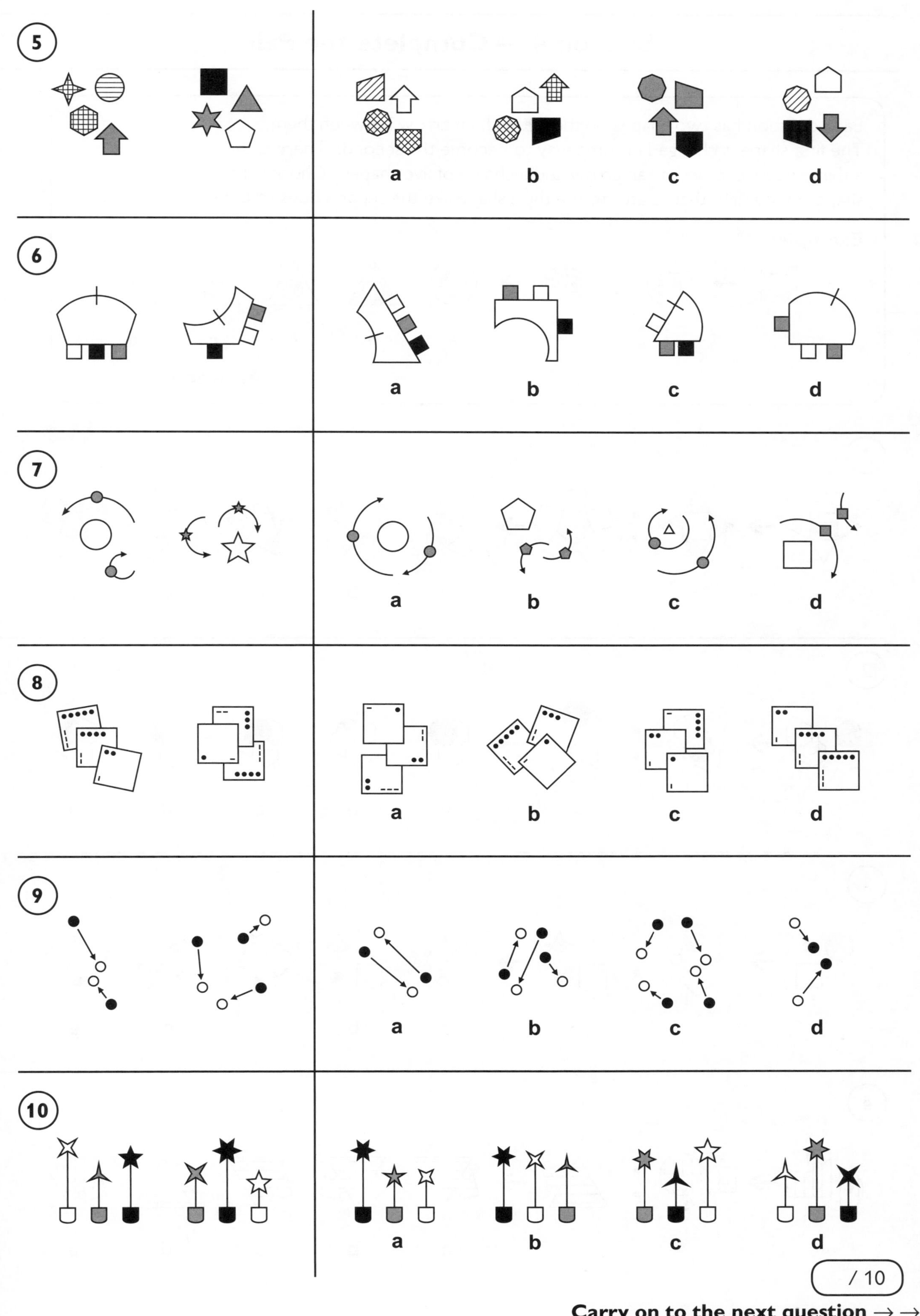

/ 10

Carry on to the next question → →

Section 4 — Complete the Pair

Each question has two shapes on the left with an arrow between them. The first shape is changed in some way to become the second. There is then a third shape followed by an arrow and a choice of five shapes. Choose the shape on the right that relates to the third shape like the second does to the first.

Example:

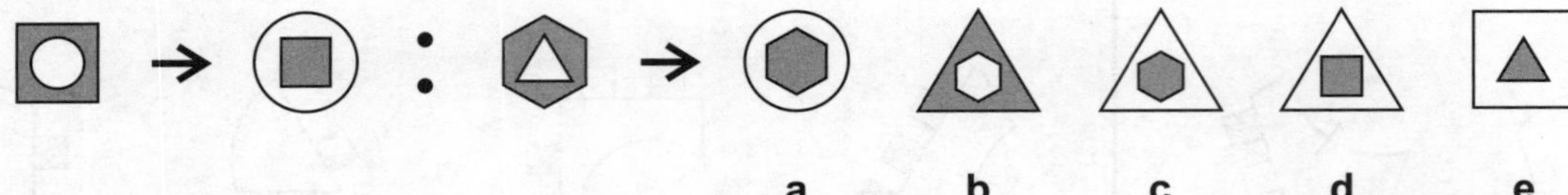

Answer: c

1

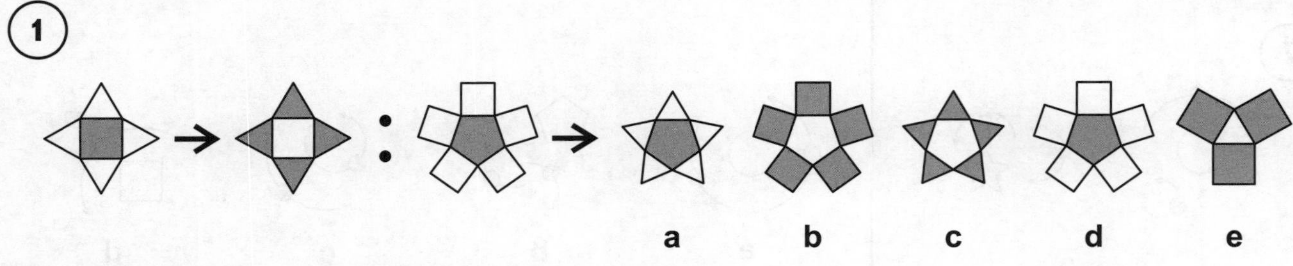

2

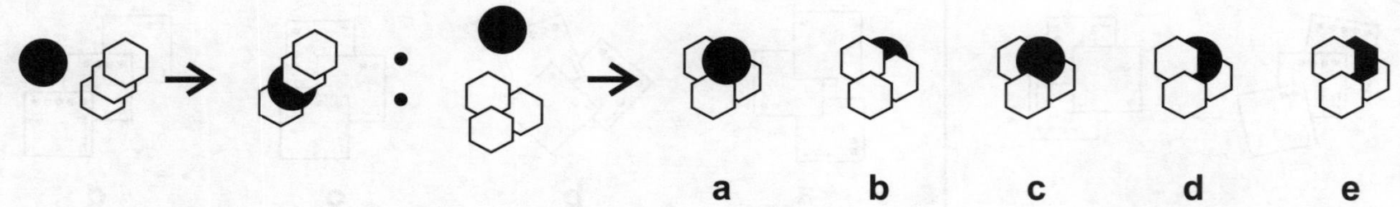

3

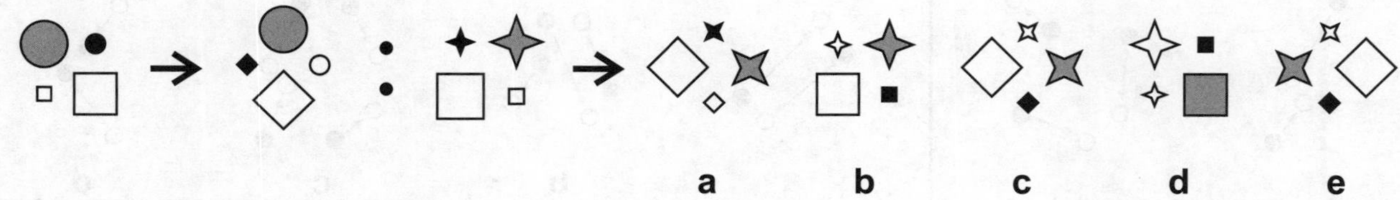

4

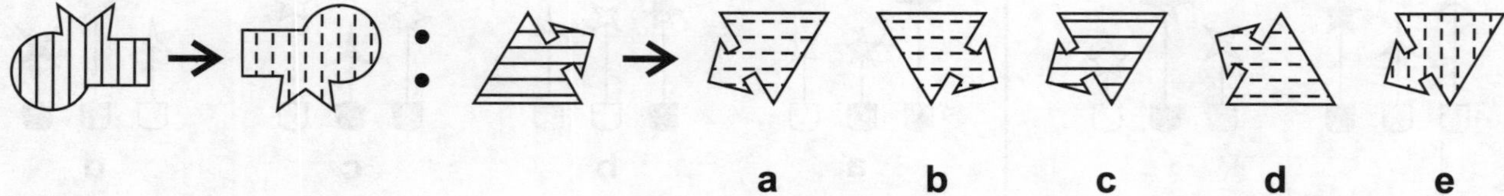

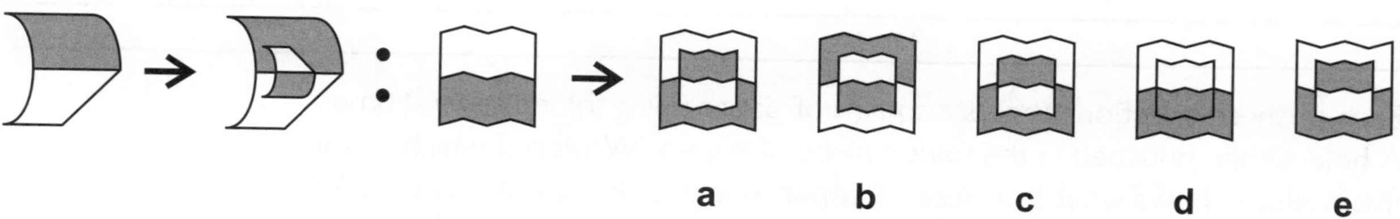

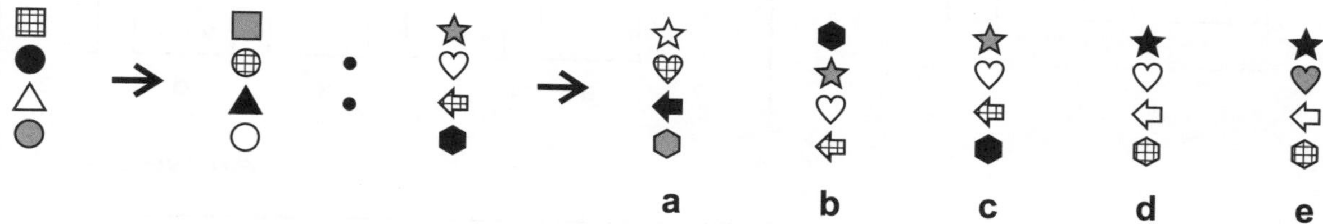

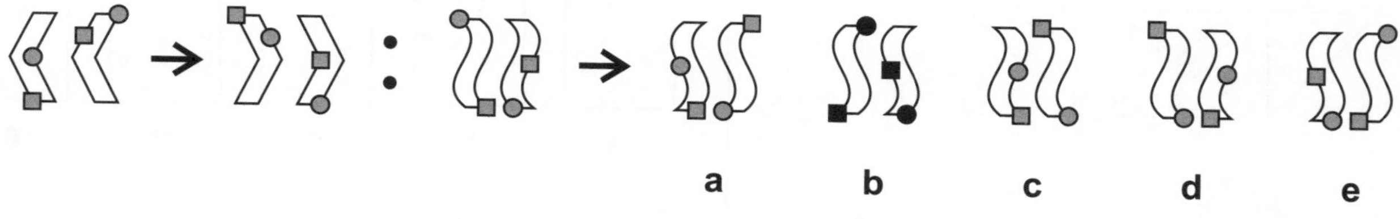

8

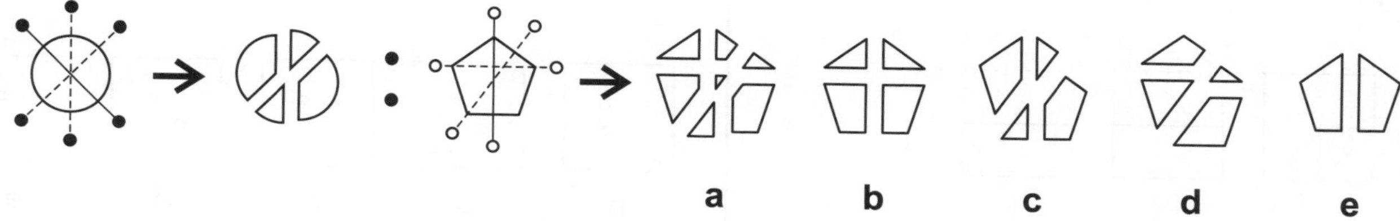

9

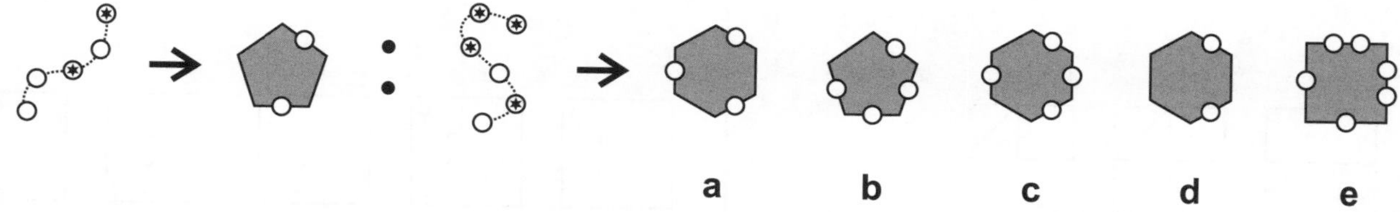

10

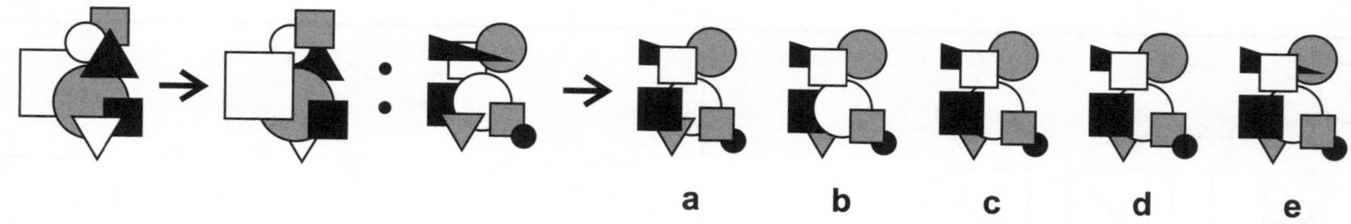

/ 10

Carry on to the next question → →

Section 5 — Fold and Punch

Each of these questions shows a square of paper being folded several times. A hole is then punched in the folded piece of paper. Work out which of the five options shows what the piece of paper would look like if it was unfolded.

Example:

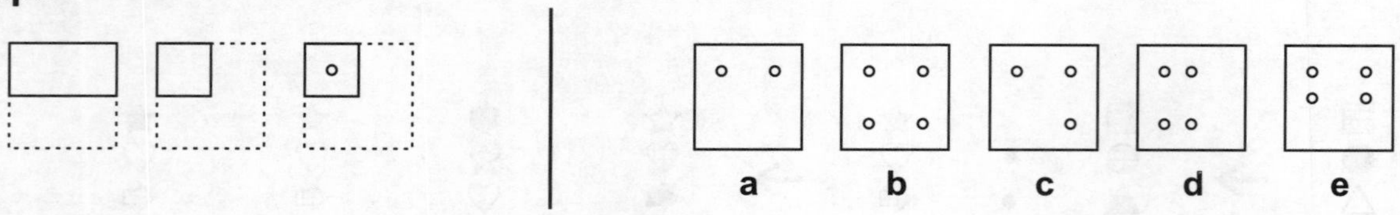

a b c d e

Answer: b

1

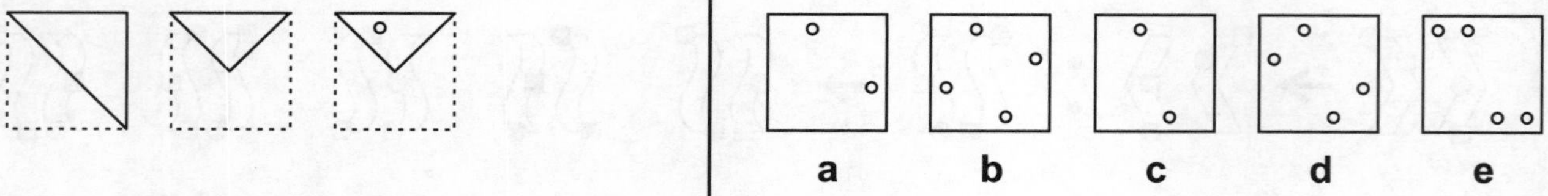

a b c d e

2

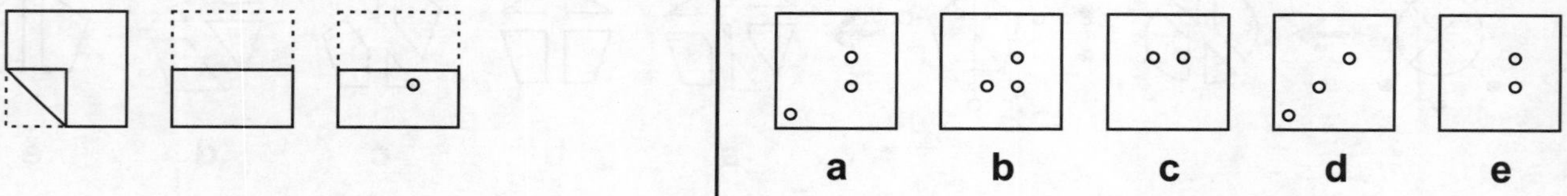

a b c d e

3

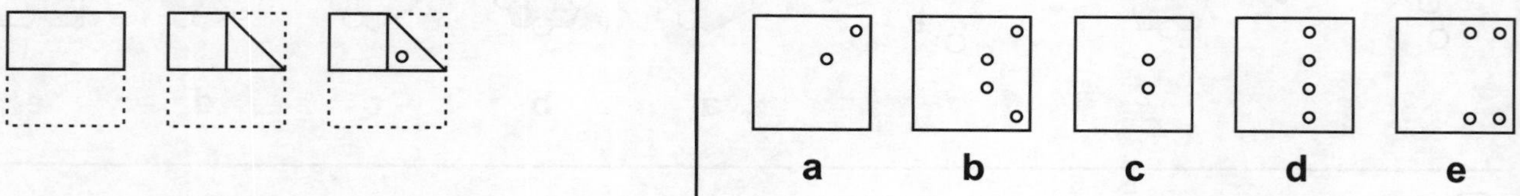

a b c d e

4

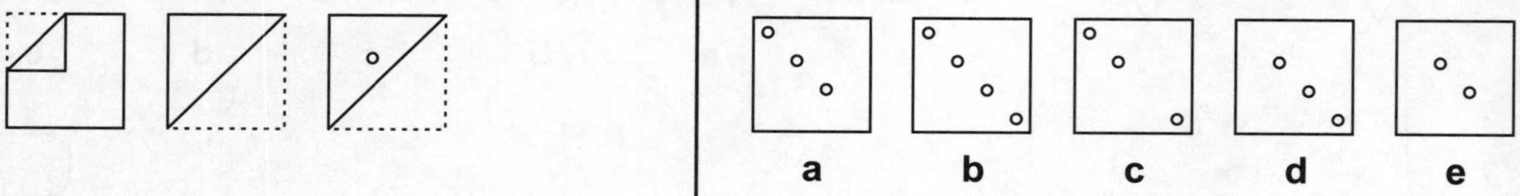

a b c d e

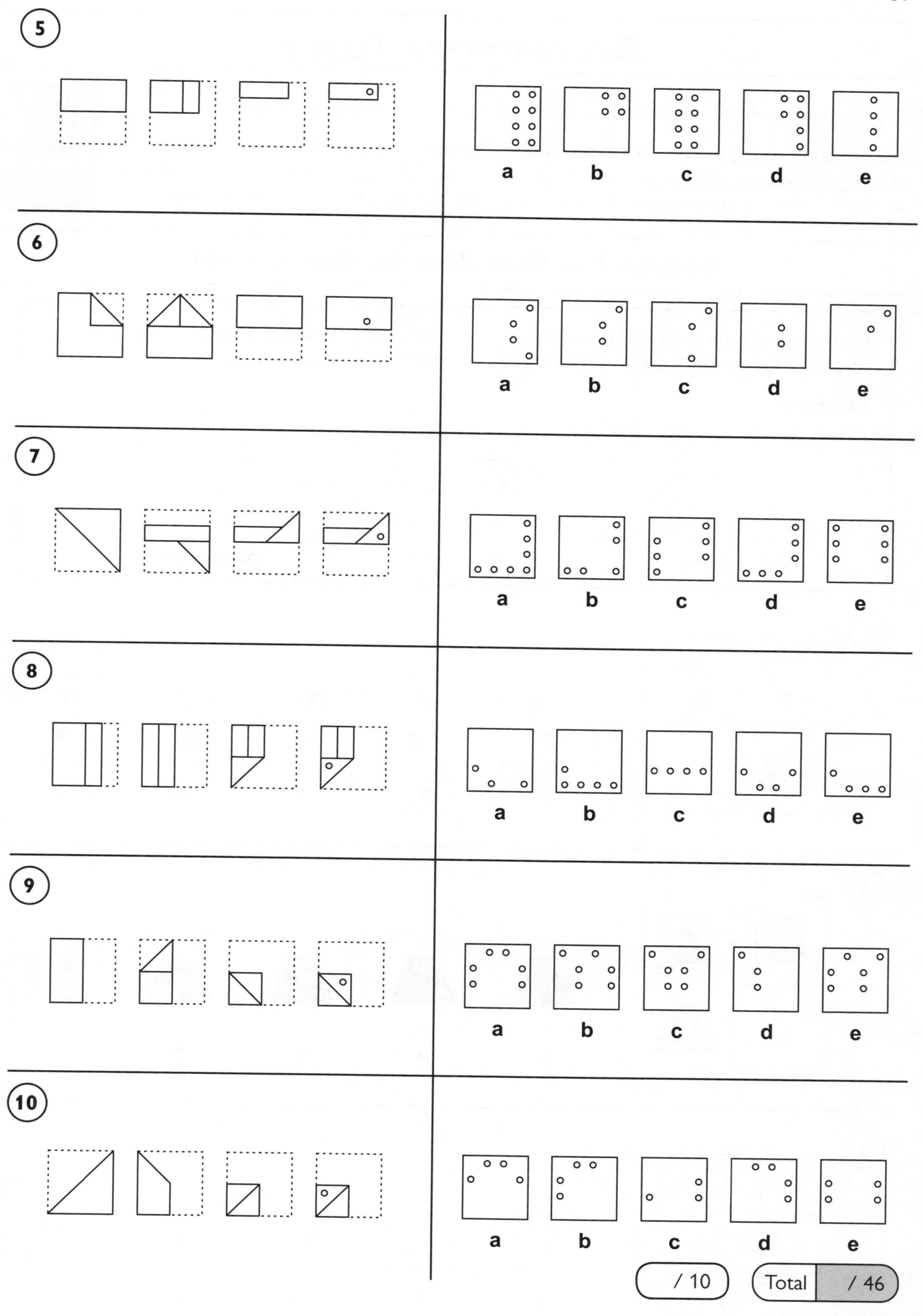

/ 10

Total / 46

End of Test

Assessment Test 5

Allow 30 minutes to do this test and work as quickly and as carefully as you can.

You can print **multiple-choice answer sheets** for these questions from our website — go to cgpbooks.co.uk/11plus/answer-sheets or scan the QR code on the right. If you'd prefer to answer them in standard write-in format, just circle the letter underneath your answer.

Section 1 — Complete the Square Grid

On the left of each question below is a big square with one small empty square. Find which of the five squares on the right should replace the empty square.

Example:

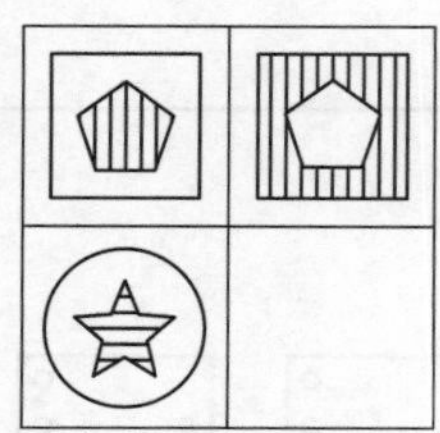

 a
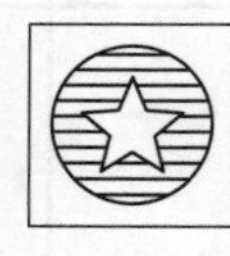 b
 c
 d
 e

Answer: b

1

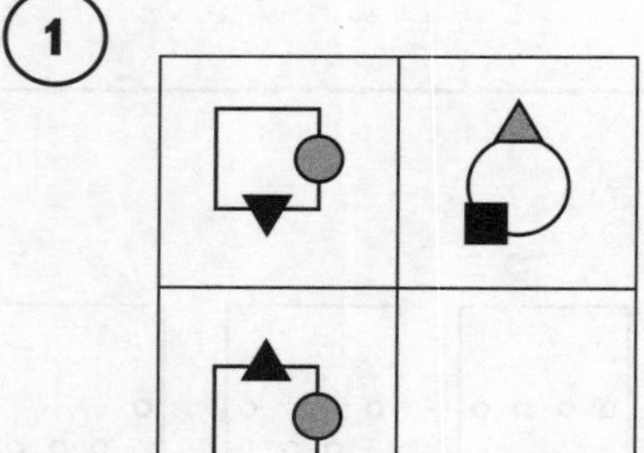

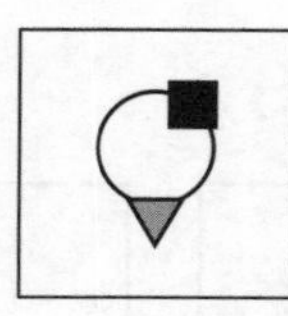 a
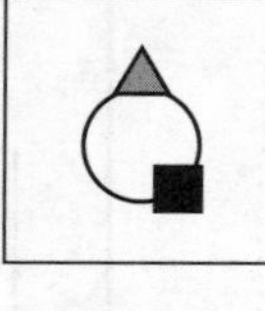 b
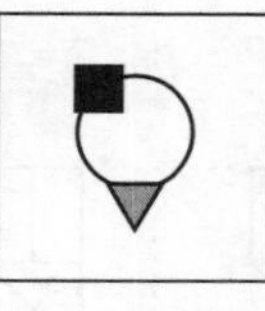 c
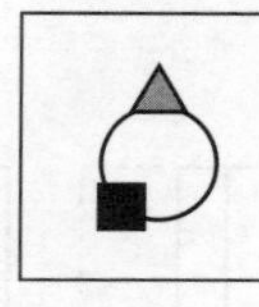 d
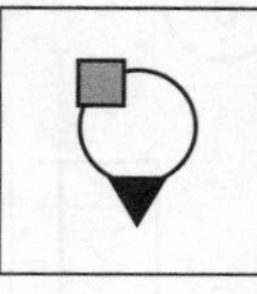 e

2

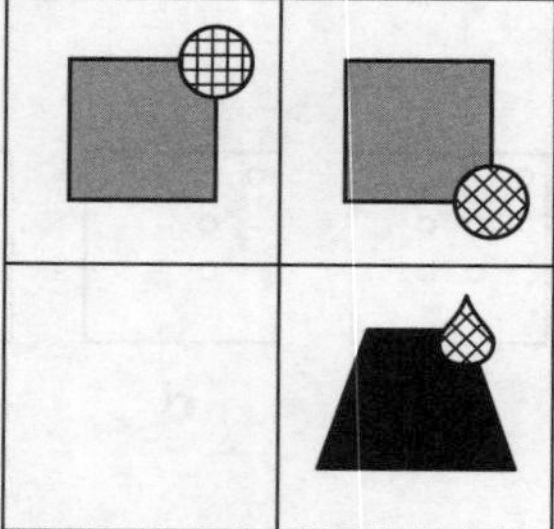

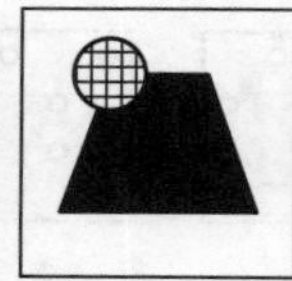 a
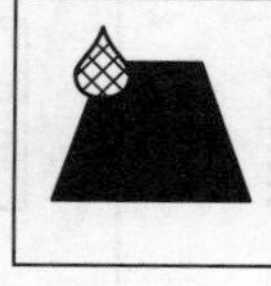 b
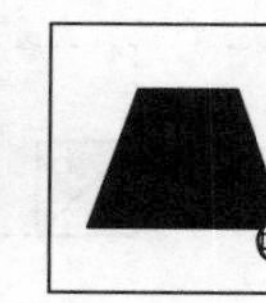
 c
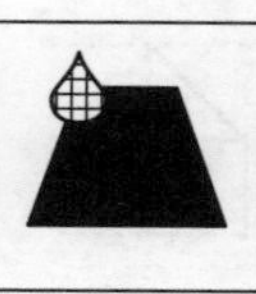 d
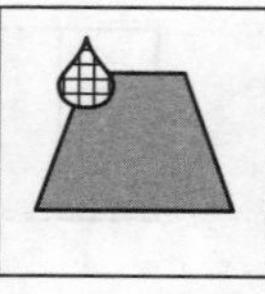 e

3

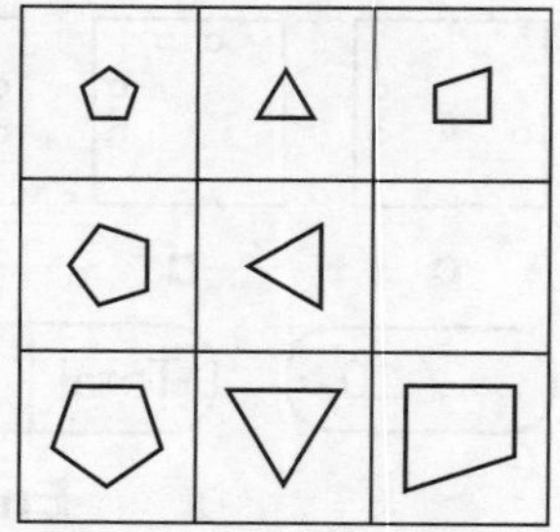

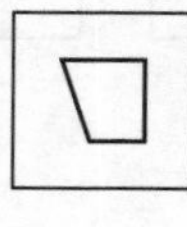 a
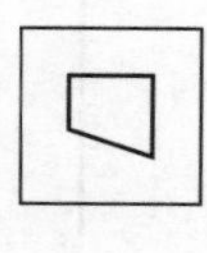 b
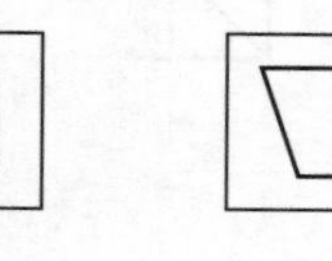
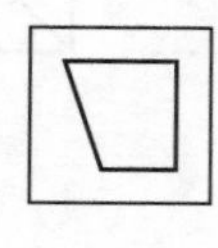 c
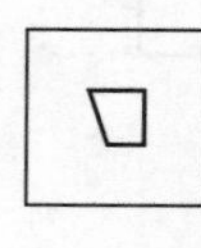 d
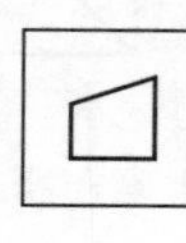 e

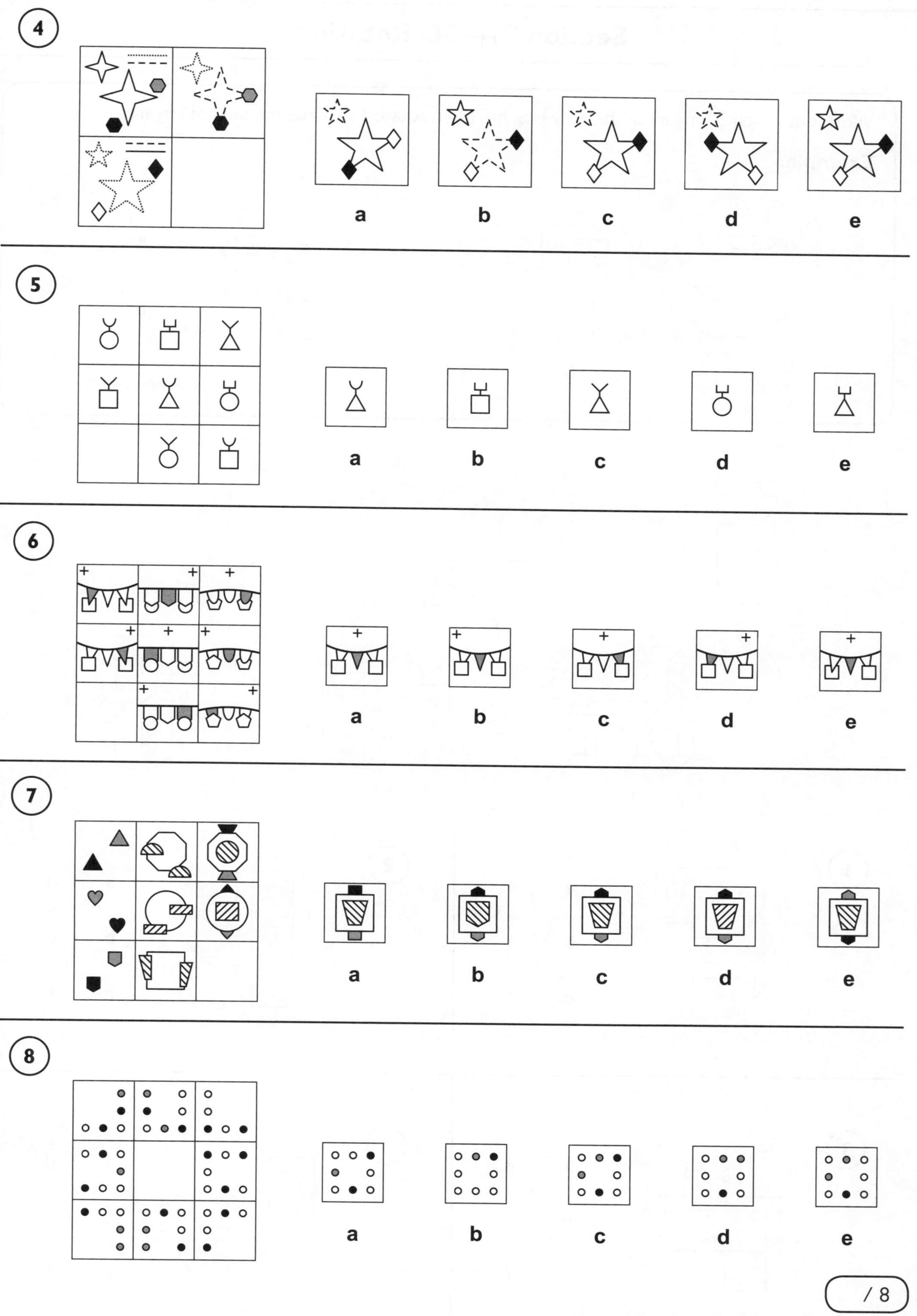

/ 8

Carry on to the next question → →

Section 2 — 3D Rotation

Work out which 3D figure in the grey box has been rotated to make the new 3D figure.

Example:

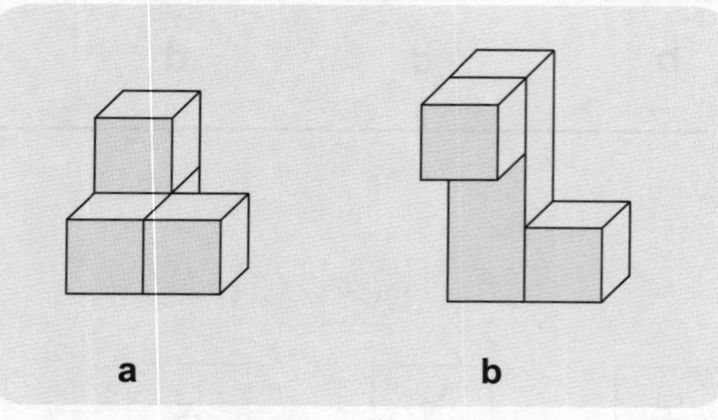

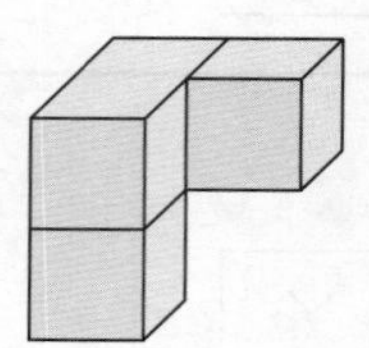

a

b

Answer: a

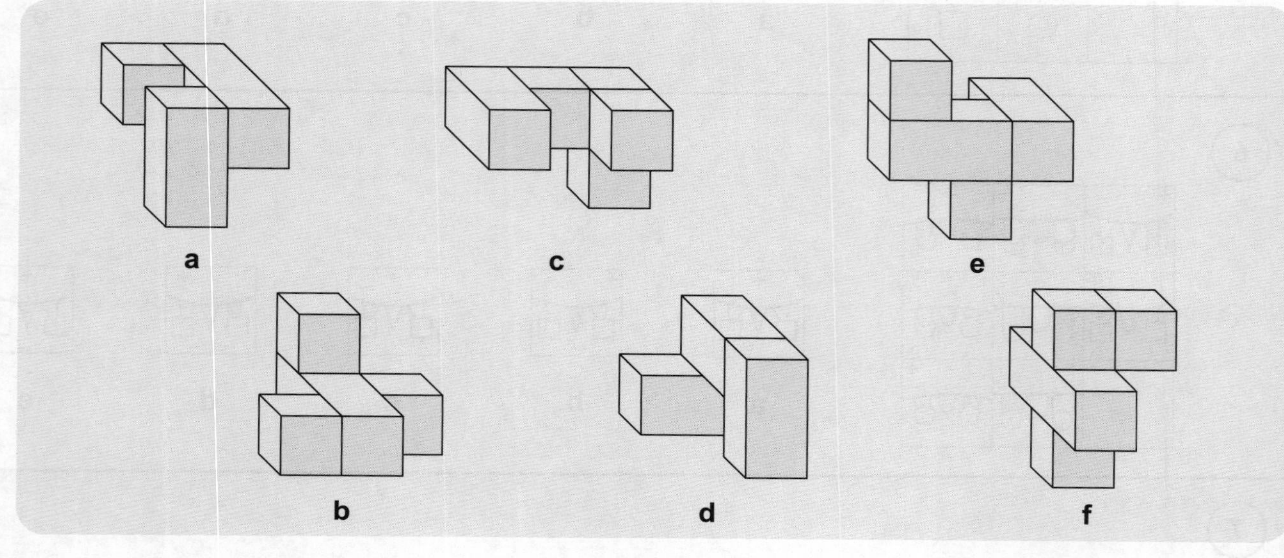

(1)

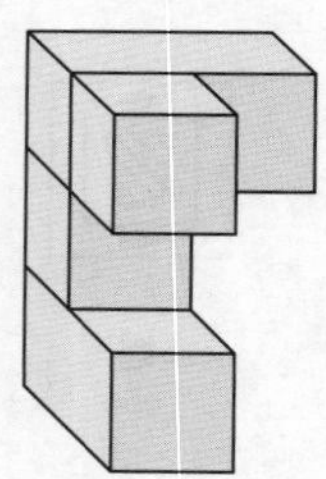

a d

b e

c f

(2)

a d

b e

c f

(3)

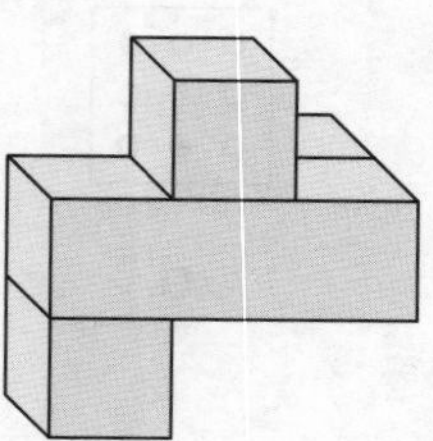

a d

b e

c f

(4)

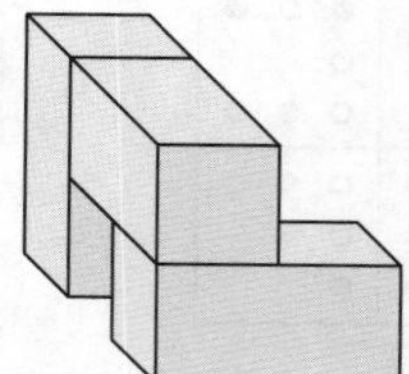

a d

b e

c f

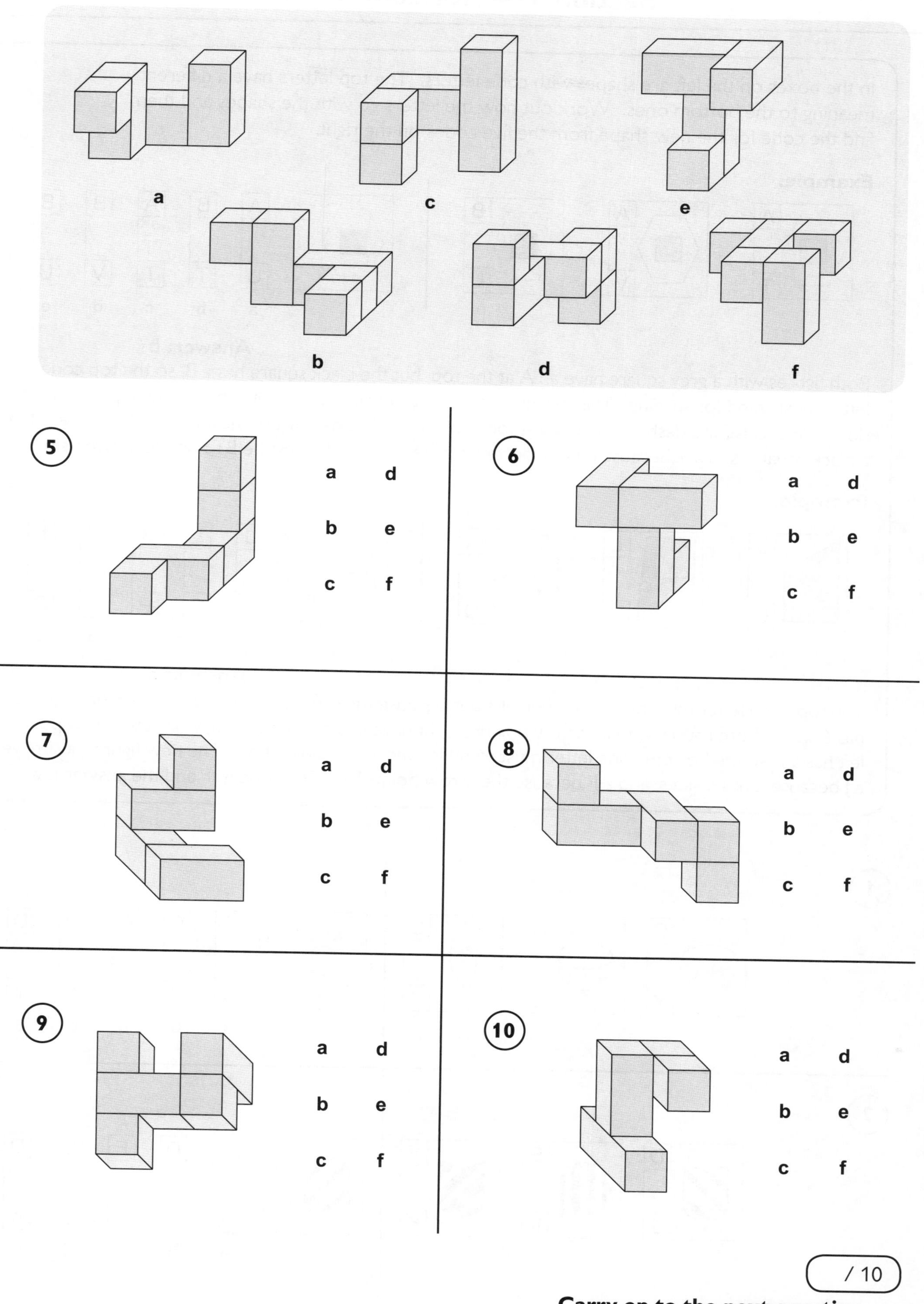

/ 10

Carry on to the next question → →

Section 3 — Horizontal Code

In the boxes on the left are shapes with code letters. The top letters have a different meaning to the bottom ones. Work out how the letters go with the shapes and then find the code for the new shape from the five codes on the right.

Example:

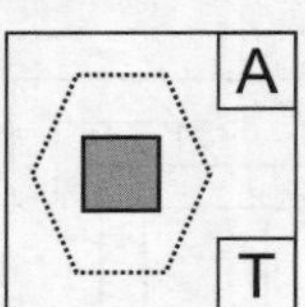
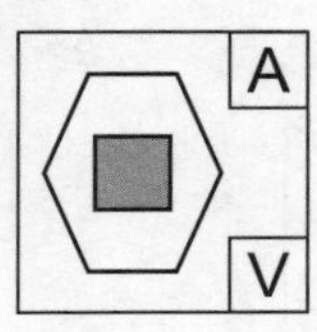
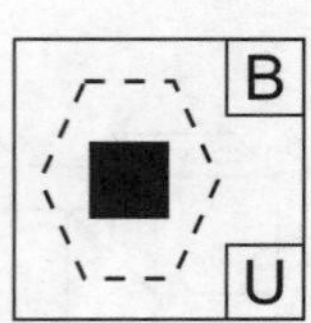
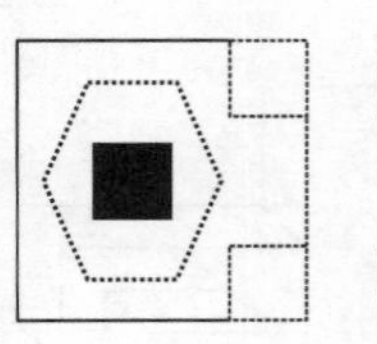
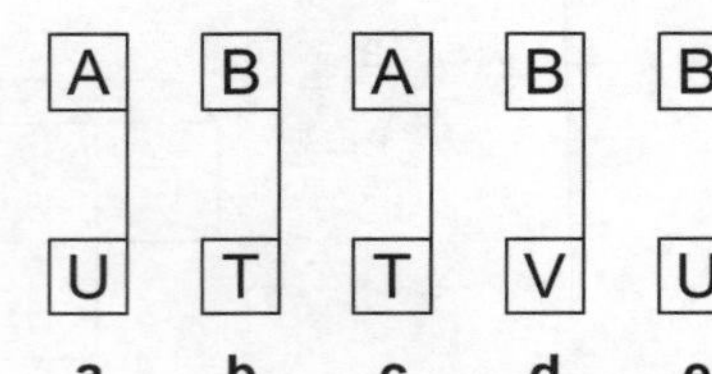

Answer: b

Both figures with a grey square have an A at the top, but the black square has a B, so the top code letter must stand for shading. This means that the bottom code letter must be for line type. T is for a dotted line, U is for a dashed line and V is for a solid line. The new figure must have a B because it has a black square, and a T because it has a dotted outline. The code must be BT and the answer is b.

Example:

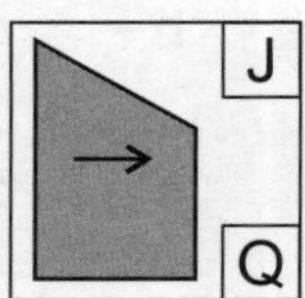
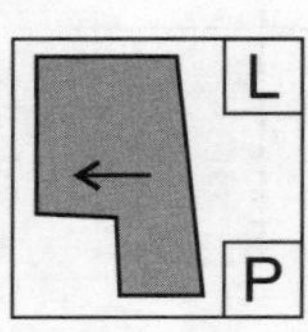
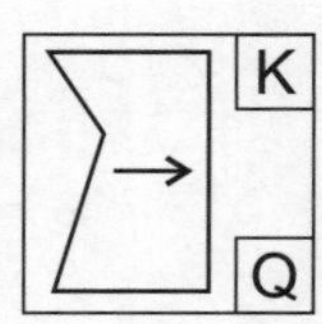
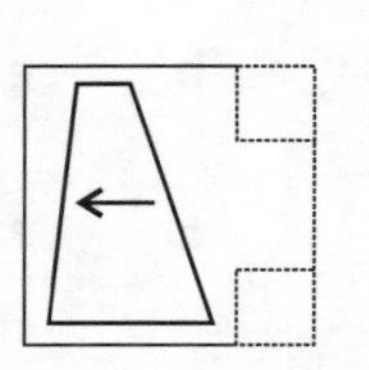
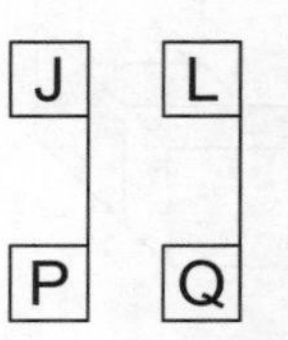
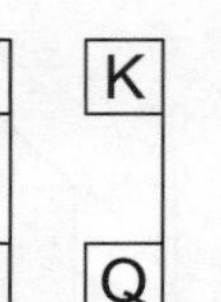

Answer: a

The top code letter must be for number of sides because the J shape has 4 sides, K has 5 sides and L has 6 sides. Both figures with an arrow pointing right have a Q at the bottom, while the arrow pointing left has a P, so the bottom code letter must stand for the arrow's direction. The new figure must have a J because it has 4 sides, and a P because the arrow points left. The code is JP and the answer is a.

1

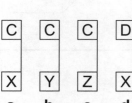

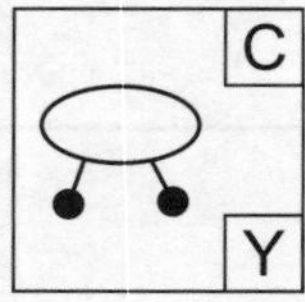
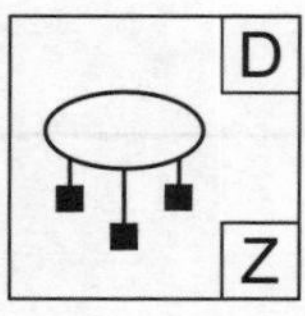
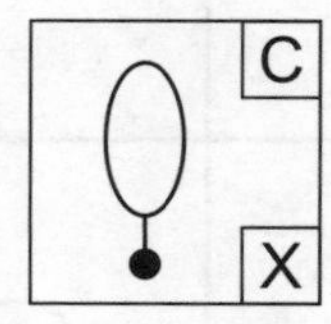
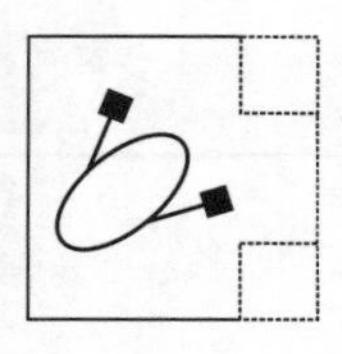
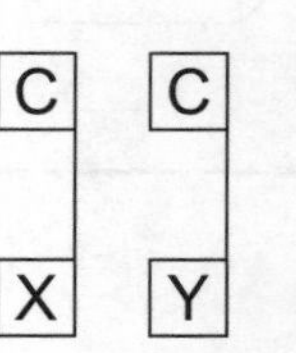
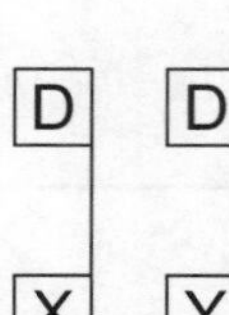

2

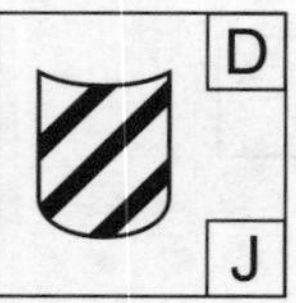

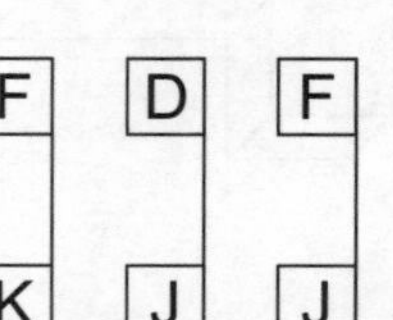
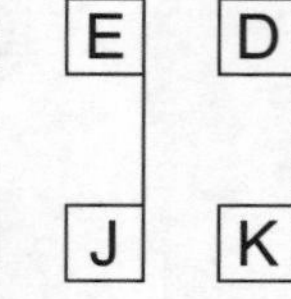

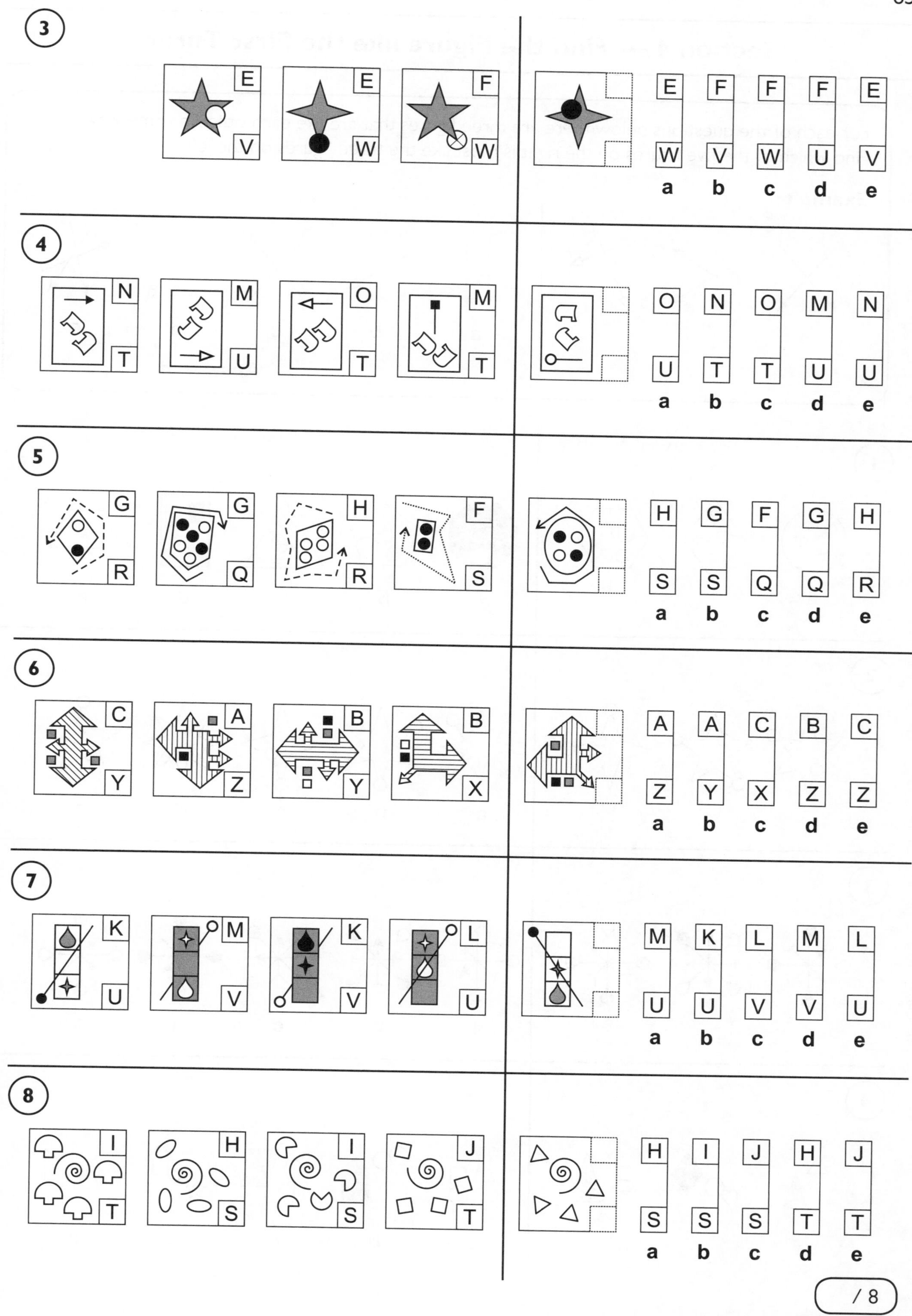

/ 8

Carry on to the next question → →

Section 4 — Find the Figure like the First Three

For each of the questions below there are three figures that are like each other in some way. Find which of the five figures on the right is most like the three figures on the left.

Example:

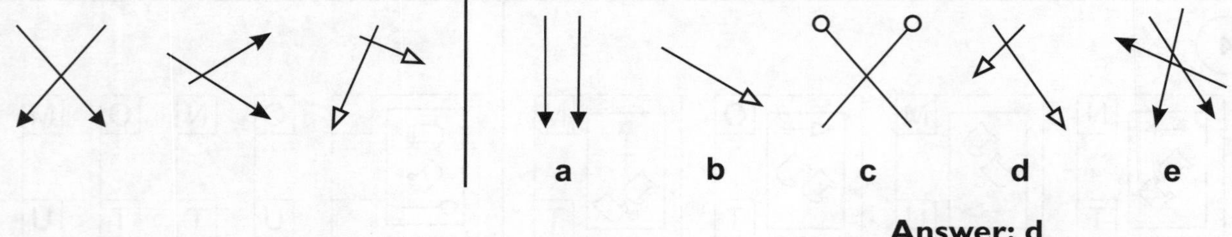

a b c d e

Answer: d

(1)

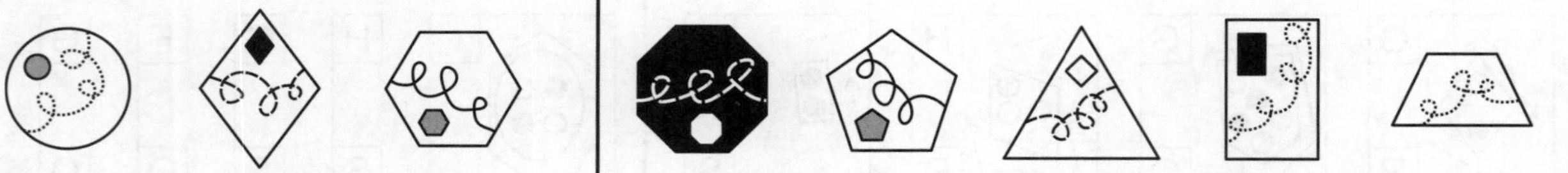

a b c d e

(2)

a b c d e

(3)

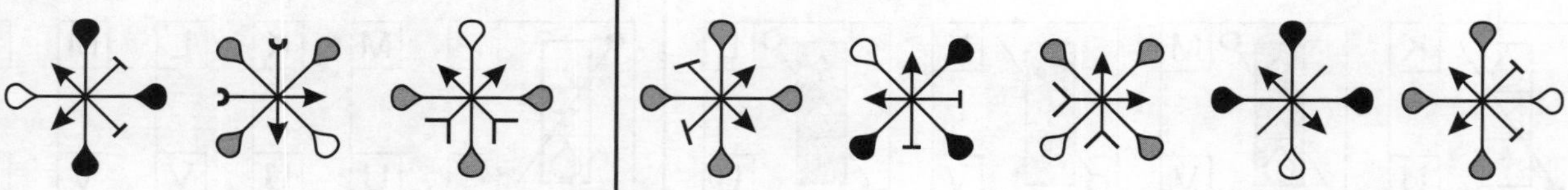

a b c d e

(4)

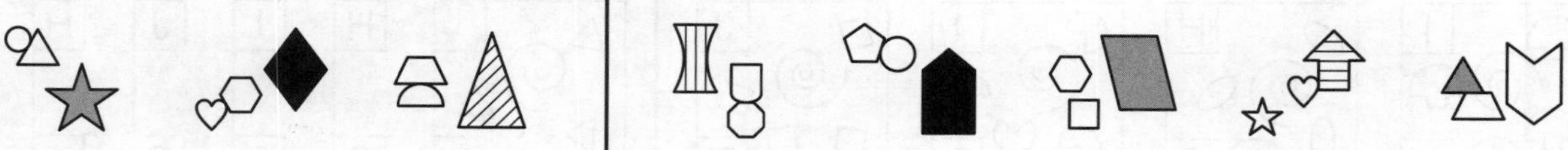

a b c d e

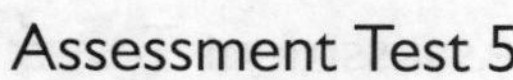

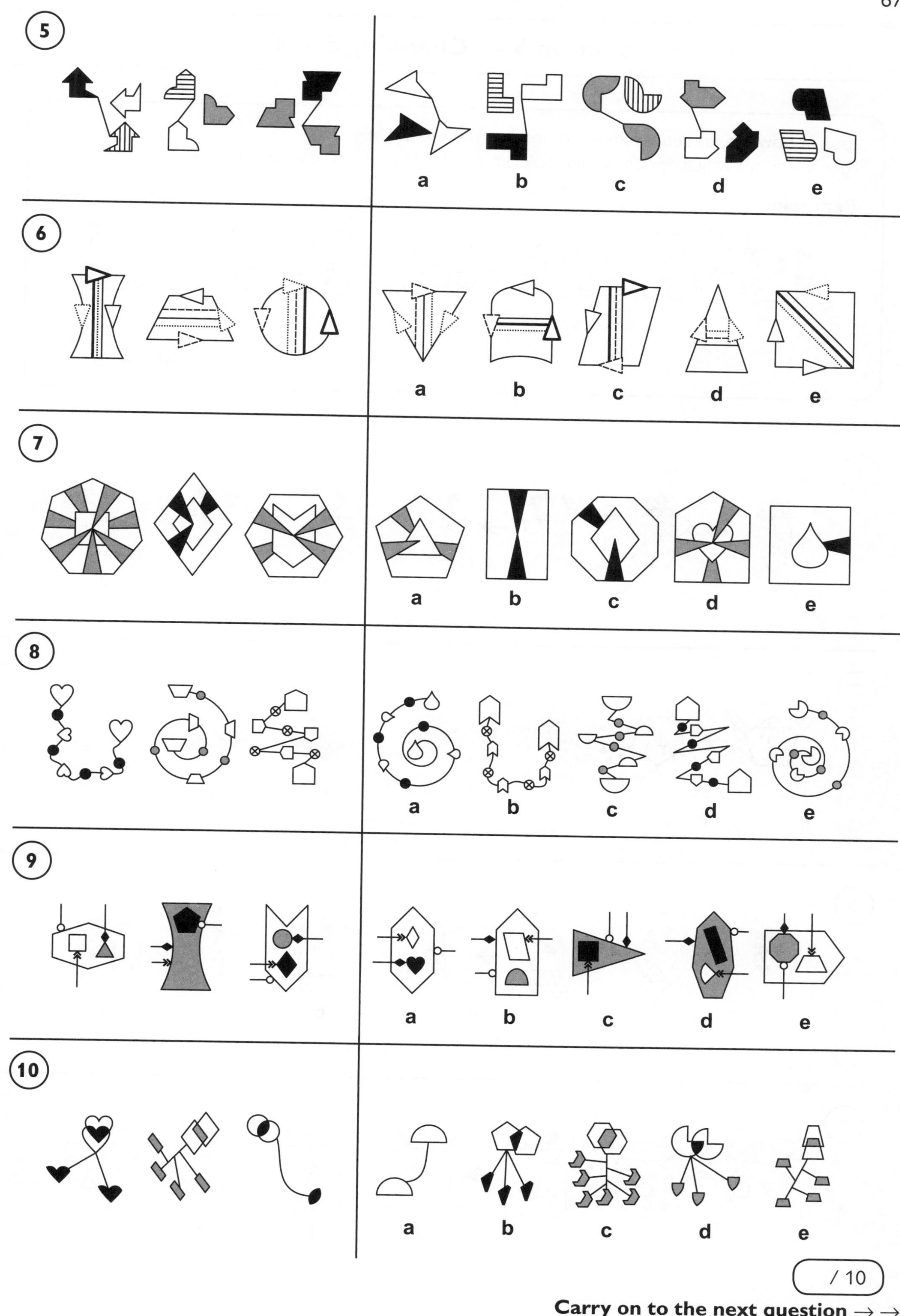

/ 10

Carry on to the next question → →

Section 5 — Changing Bugs

Look at how the first bug changes to become the second bug.
Then work out which option would look like the third bug if you changed it in the same way.

Example:

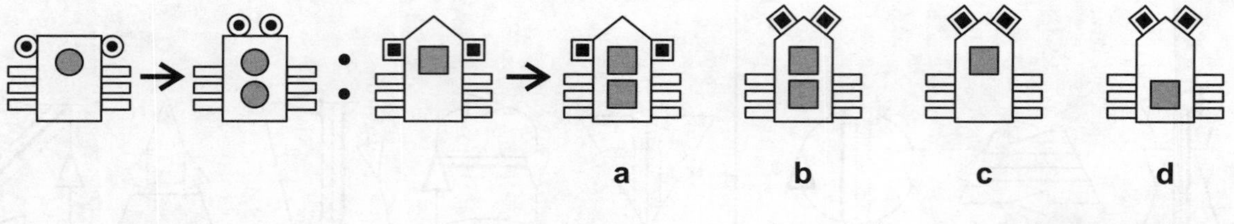

Answer: b

1

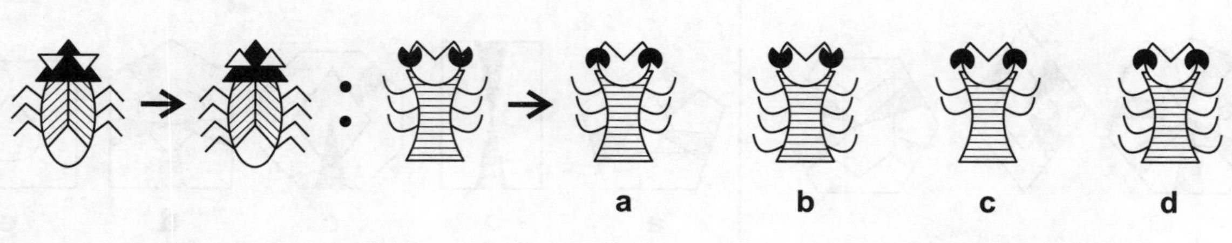

2

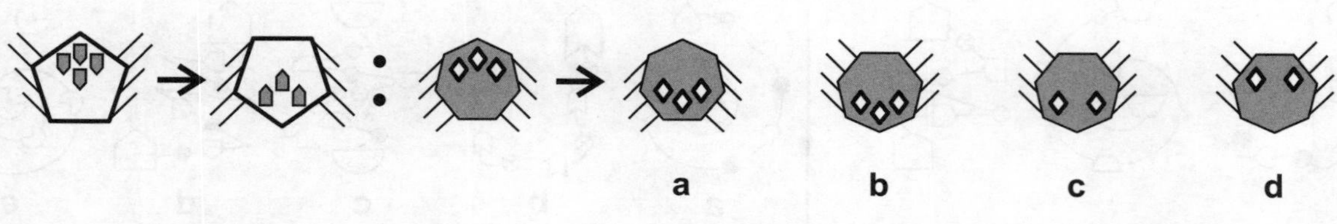

3

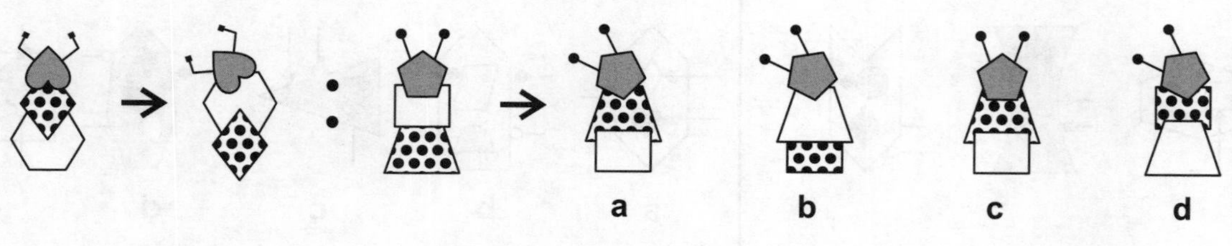

4

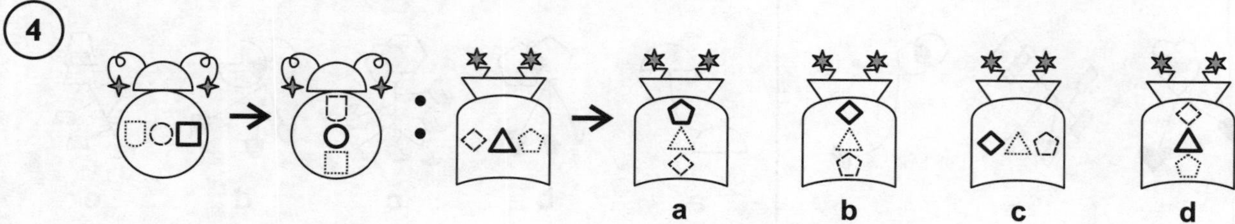

5

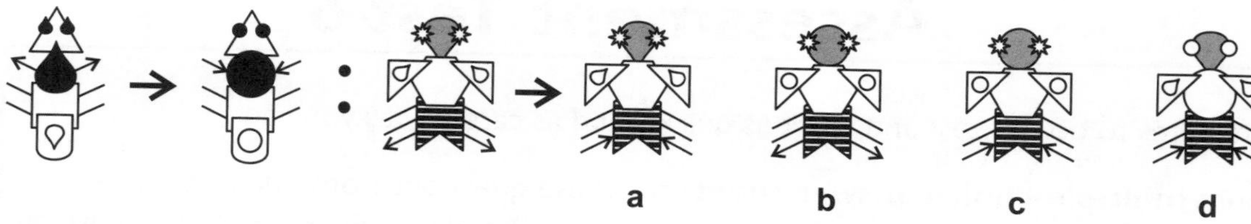

a b c d

6

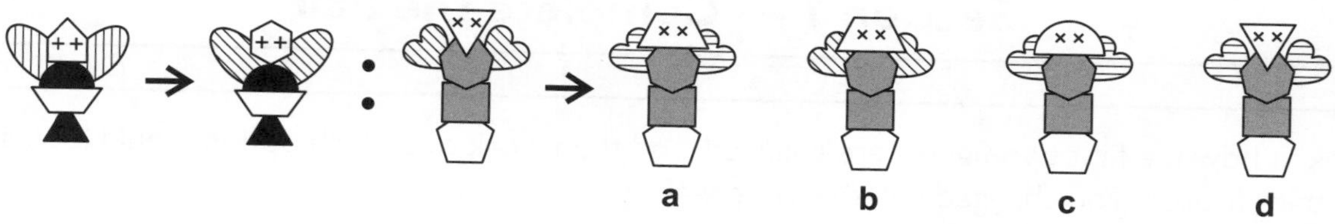

a b c d

7

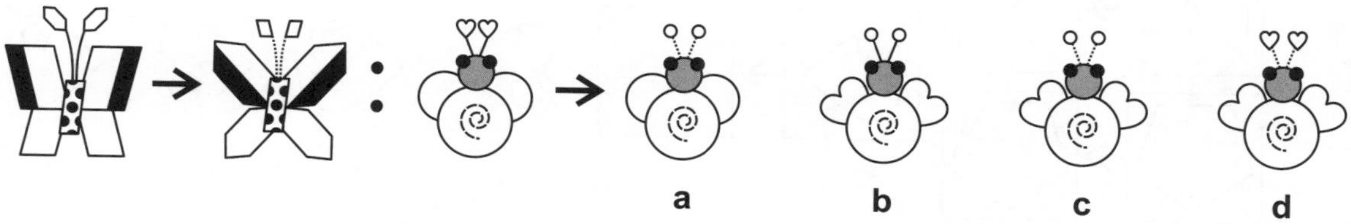

a b c d

8

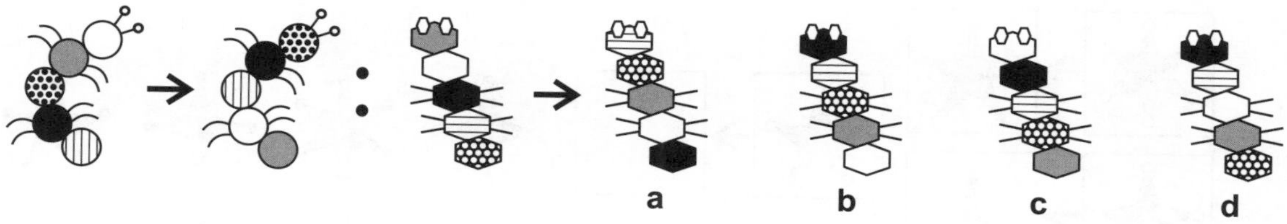

a b c d

9

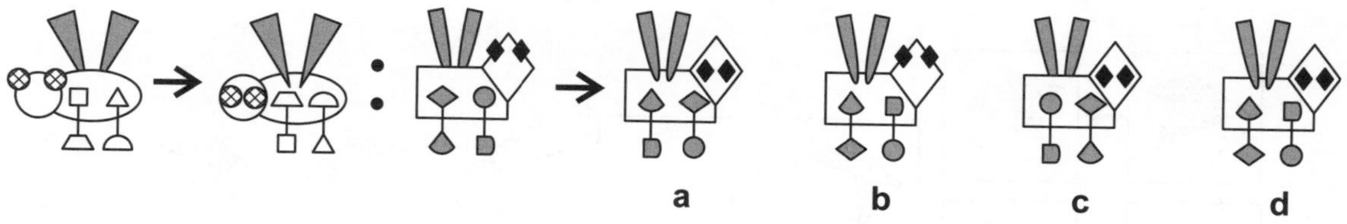

a b c d

10

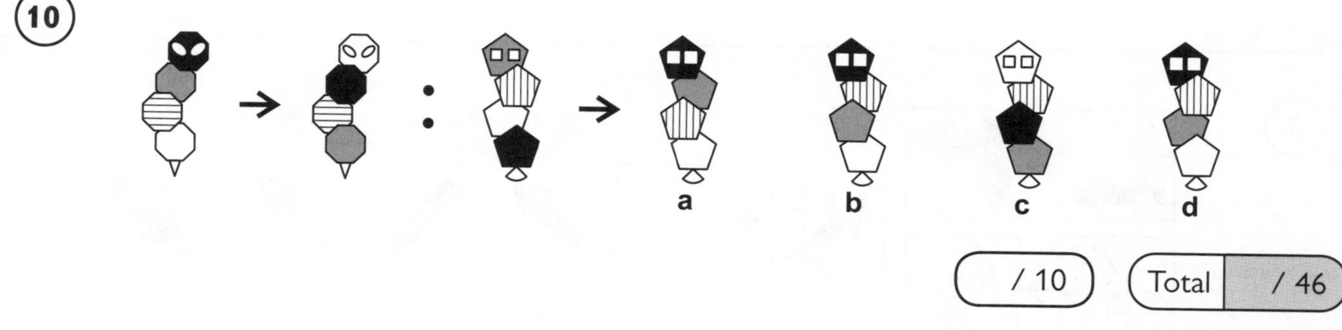

/ 10

Total / 46

End of Test

Assessment Test 6

Allow 30 minutes to do this test and work as quickly and as carefully as you can.

You can print **multiple-choice answer sheets** for these questions from our website — go to cgpbooks.co.uk/11plus/answer-sheets or scan the QR code on the right. If you'd prefer to answer them in standard write-in format, just circle the letter underneath your answer.

Section 1 — Complete the Pair

Look at how the first two figures are changed, and then work out which option would look like the third figure if you changed it in the same way.

Example:

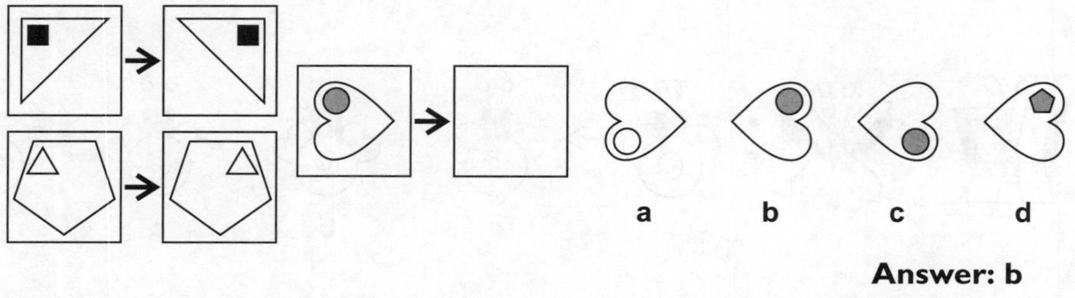

Answer: b

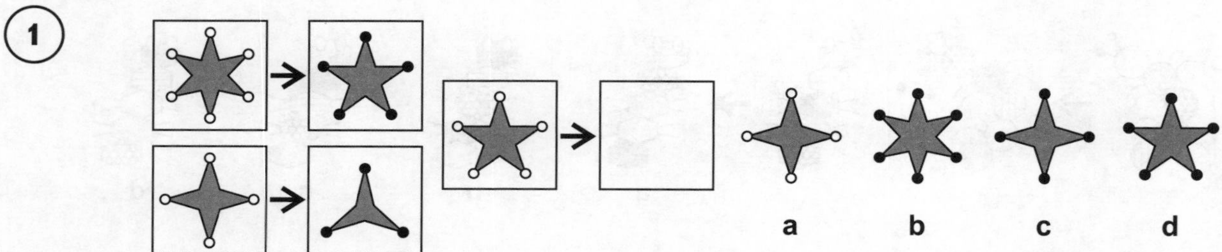

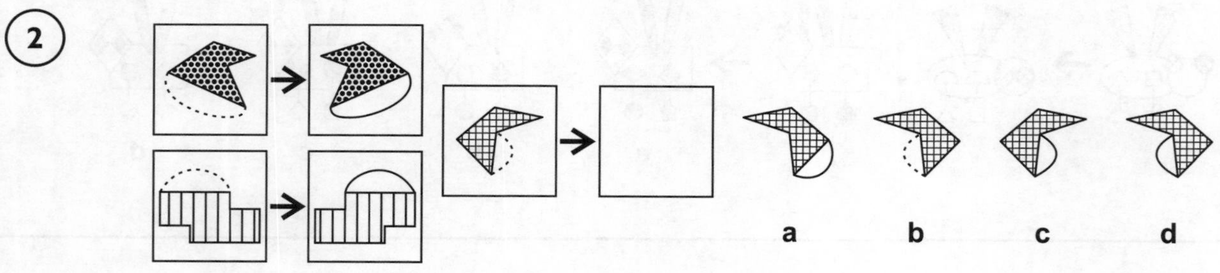

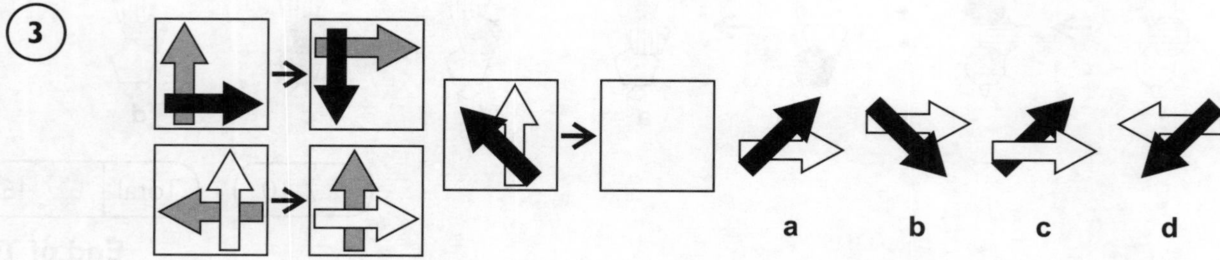

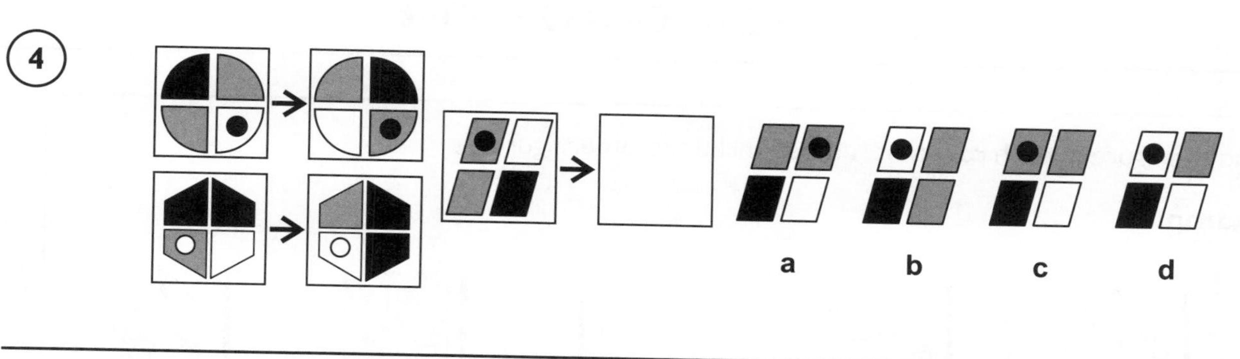

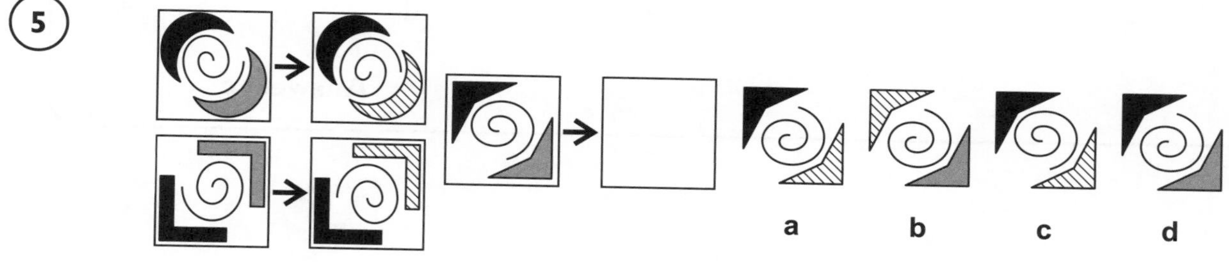

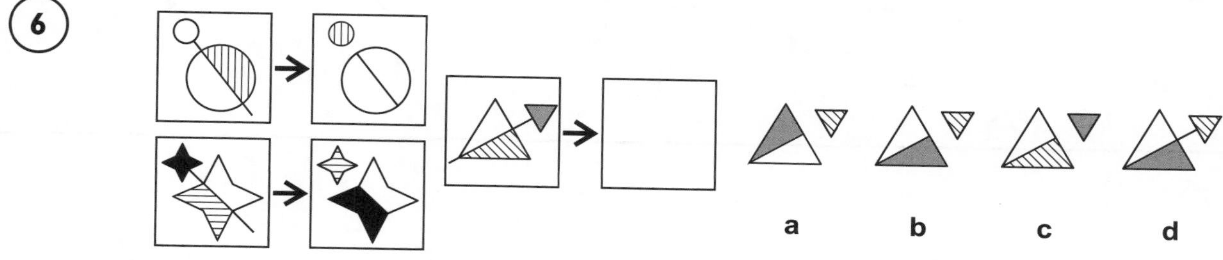

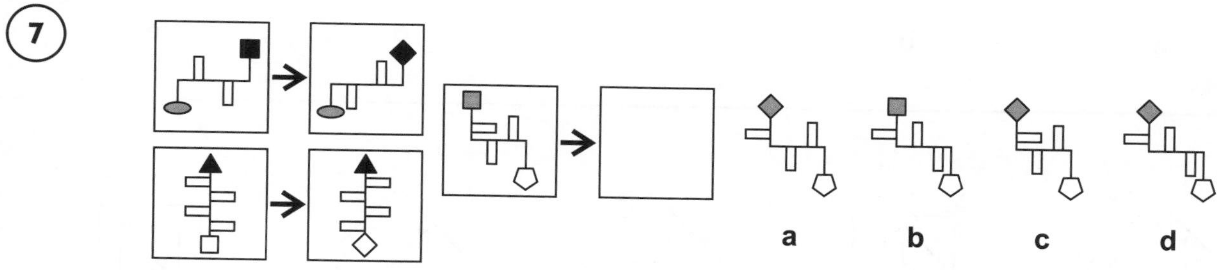

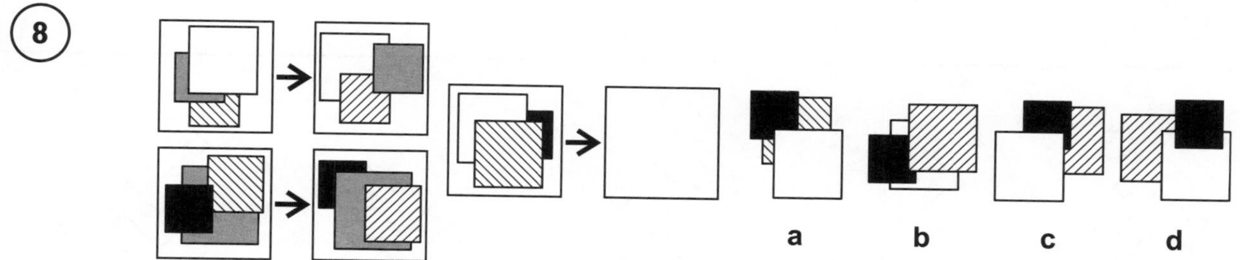

/ 8

Carry on to the next question → →

Section 2 — Odd One Out

Find the figure in each row that is most unlike the other figures.

Example:

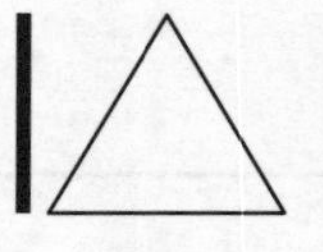
a

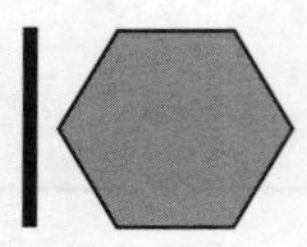
b

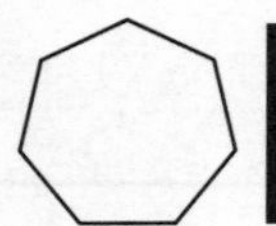
c

d

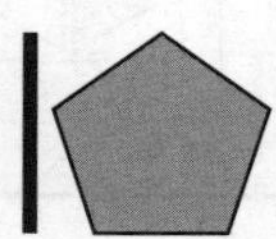
e

Answer: c

1

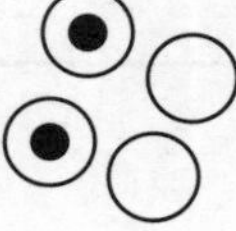
a

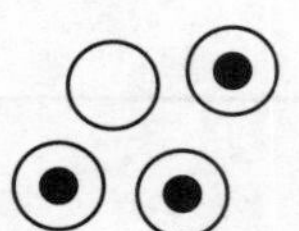
b

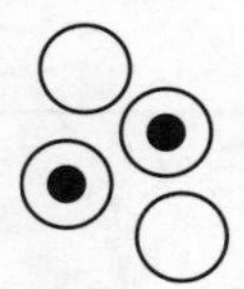
c

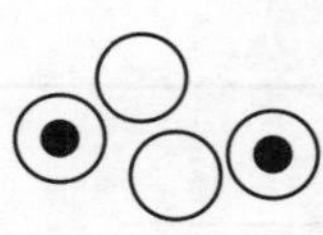
d

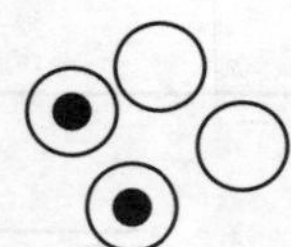
e

2

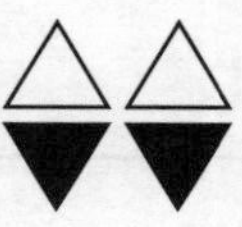
a

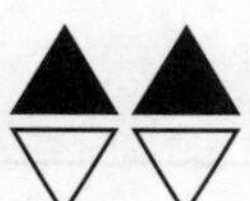
b

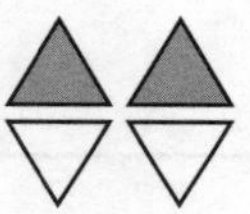
c

d

e

3

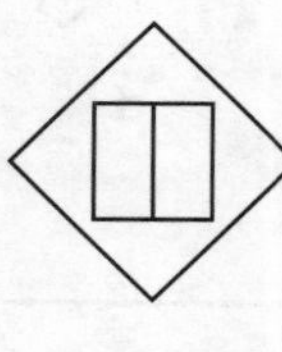
a

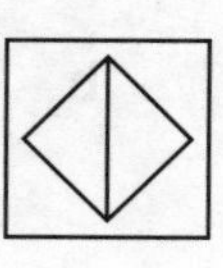
b

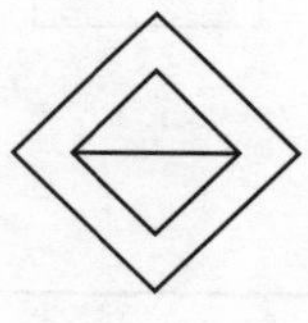
c

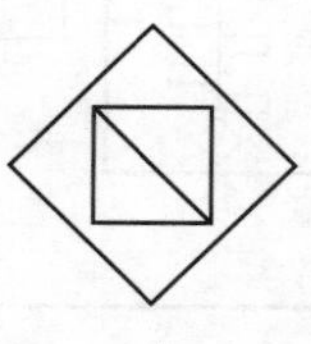
d

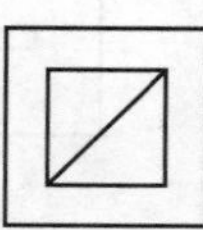
e

4

a

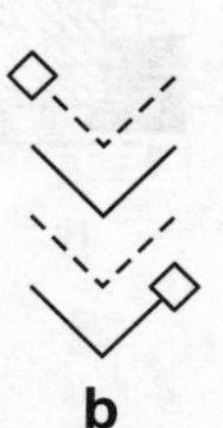
b

c

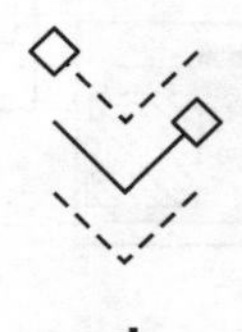
d

e

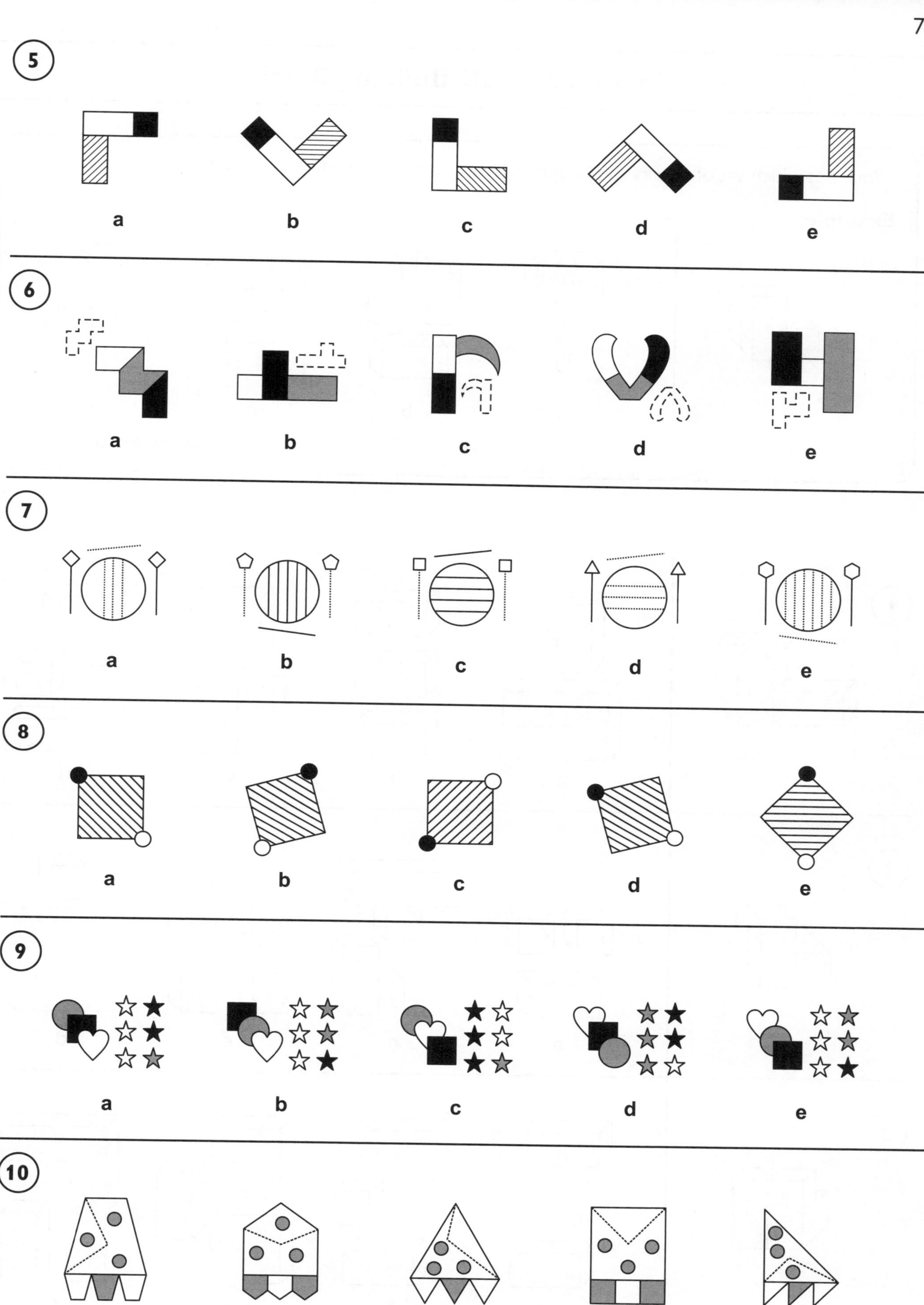

/ 10

Carry on to the next question → →

Section 3 — 3D Building Blocks

Work out which set of blocks can be put together to make the 3D figure on the left.

Example:

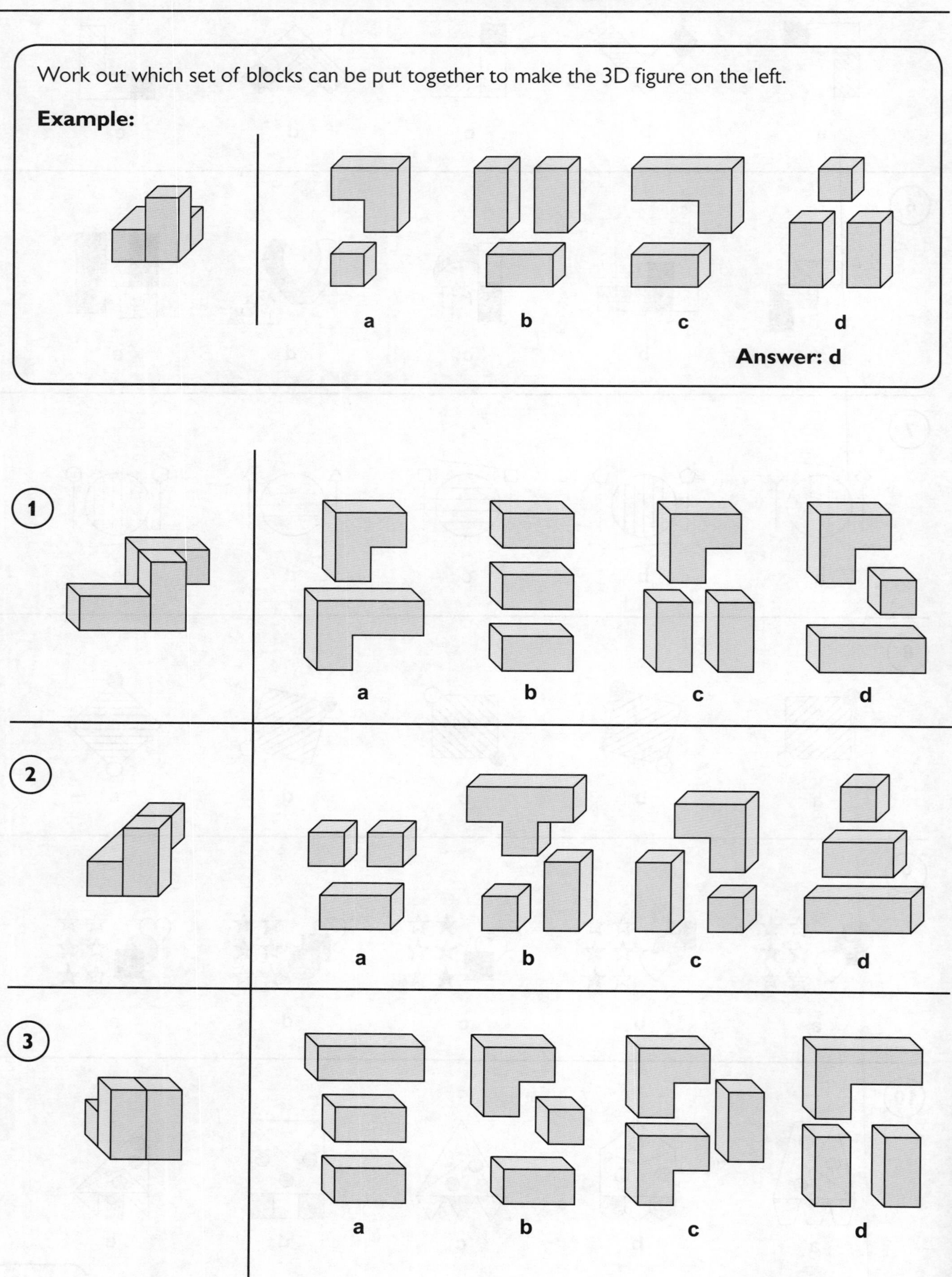

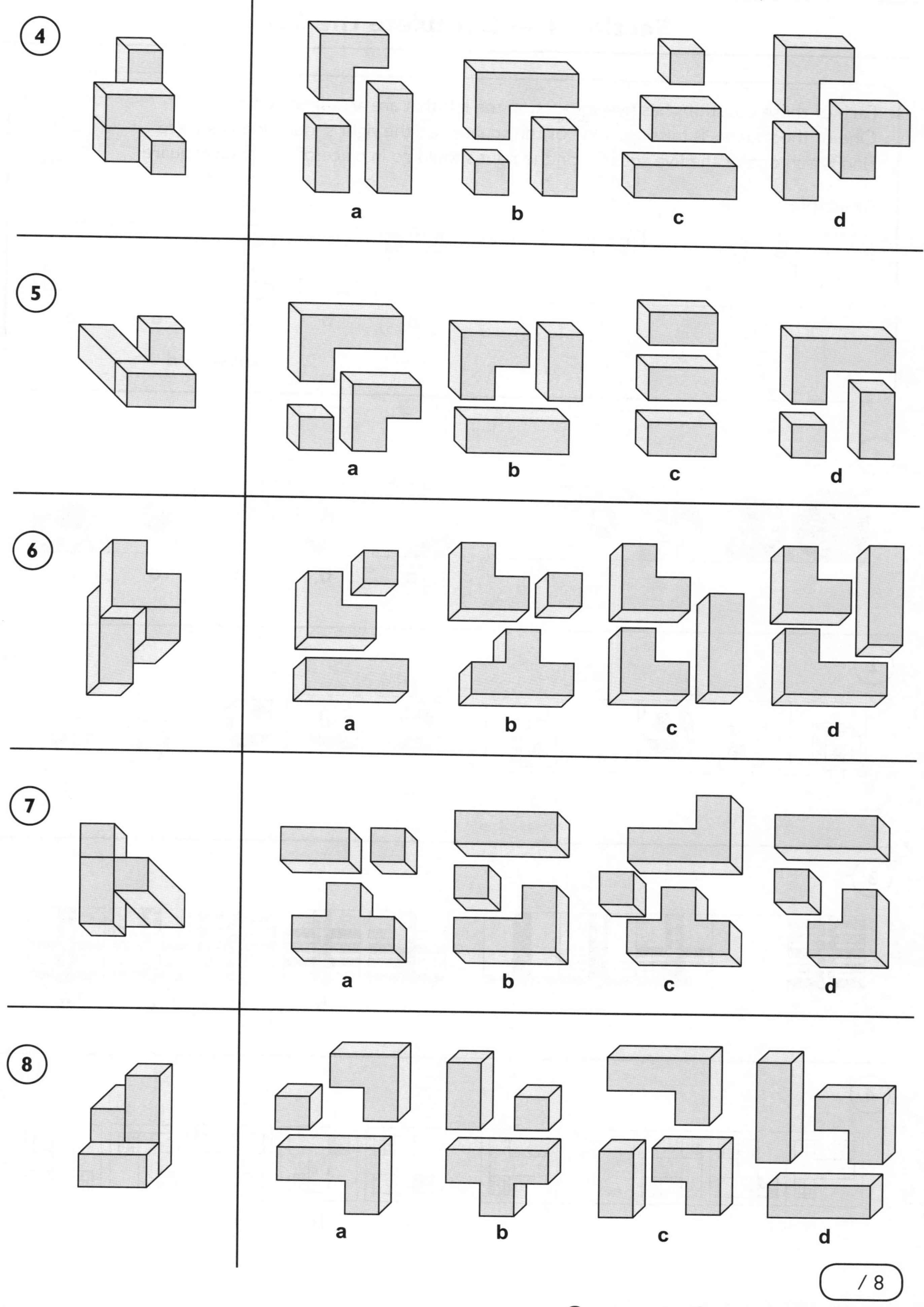

/ 8

Carry on to the next question → →

Section 4 — Complete the Series

Each of these questions has five squares on the left that are arranged in order.
One of the squares is missing. One of the squares on the right should go in its place.
Find which one of the five squares on the right should go in place of the empty square.

Example:

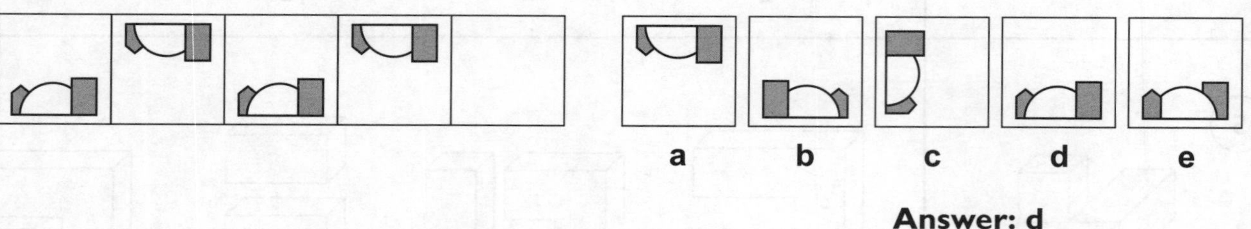

Answer: d

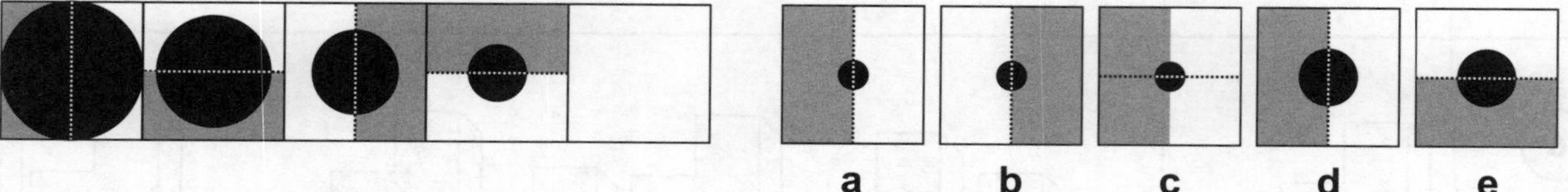

2

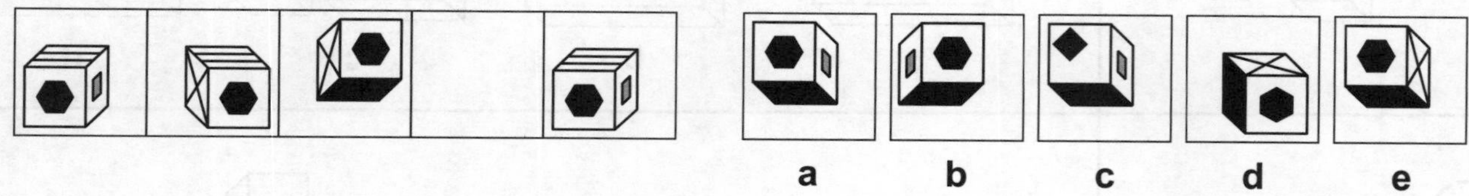

3

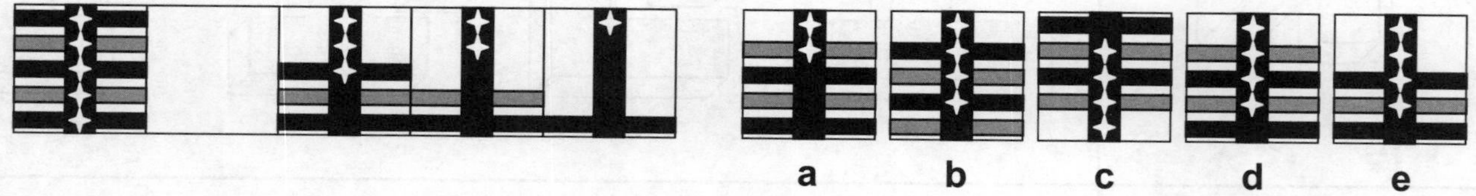

4

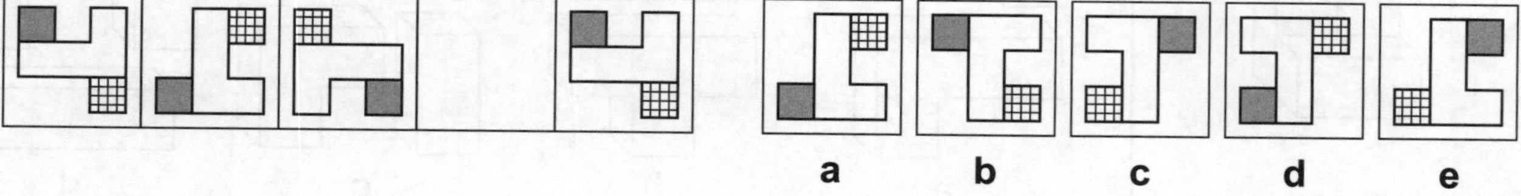

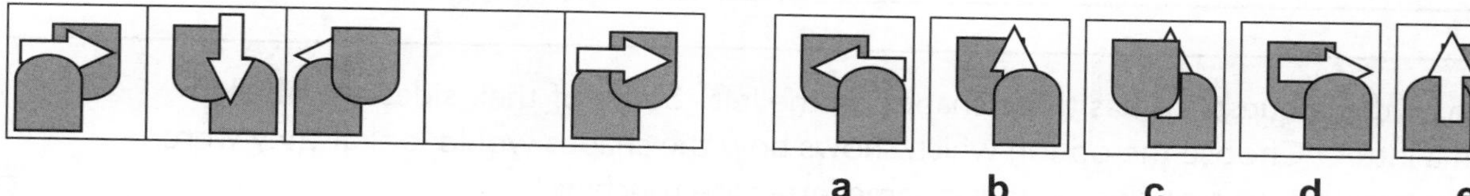

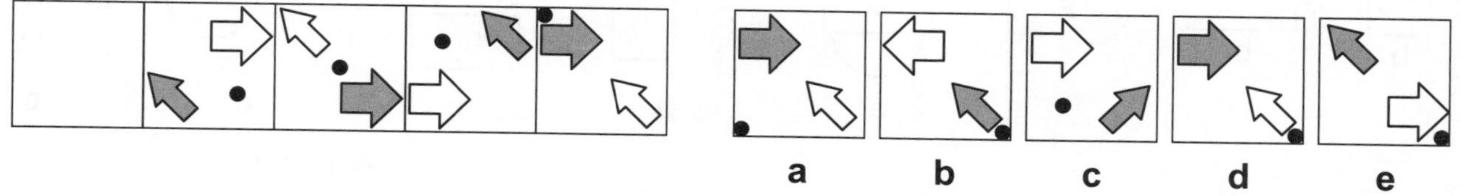

7

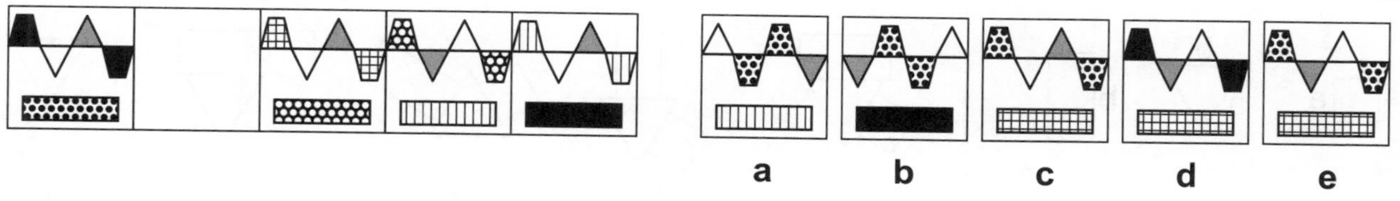

8

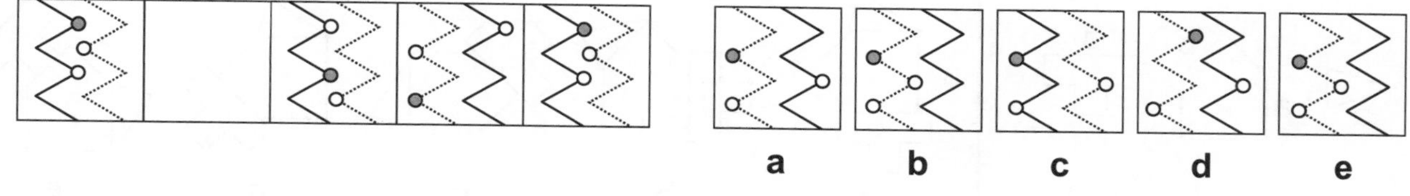

9

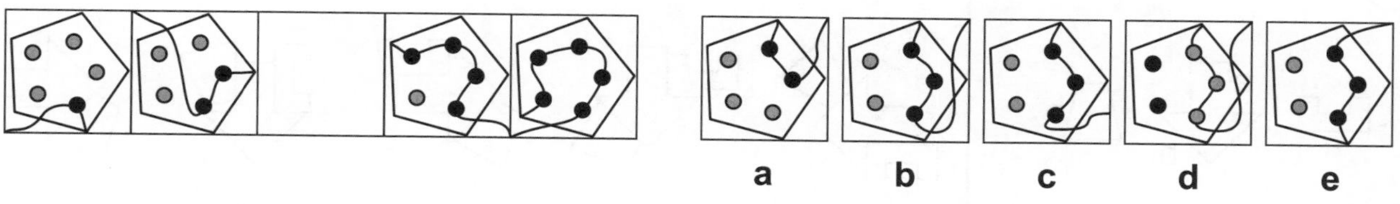

10

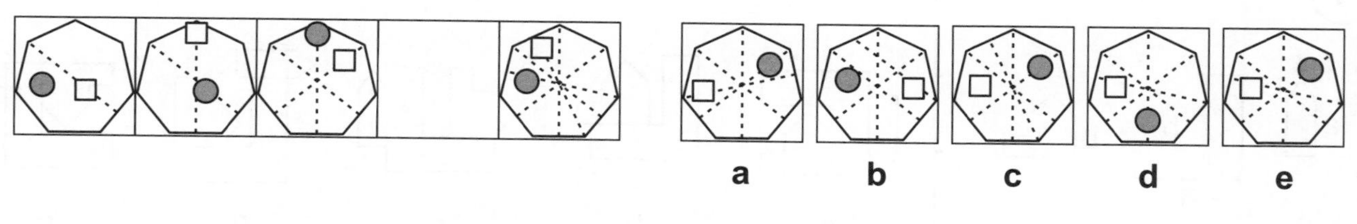

/ 10

Carry on to the next question →→

Section 5 — Connecting Shapes

Each of these questions has three shapes on the left. Some of their sides are labelled with a letter. Choose the option which shows how the shapes would look if they were joined together so that sides with the same letter are touching.

Example:

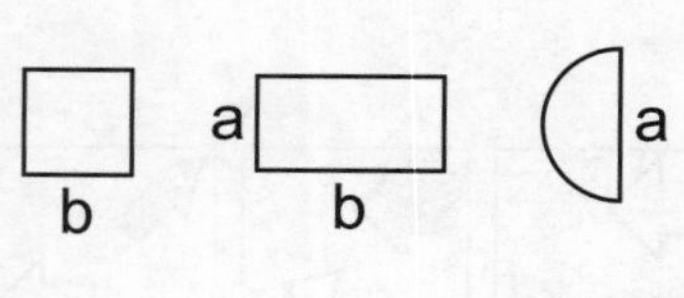

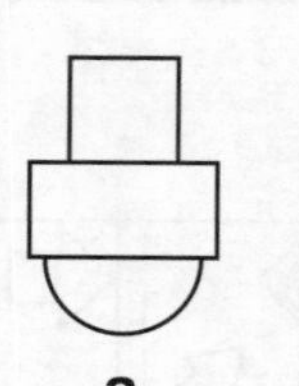

a

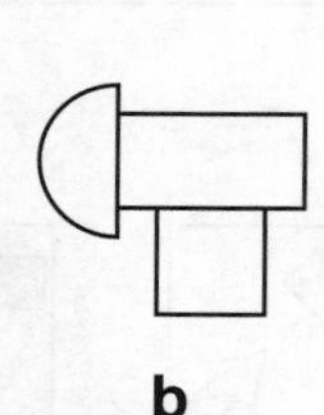

b

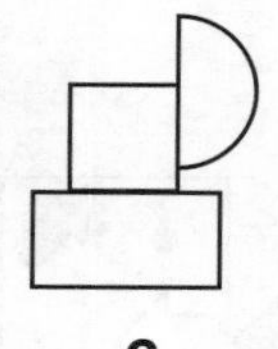

c

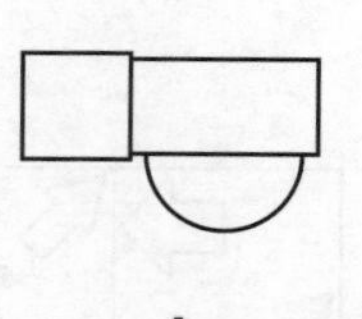

d

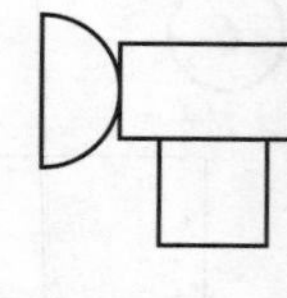

e

Answer: b

1

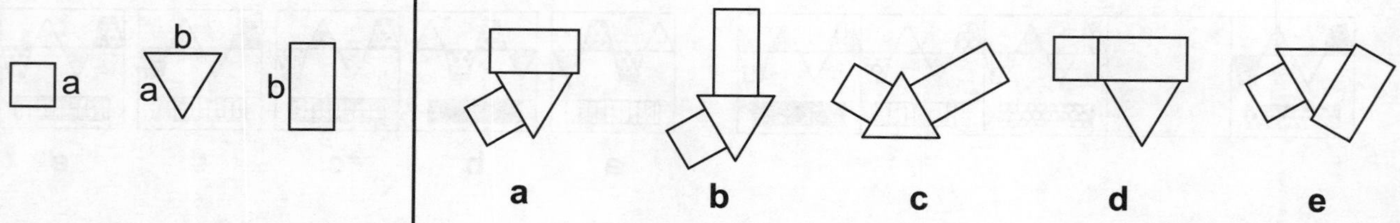

a b a b a b c d e

2

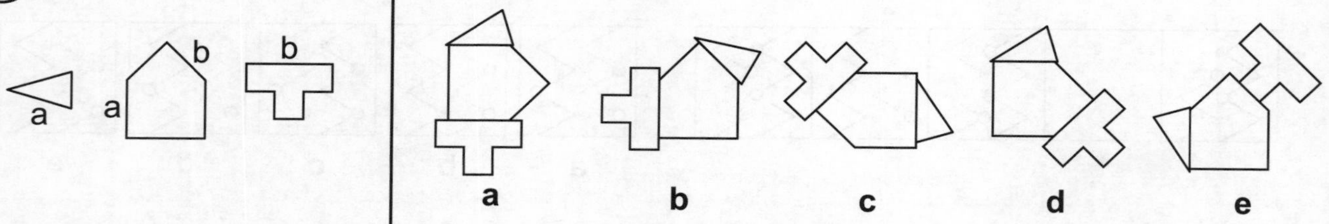

a a b b a b c d e

3

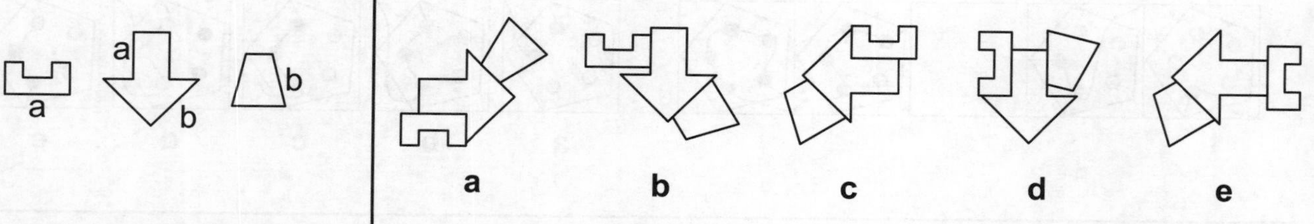

a a b b a b c d e

4

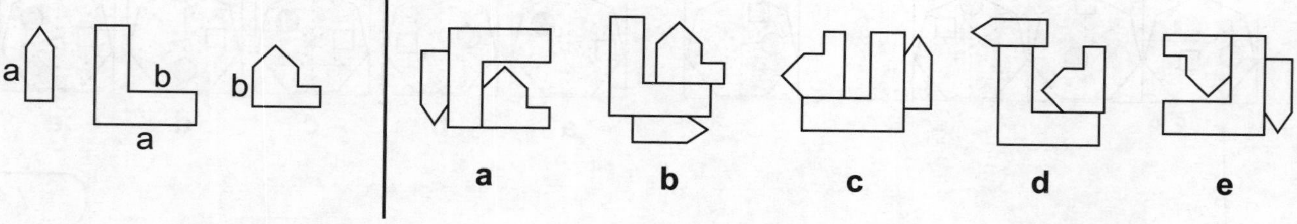

a b a b a b c d e

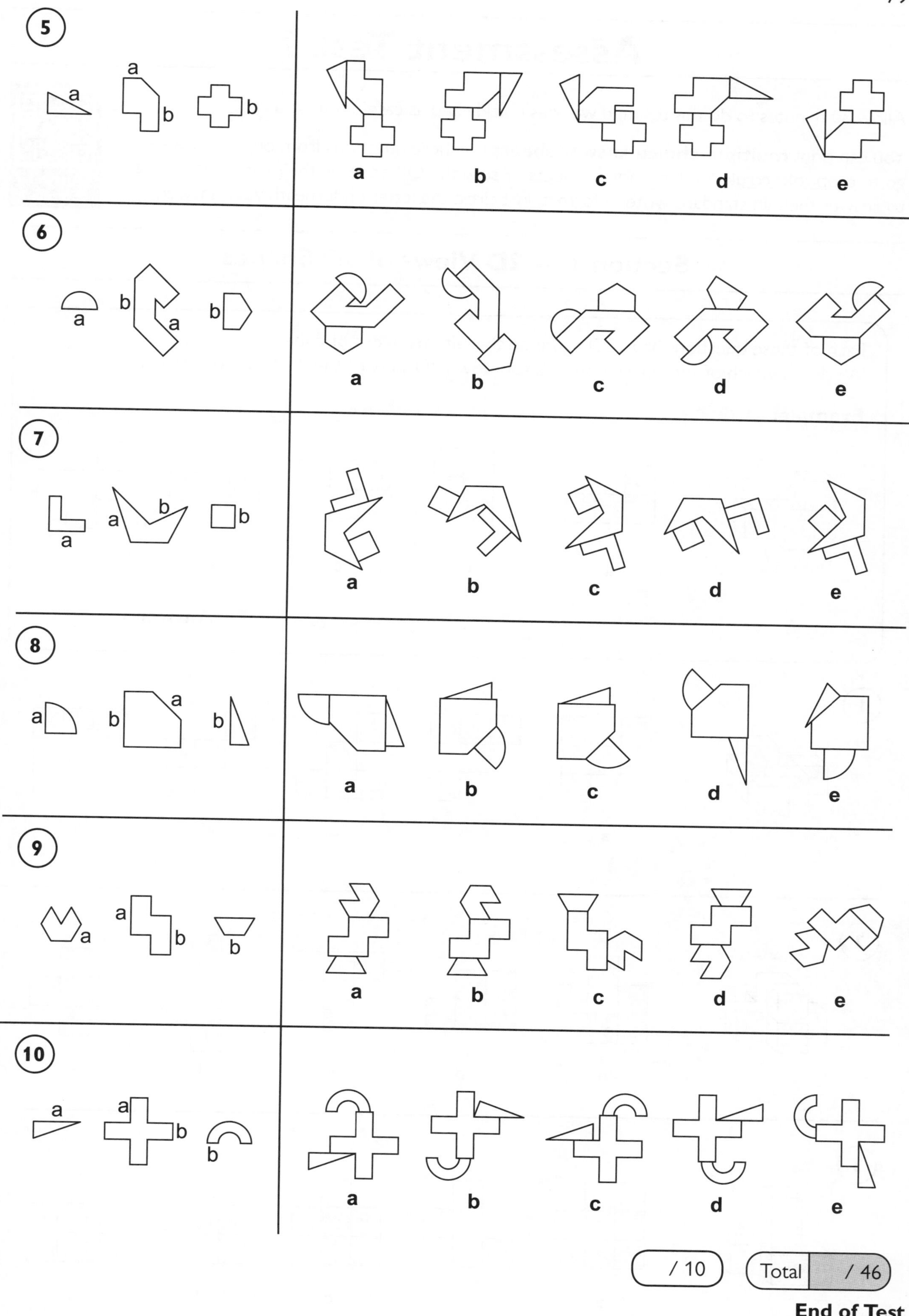

/ 10

Total / 46

End of Test

Assessment Test 7

Allow 30 minutes to do this test and work as quickly and as carefully as you can.

You can print **multiple-choice answer sheets** for these questions from our website — go to cgpbooks.co.uk/11plus/answer-sheets or scan the QR code on the right. If you'd prefer to answer them in standard write-in format, just circle the letter underneath your answer.

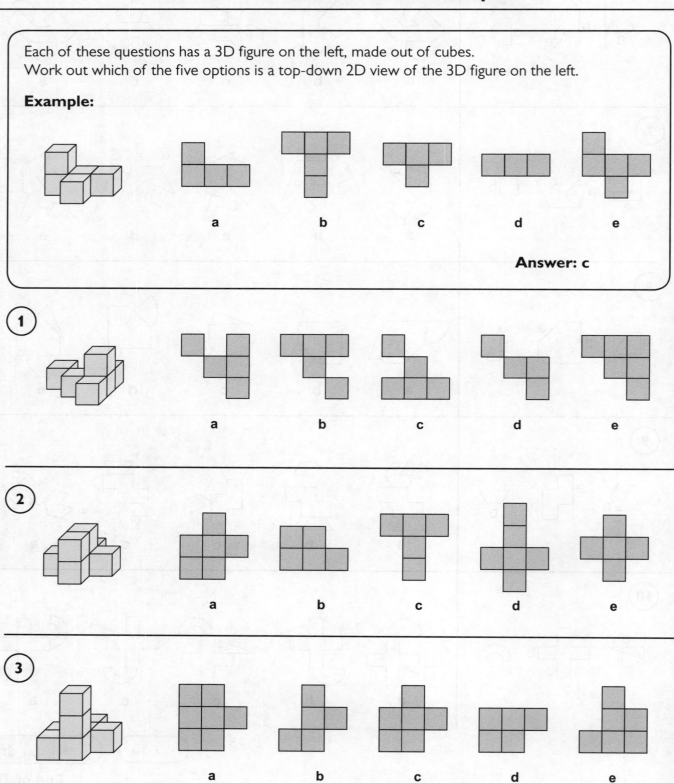

Section 1 — 2D Views of 3D Shapes

Each of these questions has a 3D figure on the left, made out of cubes.
Work out which of the five options is a top-down 2D view of the 3D figure on the left.

Example:

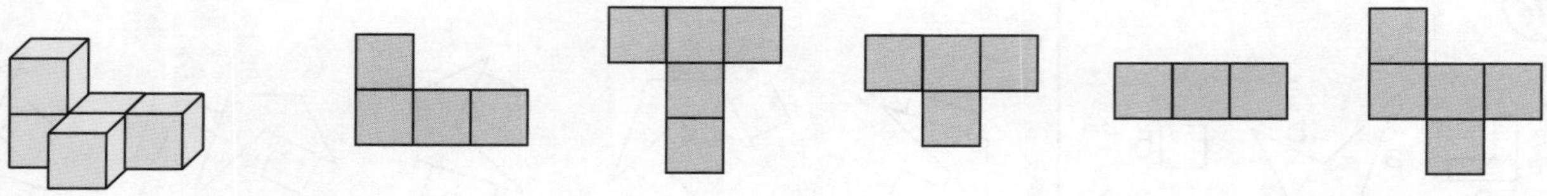

a b c d e

Answer: c

1

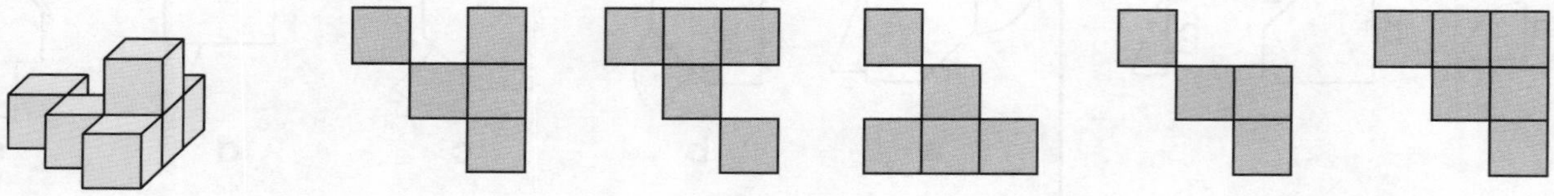

a b c d e

2

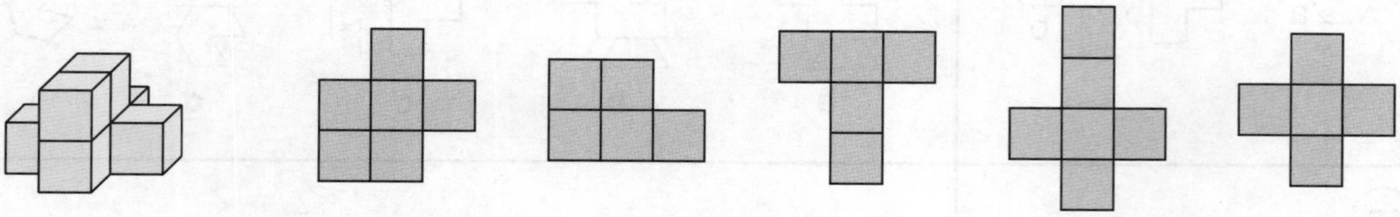

a b c d e

3

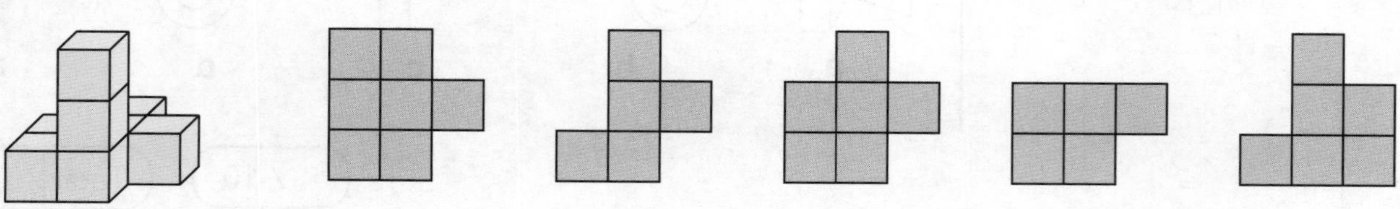

a b c d e

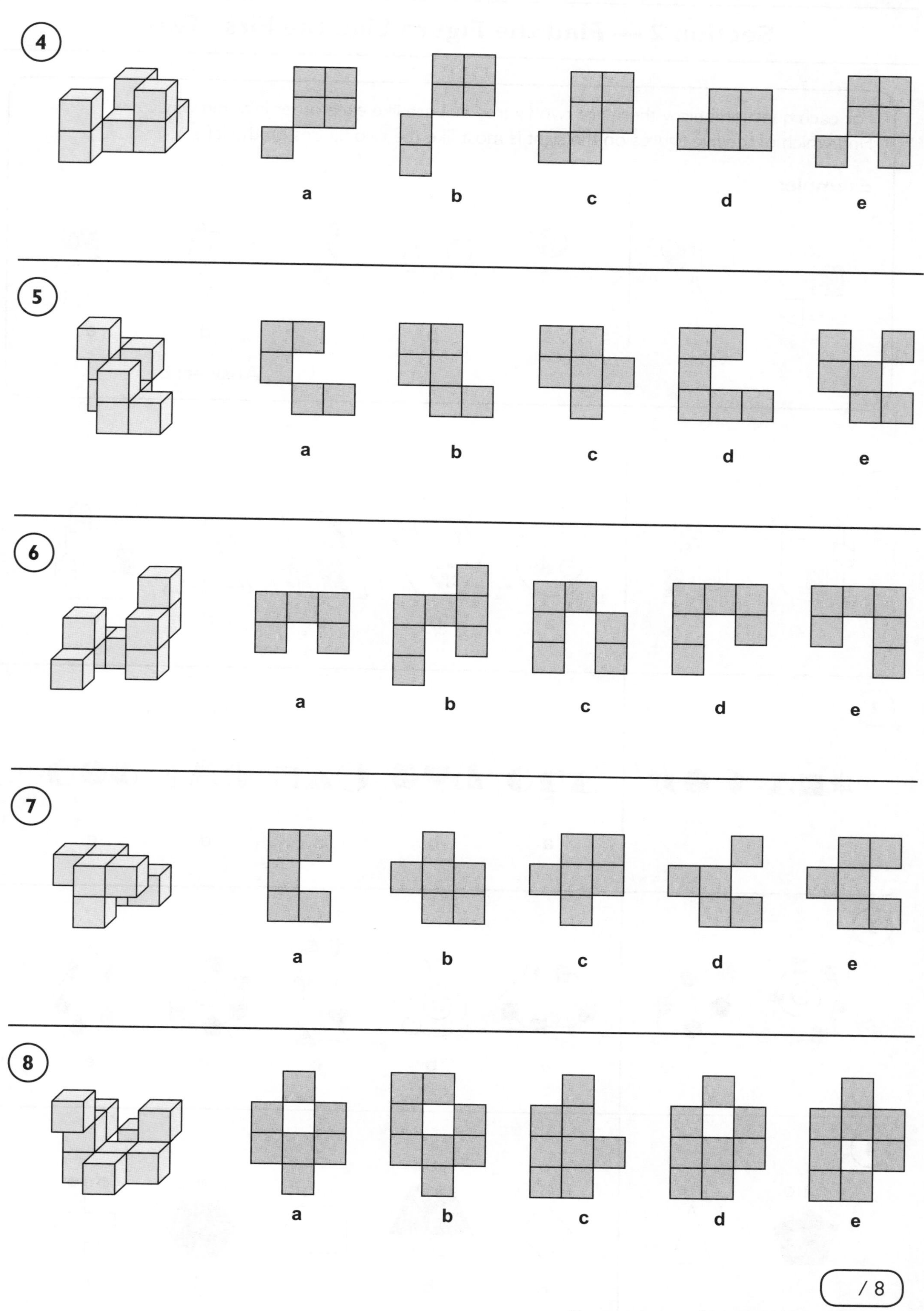

/ 8

Carry on to the next question → →

Section 2 — Find the Figure Like the First Two

For each question below there are two figures that are like each other in some way.
Find which of the five figures on the right is most like the two figures on the left.

Example:

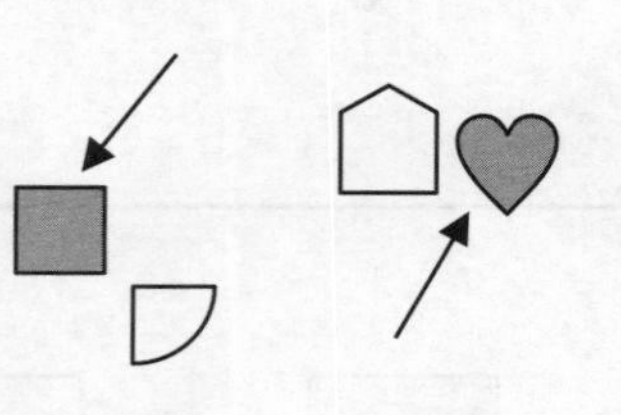

a

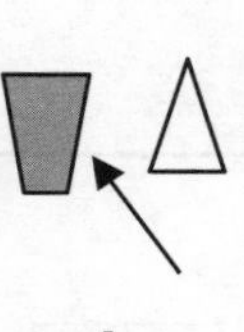
b

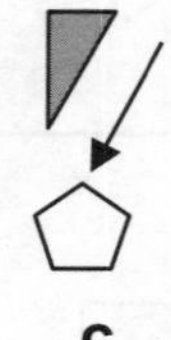
c

d

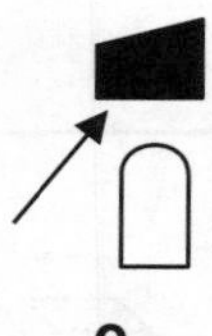
e

Answer: b

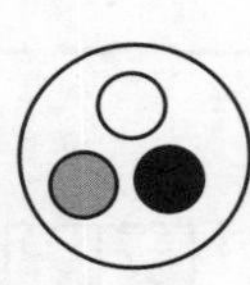
a

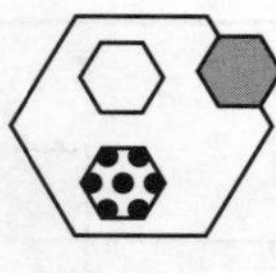
b

c

d

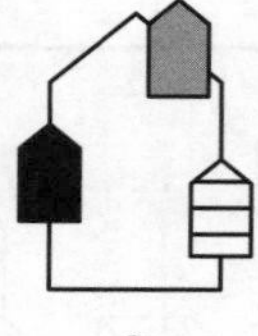
e

(2)

a

b

c

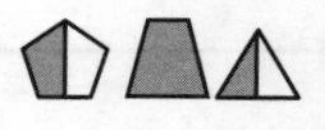
d

e

(3)

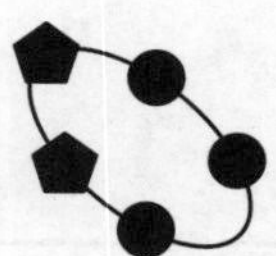

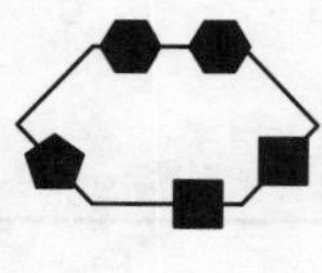
a

b

c

d

e

(4)

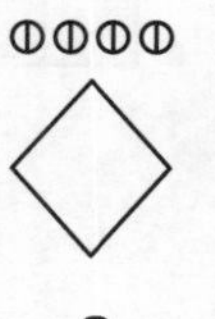
a

b

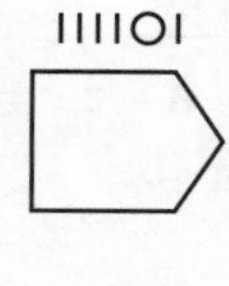
c

d

e

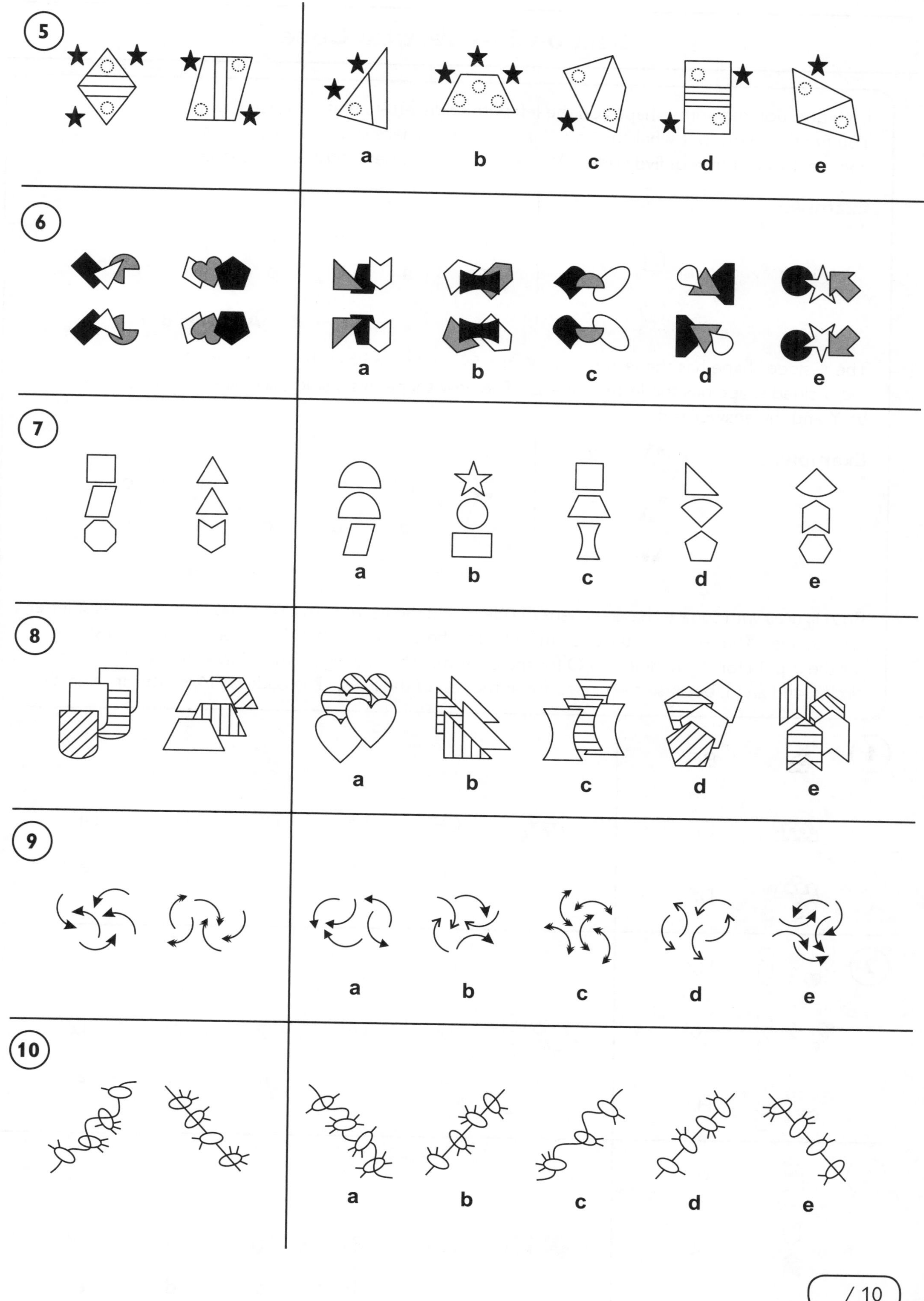

/ 10

Carry on to the next question → →

Section 3 — Vertical Code

Each question has some shapes on the left with code letters that describe them. You need to work out what the code letters mean. There is then a shape on its own next to a choice of five codes. Work out which code describes this shape.

Example:

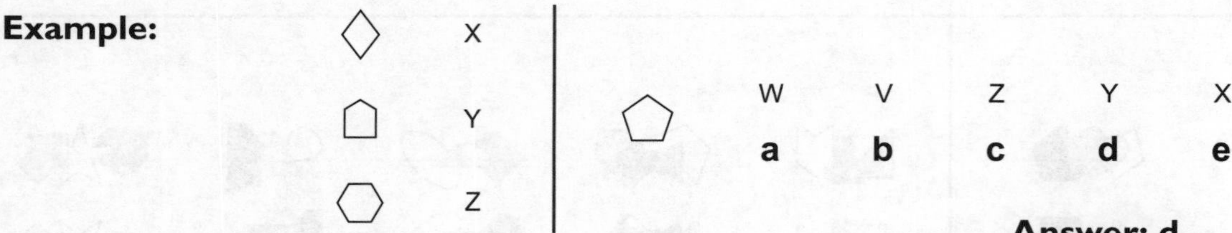

Answer: d

The 4-sided shape has the letter code X, the 5-sided shape has the letter code Y and the 6-sided shape has the letter code Z. The new shape has 5 sides, so the code must be Y and the answer is d.

Example:

EM

FO

EN

FN	EO	FM	MN	FO
a	**b**	**c**	**d**	**e**

Answer: c

Both figures with squares have the letter code E, and the figure with circles has an F, so the first letter is for shape. The second letter code must be for the position of the shapes on the lines. M stands for the top, N for the middle and O for the bottom. The new figure must have an F, as there are circles, and an M, because the circles are at the top of the lines. The code is FM, so the answer is c.

1

BE

CE

DF

CE	BF	CF	EF	DE
a	**b**	**c**	**d**	**e**

2

HX

IY

HZ

IX	HY	IZ	IY	HX
a	**b**	**c**	**d**	**e**

3

RT

SU

RV

RU	ST	RT	SU	SV
a	**b**	**c**	**d**	**e**

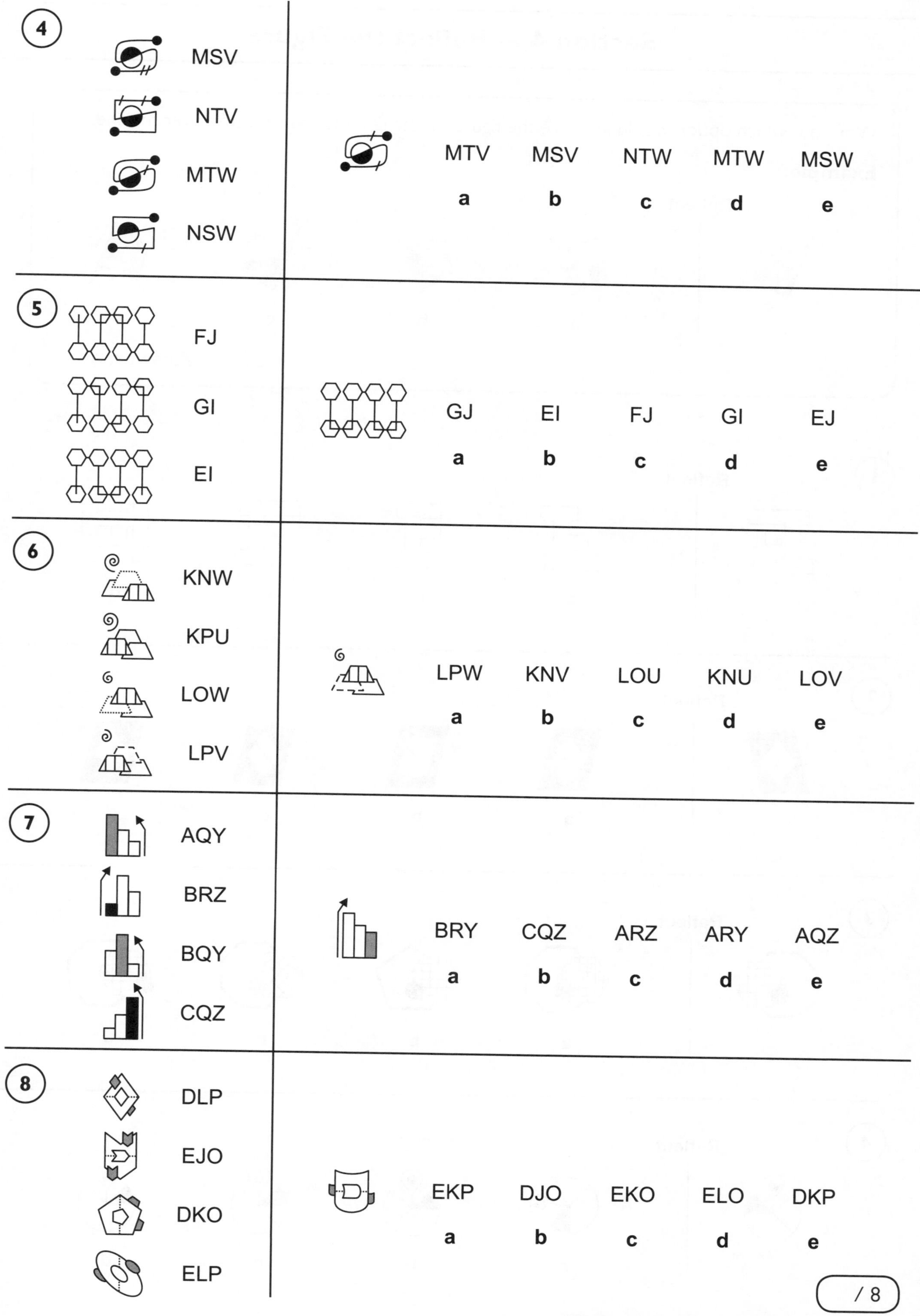

/ 8

Carry on to the next question → →

Section 4 — Reflect the Figure

Work out which option would look like the figure on the left if it was reflected over the line.

Example:

Reflect

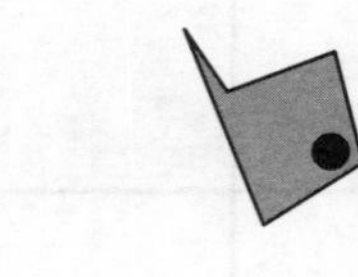
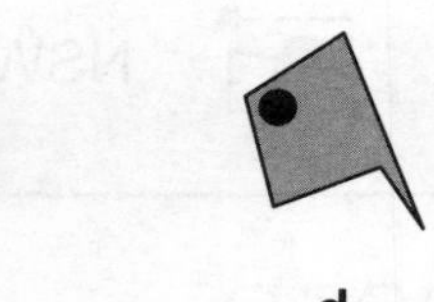

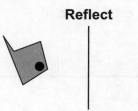

a b c d

Answer: a

(1) Reflect

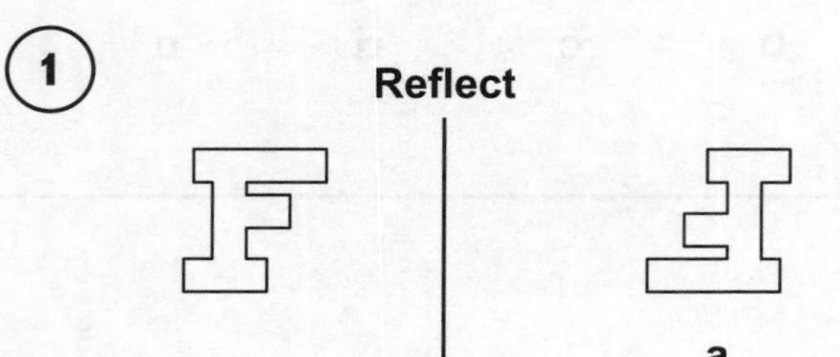
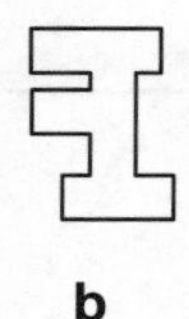
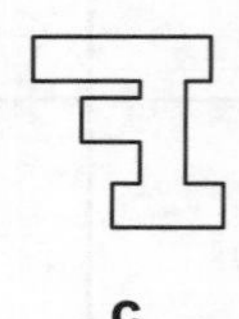
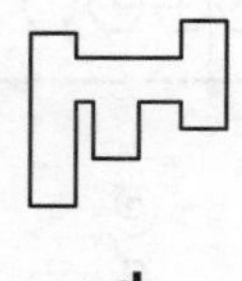

a b c d

(2) Reflect

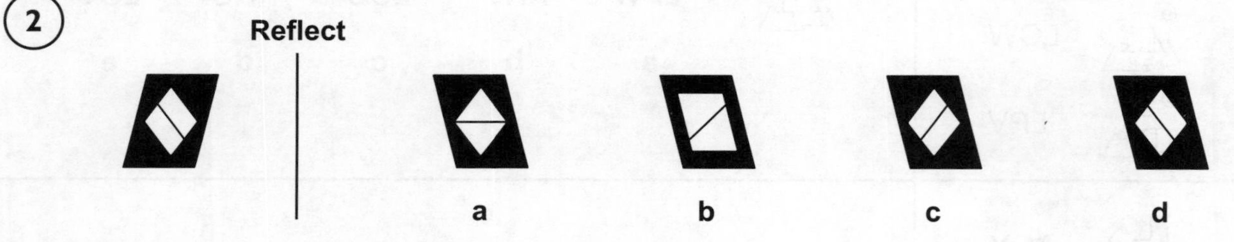

a b c d

(3) Reflect

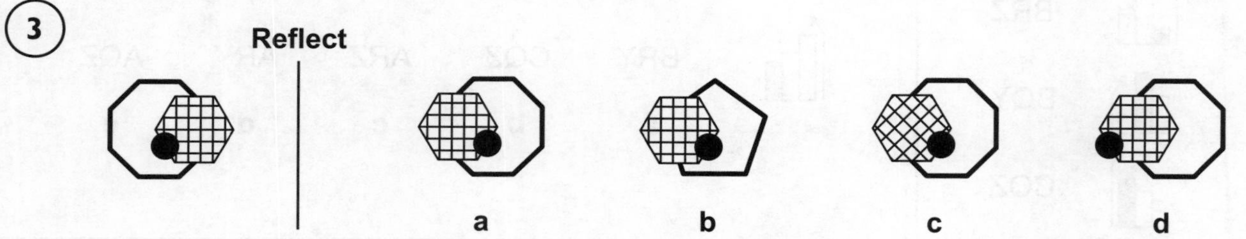

a b c d

(4) Reflect

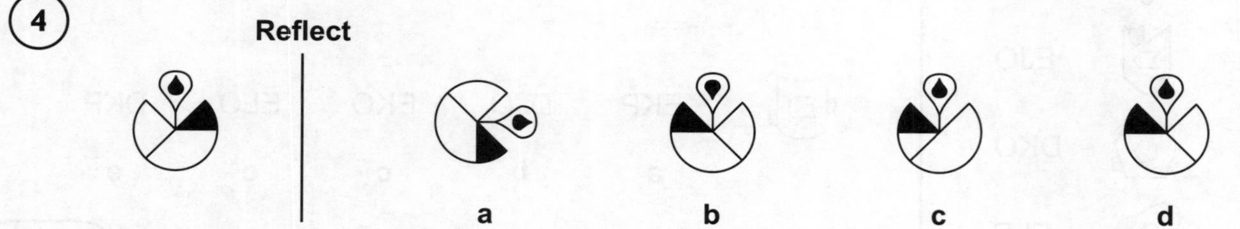

a b c d

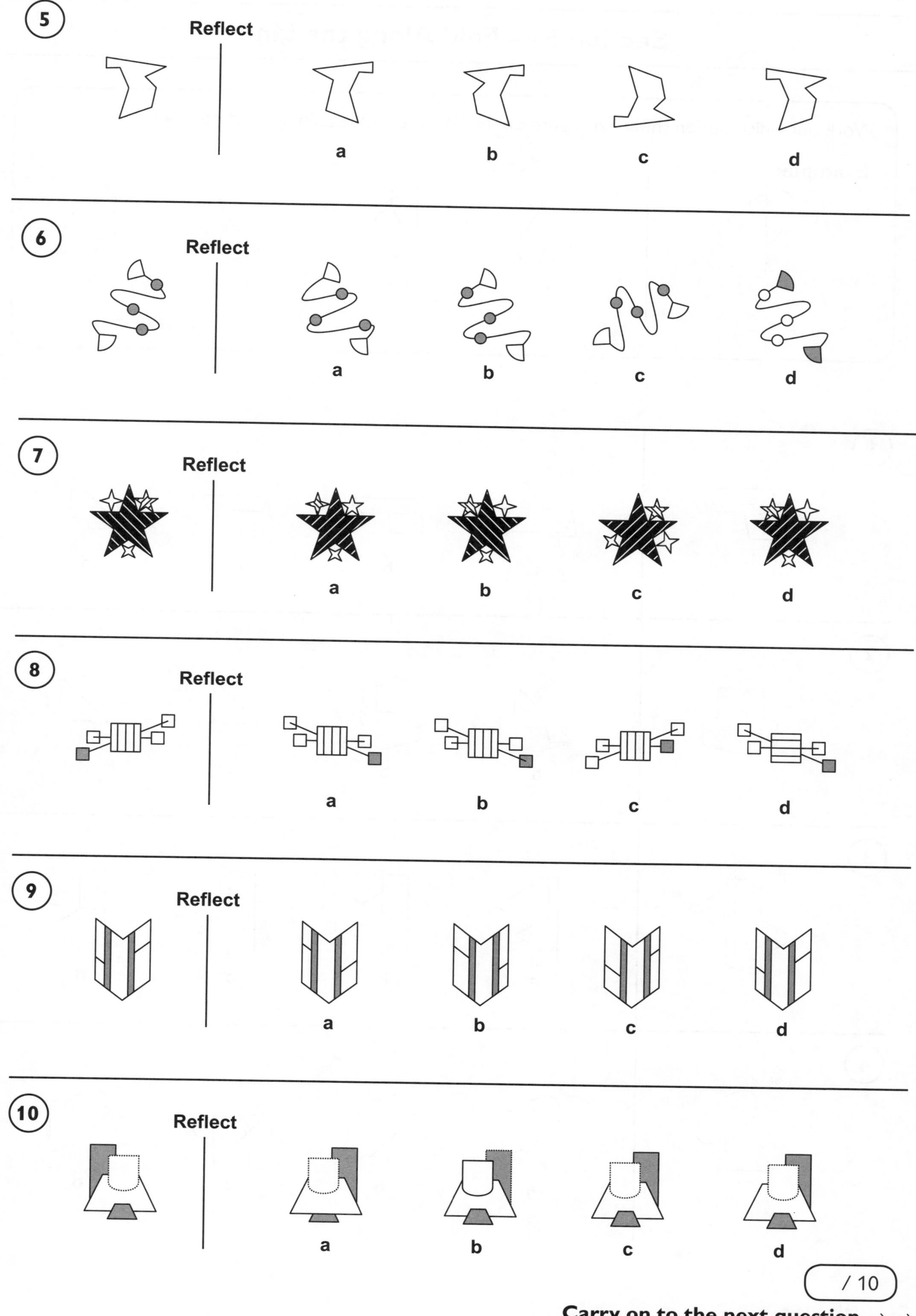

/ 10

Carry on to the next question → →

Section 5 — Fold Along the Line

Work out which option shows the figure on the left when folded along the dotted line.

Example:

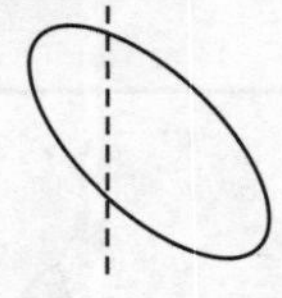

a

b

c

d

Answer: b

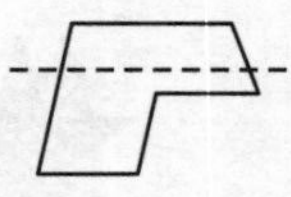

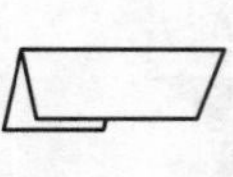
a

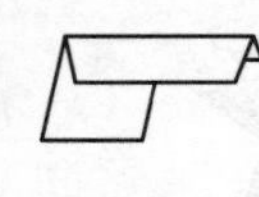
b

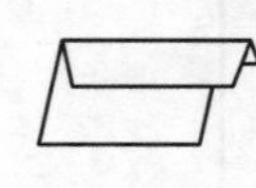
c

d

(2)

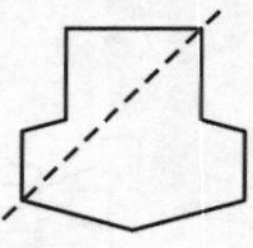

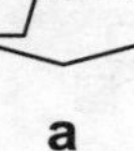
a

b

c

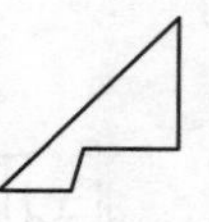
d

(3)

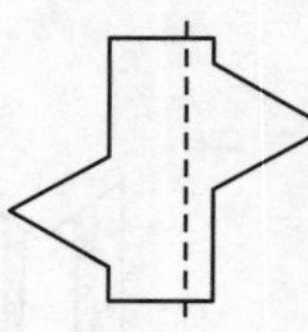

a

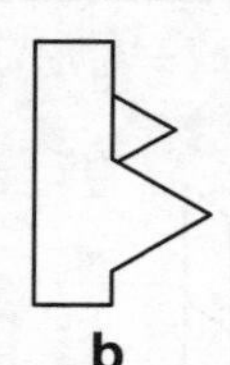
b

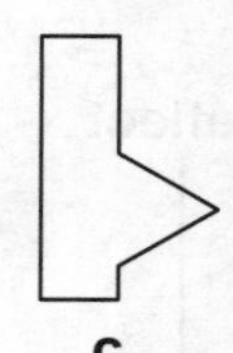
c

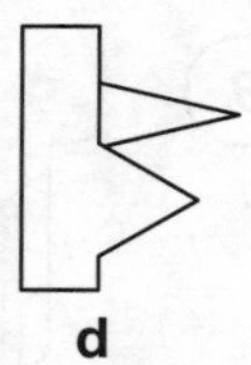
d

(4)

a

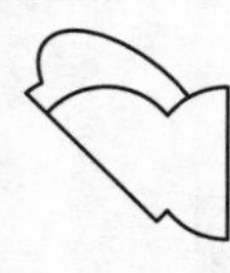
b

c

d

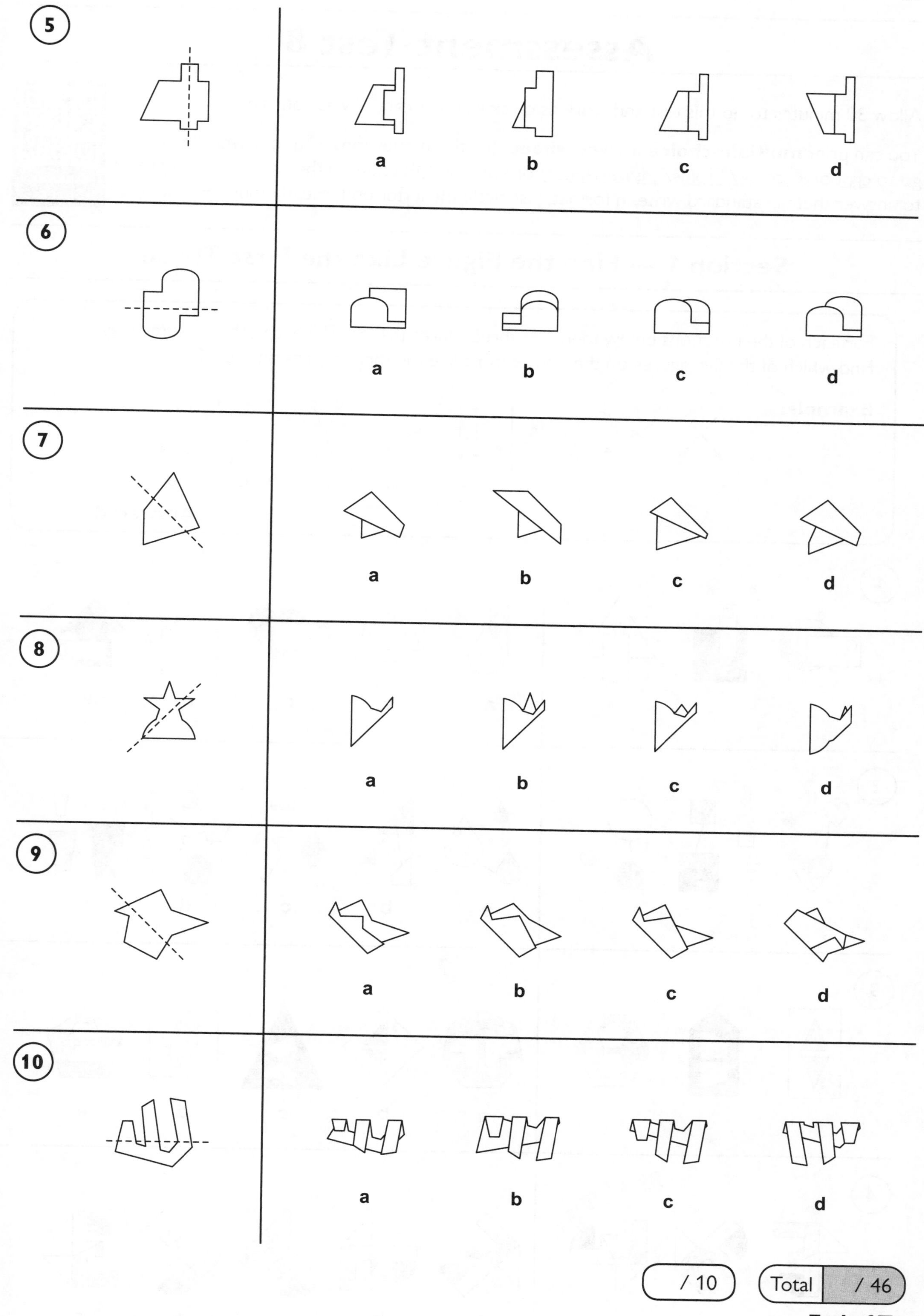

/ 10

Total / 46

End of Test

Assessment Test 8

Allow 30 minutes to do this test and work as quickly and as carefully as you can.

You can print **multiple-choice answer sheets** for these questions from our website — go to cgpbooks.co.uk/11plus/answer-sheets or scan the QR code on the right. If you'd prefer to answer them in standard write-in format, just circle the letter underneath your answer.

Section 1 — Find the Figure Like the First Three

For each of the questions below there are three figures that are like each other in some way. Find which of the five figures on the right is most like the three figures on the left.

Example:

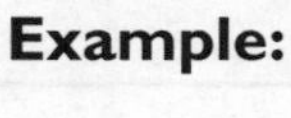

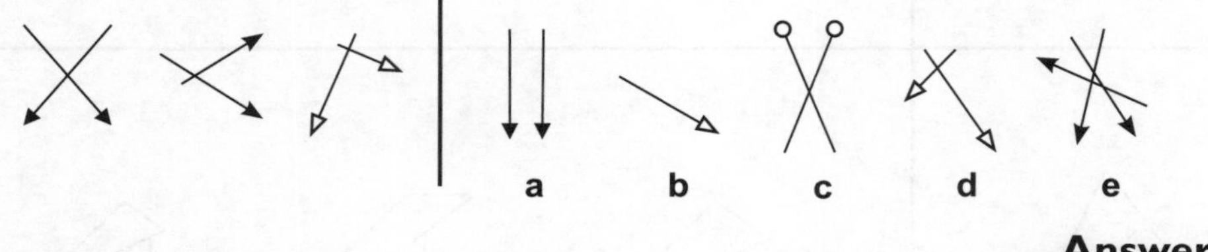

a b c d e

Answer: d

1

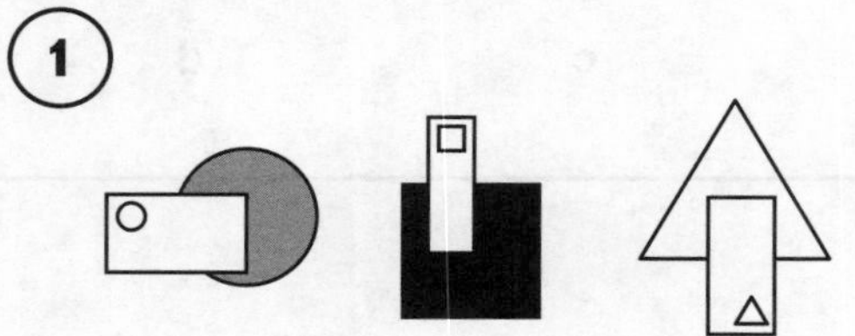

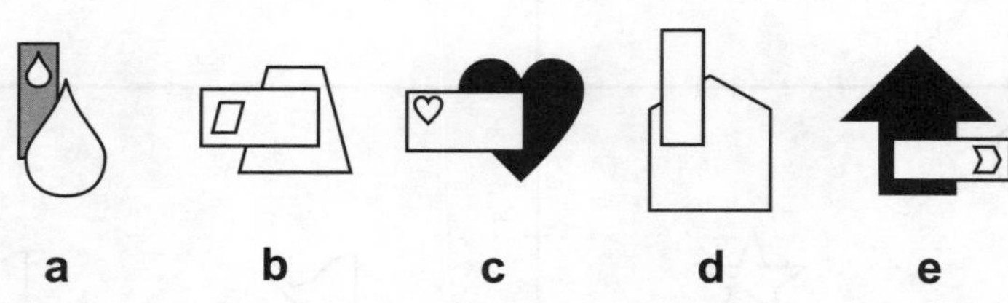

a b c d e

2

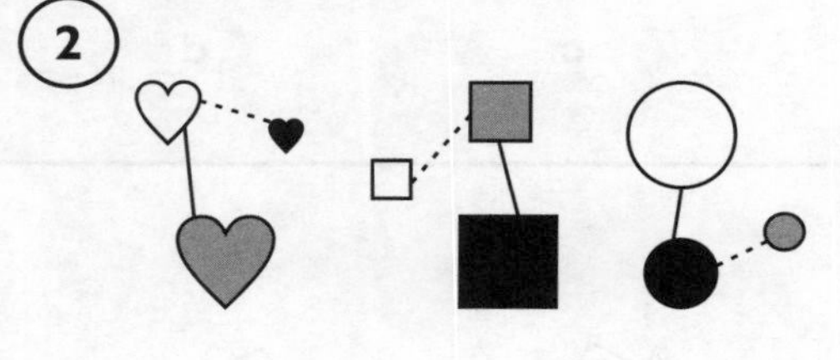

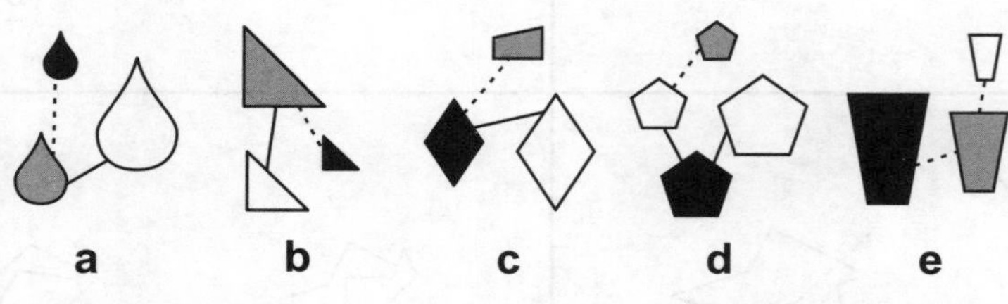

a b c d e

3

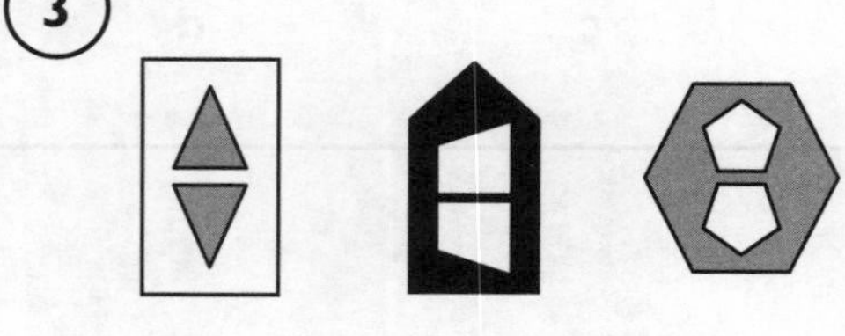

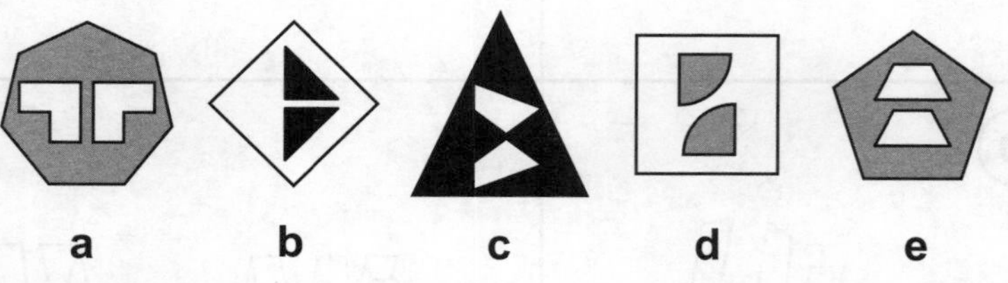

a b c d e

4

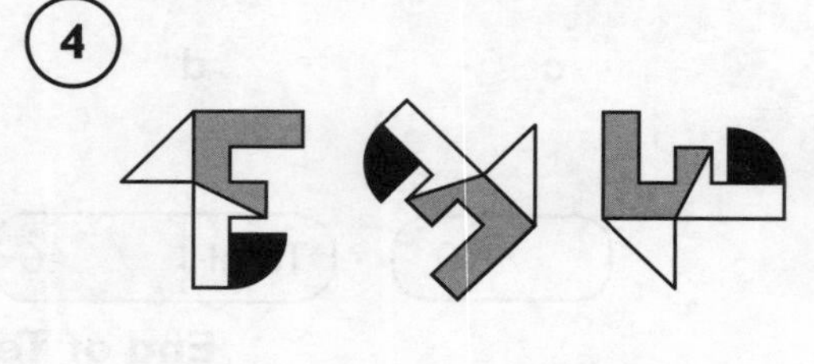

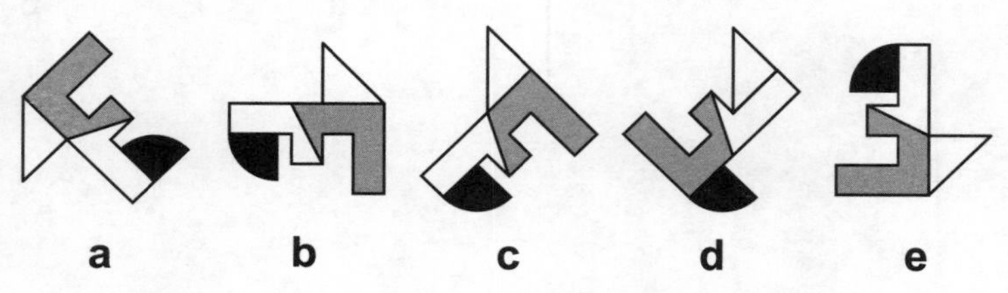

a b c d e

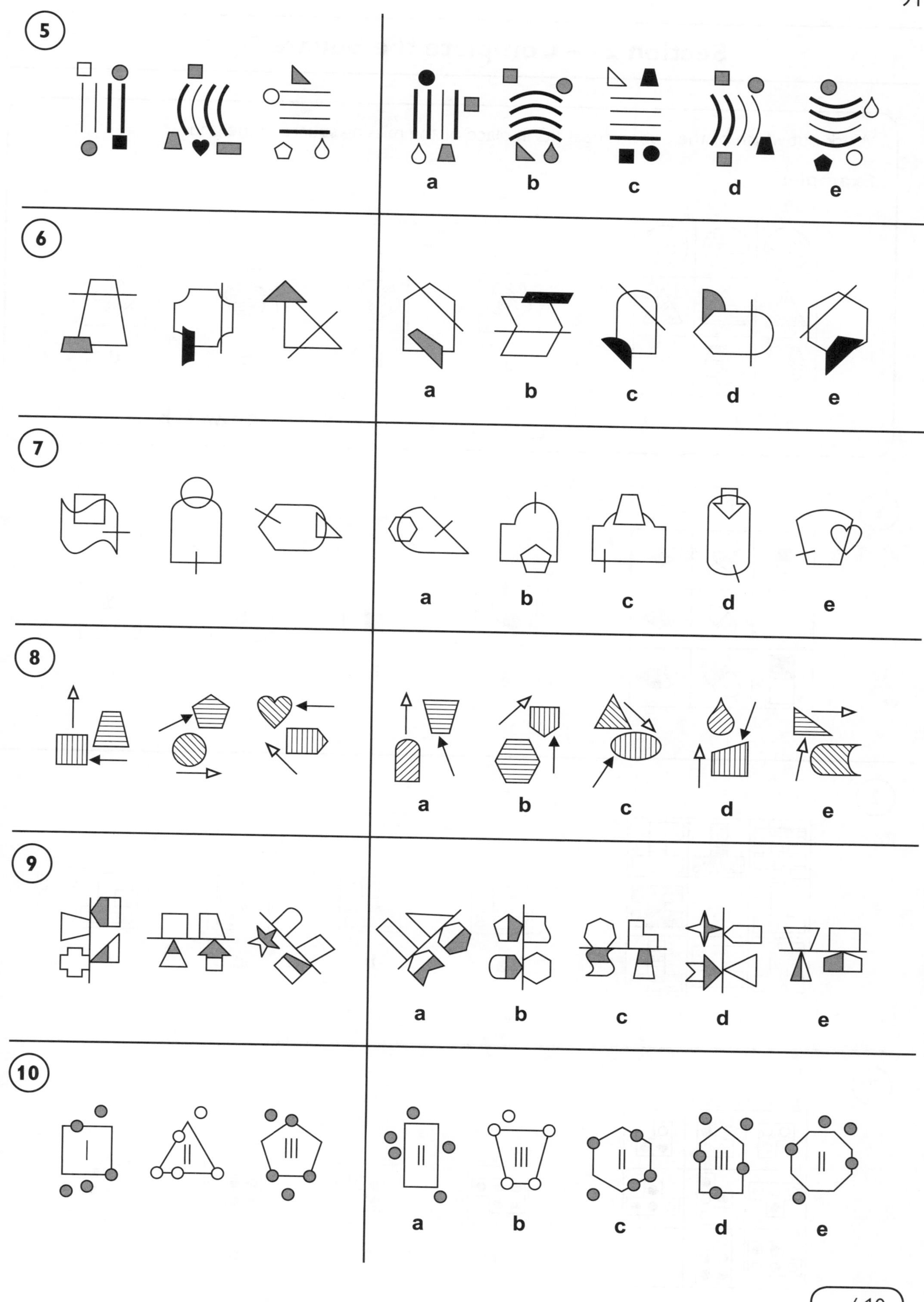

/ 10

Carry on to the next question → →

Section 2 — Complete the Square Grid

Work out which of the options best fits in place of the missing square in the grid.

Example:

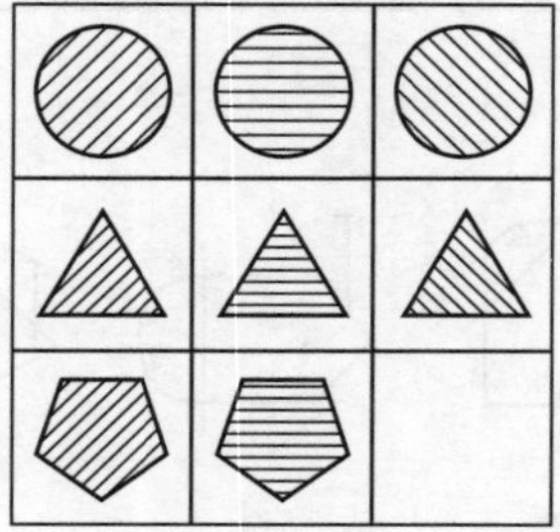

a

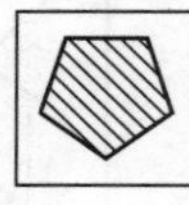
b

c

d

Answer: b

1

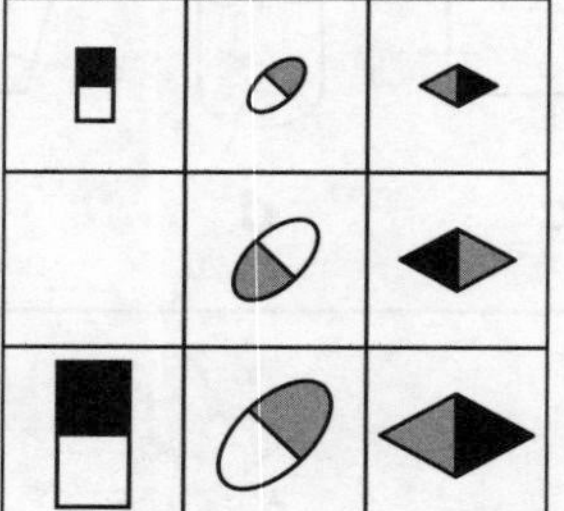

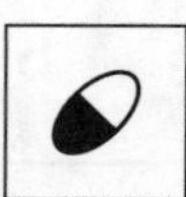
a

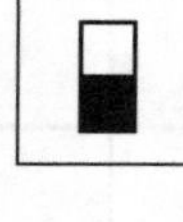
b

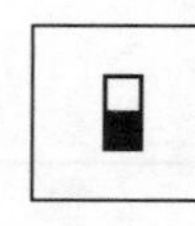
c

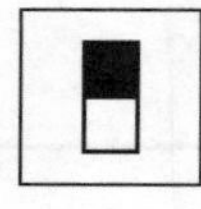
d

2

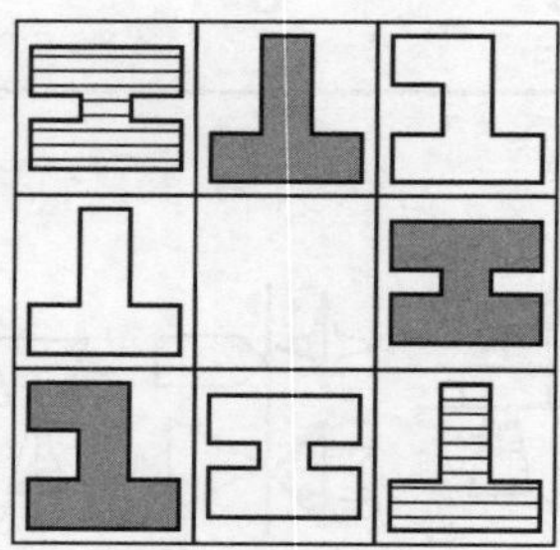

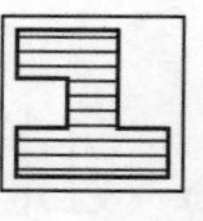
a

b

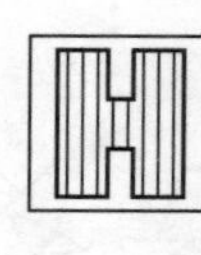
c

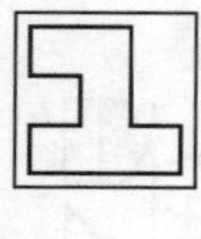
d

3

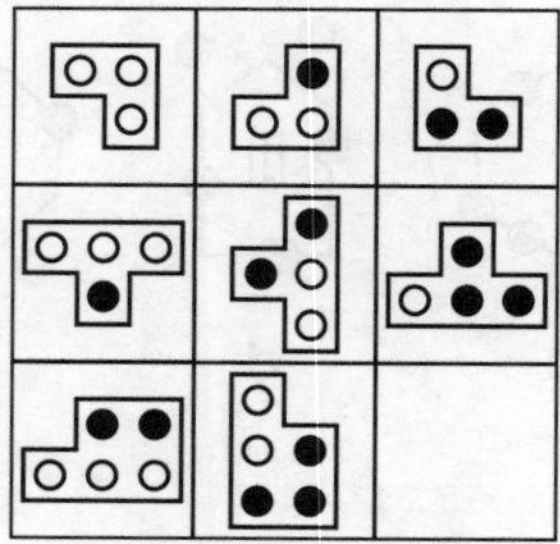

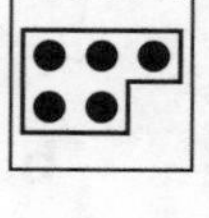
a

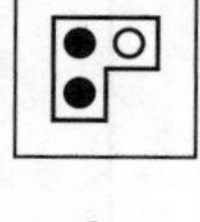
b

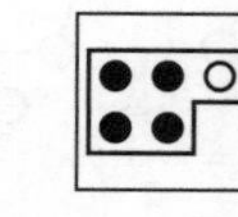
c

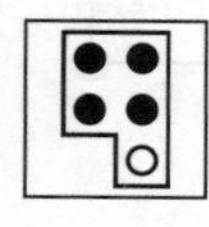
d

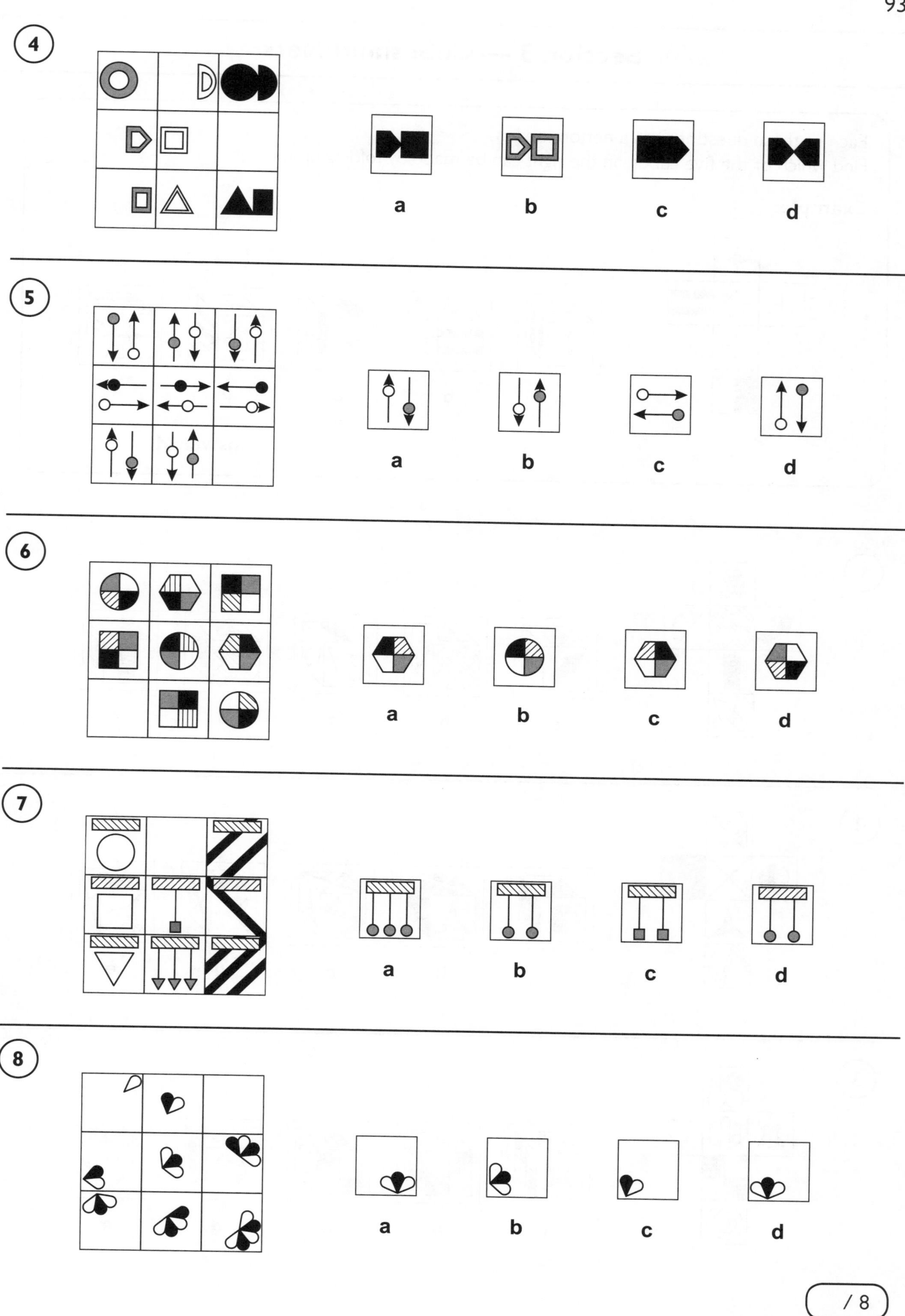

/ 8

Carry on to the next question → →

Section 3 — Cubes and Nets

Each of these questions has a net on the left.
Find which of the five cubes on the right can be made by folding up the net.

Example:

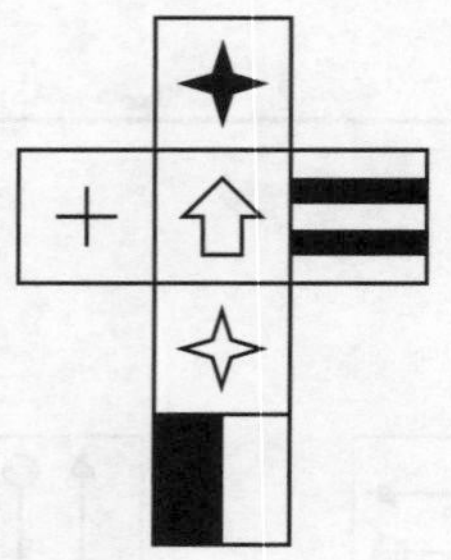

a

b

c

d

e

Answer: d

1

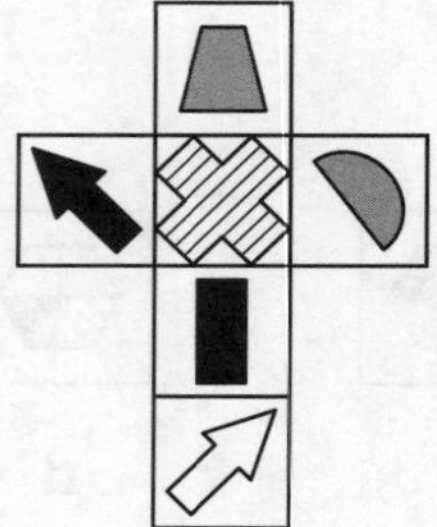

a

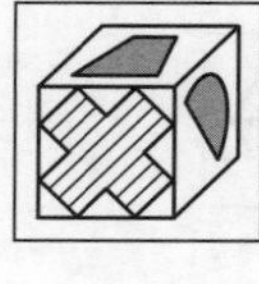
b

c

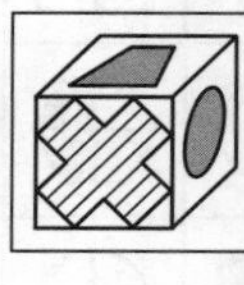
d

e

2

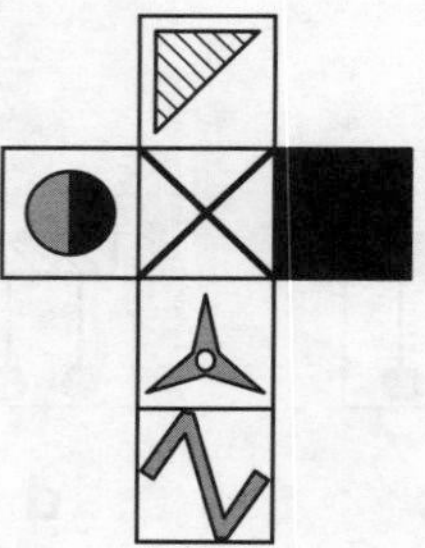

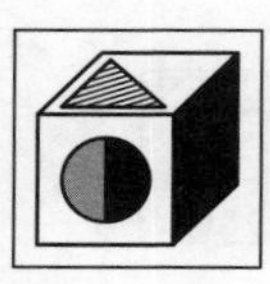
a

b

c

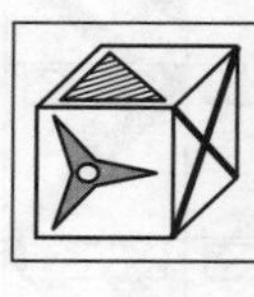
d

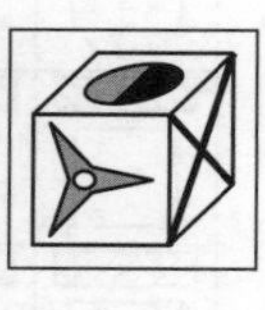
e

3

a

b

c

d

e

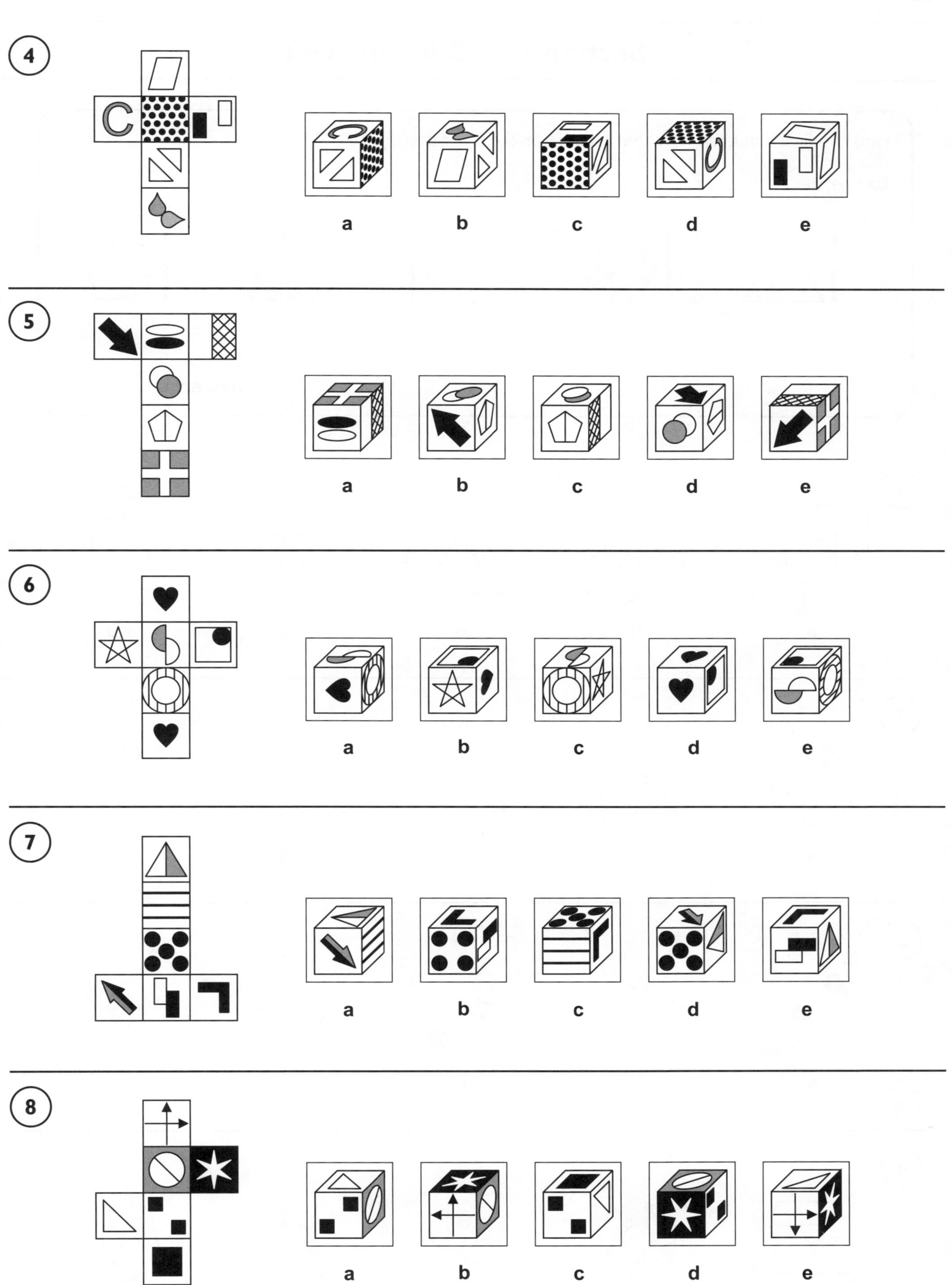

/ 8

Carry on to the next question → →

Section 4 — Odd One Out

Find the figure in each row that is most unlike the other figures.

Example:

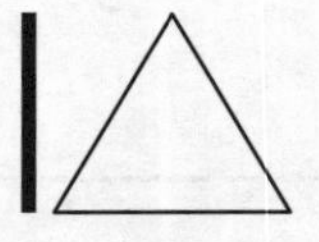
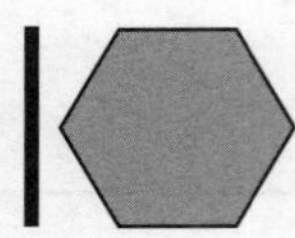
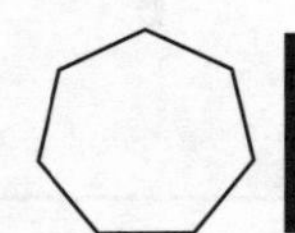
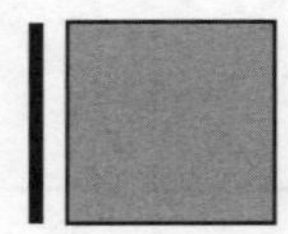
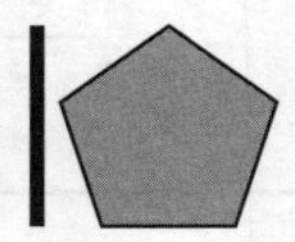

a b c d e

Answer: c

1

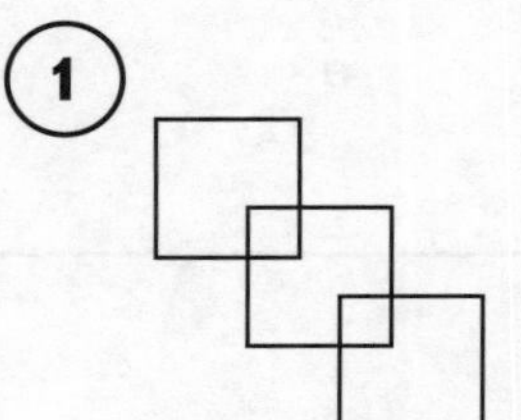

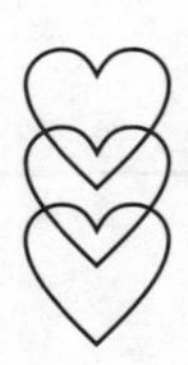
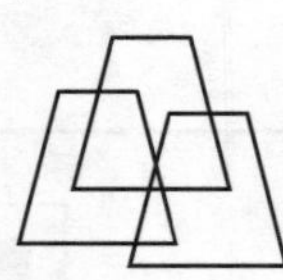

a b c d e

2

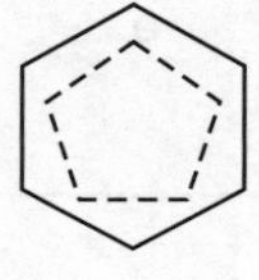
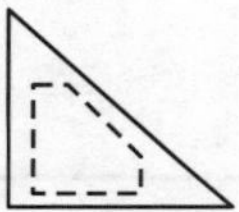
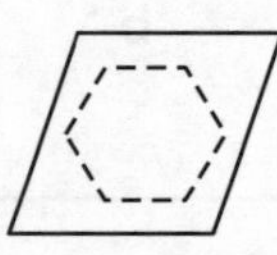

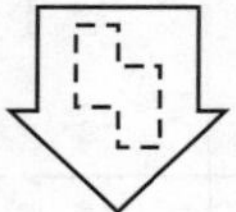

a b c d e

3

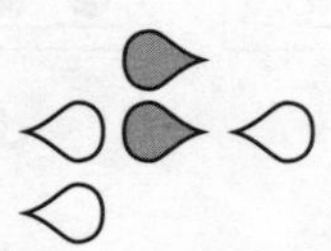

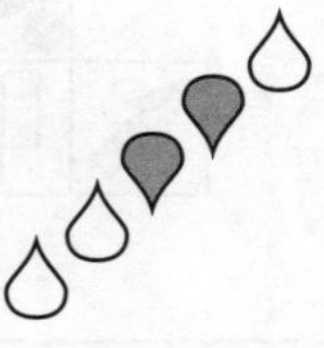

a b c d e

4

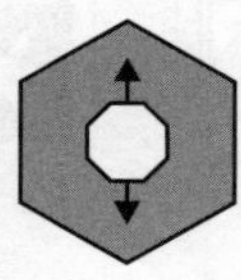
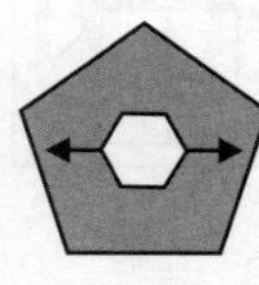
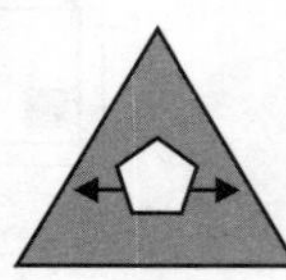
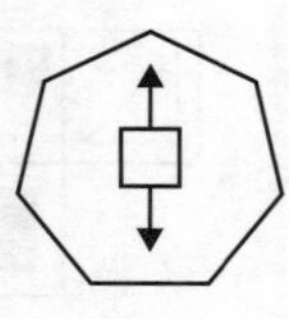

a b c d e

(5)

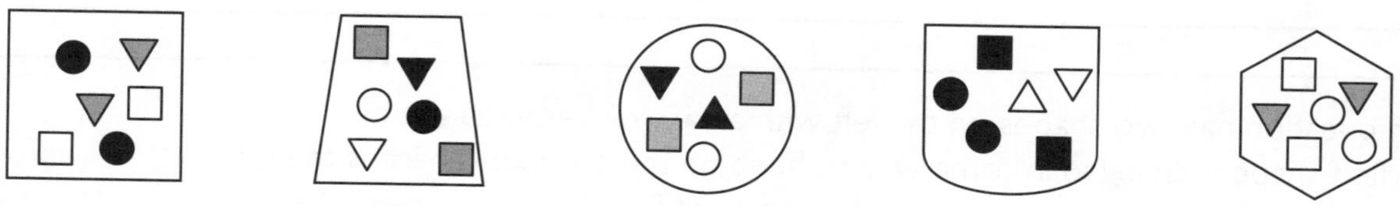

a b c d e

(6)

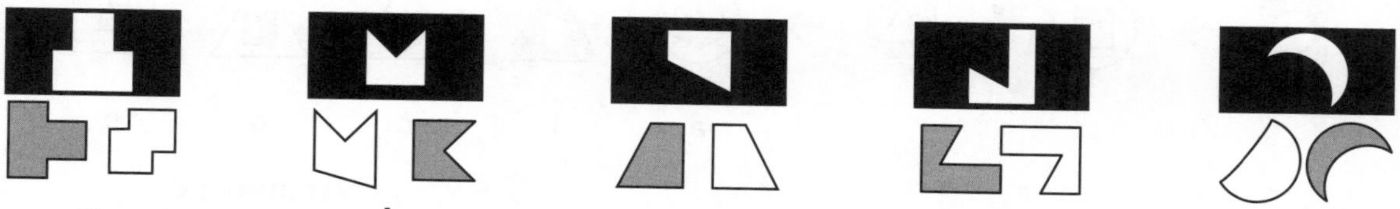

a b c d e

(7)

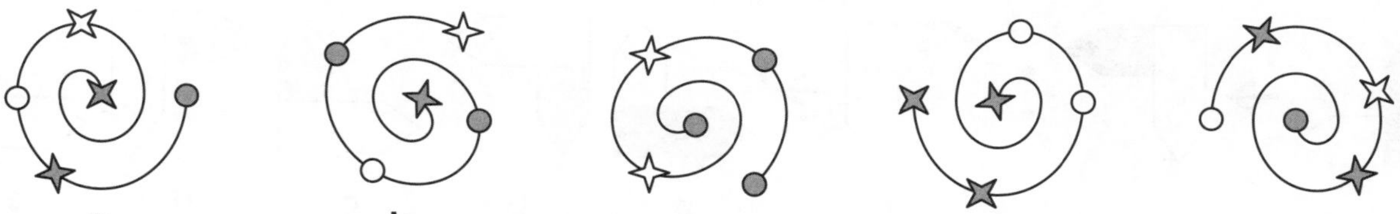

a b c d e

(8)

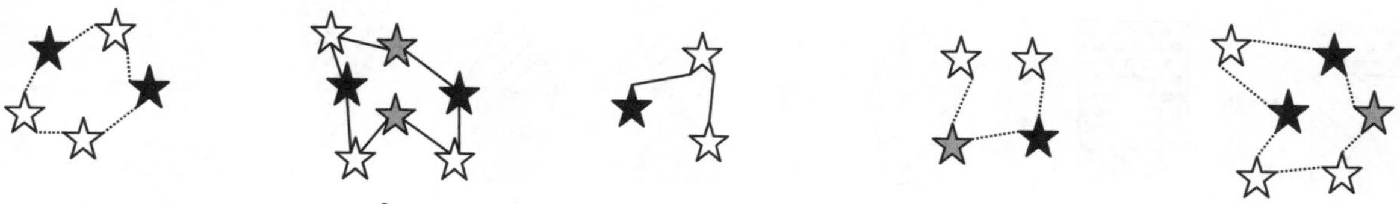

a b c d e

(9)

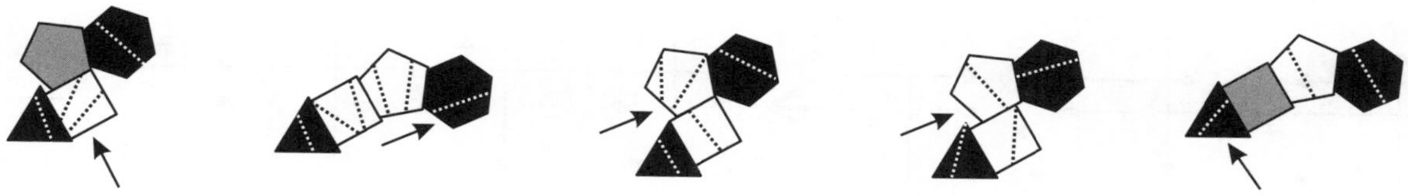

a b c d e

(10)

a b c d e

/ 10

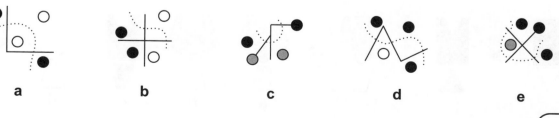

Carry on to the next question → →

Section 5 — Complete the Pair

Each question has two shapes on the left with an arrow between them. The first shape is changed in some way to become the second. There is then a third shape followed by an arrow and a choice of five shapes. Choose the shape on the right that relates to the third shape like the second does to the first.

Example:

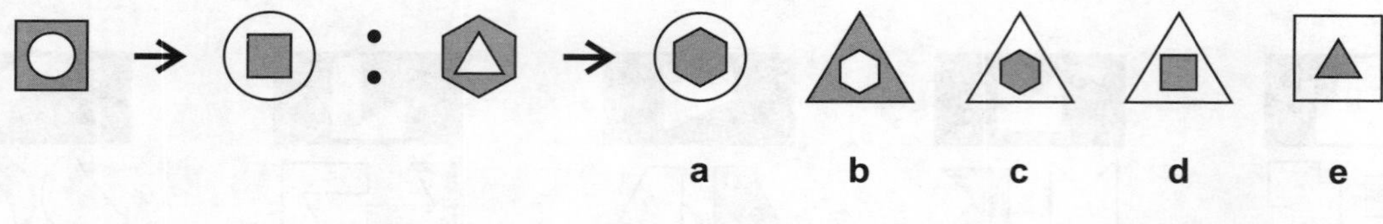

Answer: c

1

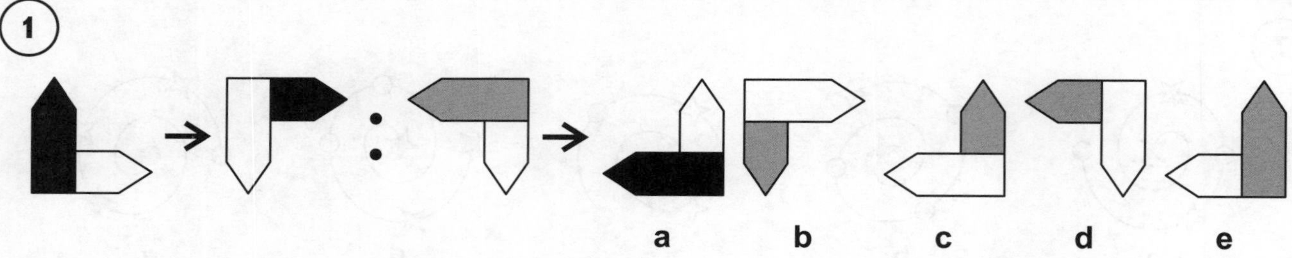

2

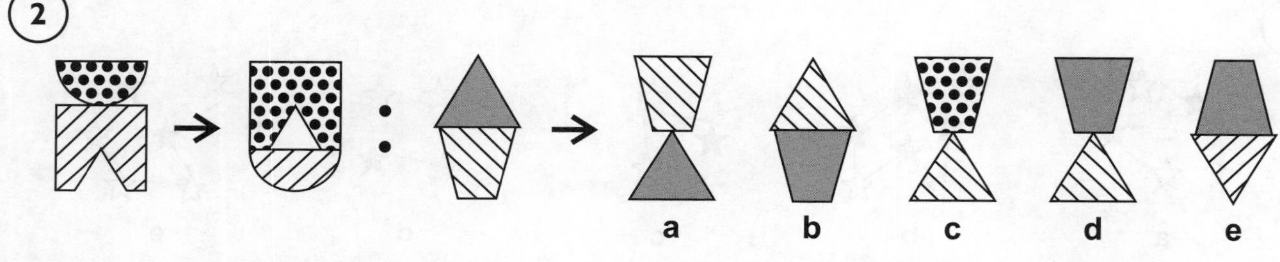

3

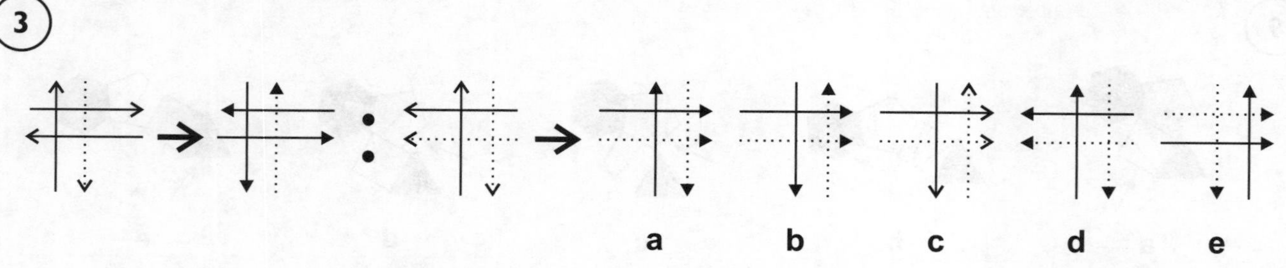

4

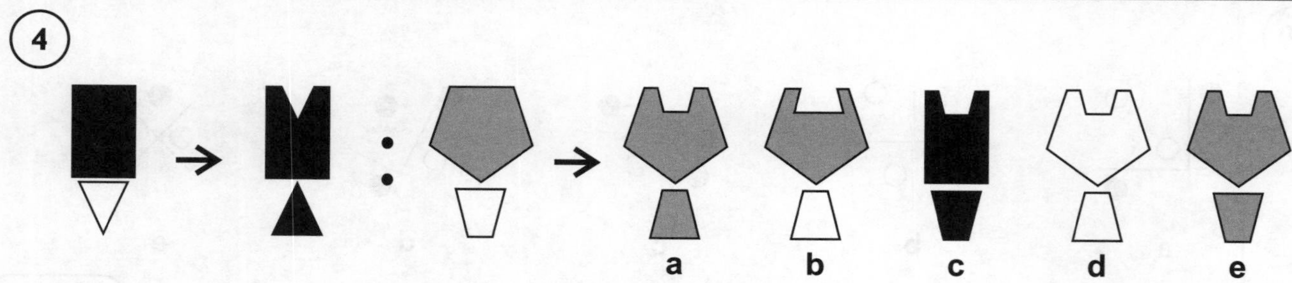

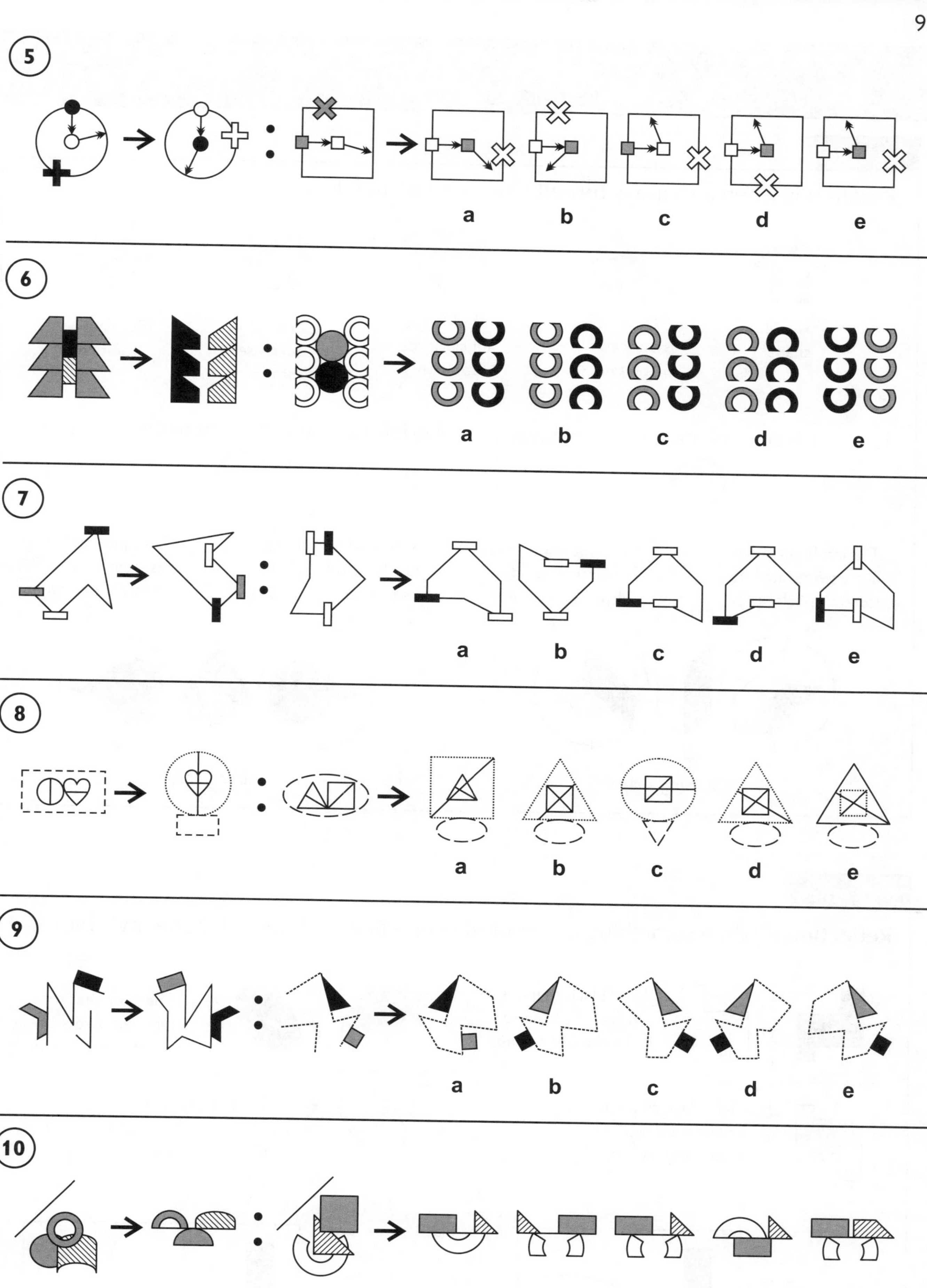

/ 10

Total / 46

End of Test

Glossary

Rotation

Rotation is when a shape is **turned** clockwise or anticlockwise.

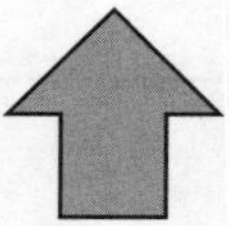
Example shape

90 degrees clockwise rotation

45 degrees anticlockwise rotation

135 degrees clockwise rotation

180 degrees rotation

The hands on a clock move **clockwise**.

Anticlockwise is the **opposite** direction.

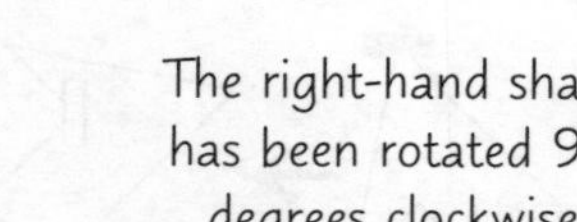

The left-hand shape has been rotated 45 degrees anticlockwise.

The right-hand shape has been rotated 45 degrees clockwise.

Starting shape

The left-hand shape has been rotated 90 degrees anticlockwise.

The right-hand shape has been rotated 90 degrees clockwise.

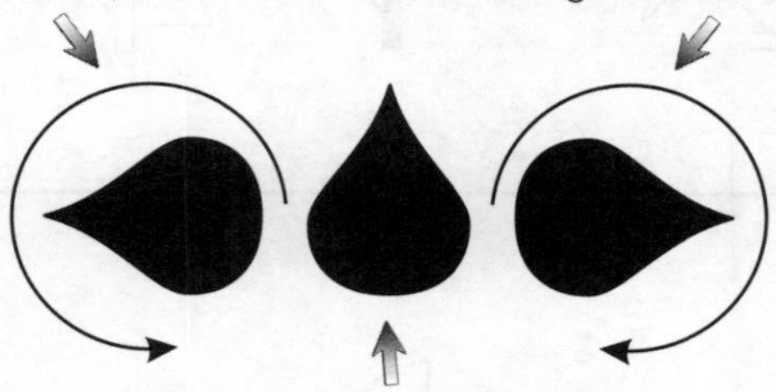
Starting shape

Reflection

Reflection is when something is **mirrored** over a line (this line might be invisible).

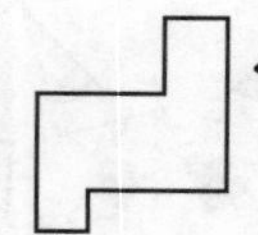
The black shape is reflected across to make the white shape.

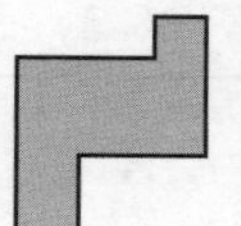
The black shape is reflected down to make the grey shape.

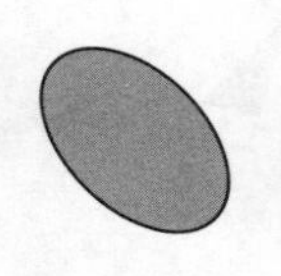

The grey shape is reflected across to make the black shape.

The grey shape is reflected down to make the white shape.

This black shape has been reflected and rotated to make the white shape.

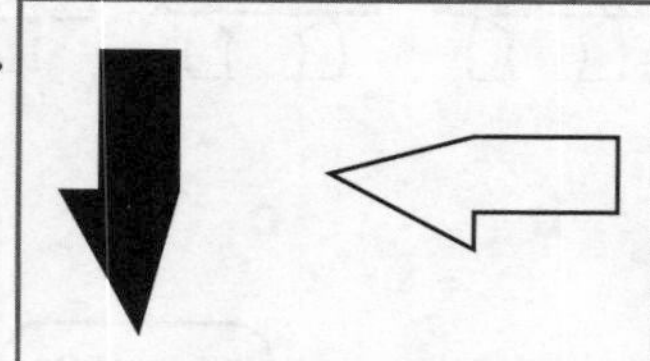

The black shape has been reflected over an invisible line (to make the dashed shape). Then it has been rotated 90 degrees clockwise.

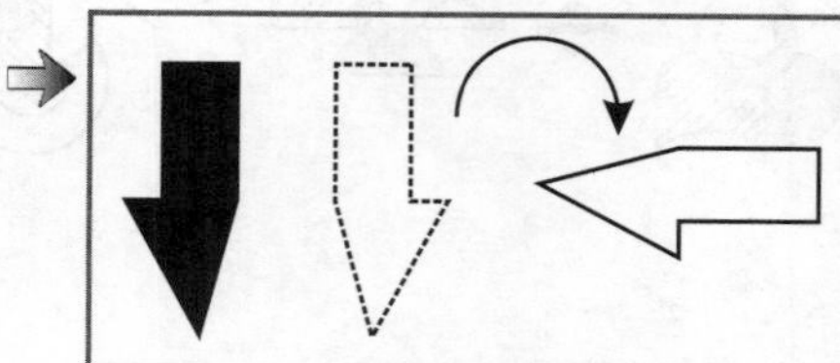

3D Rotation

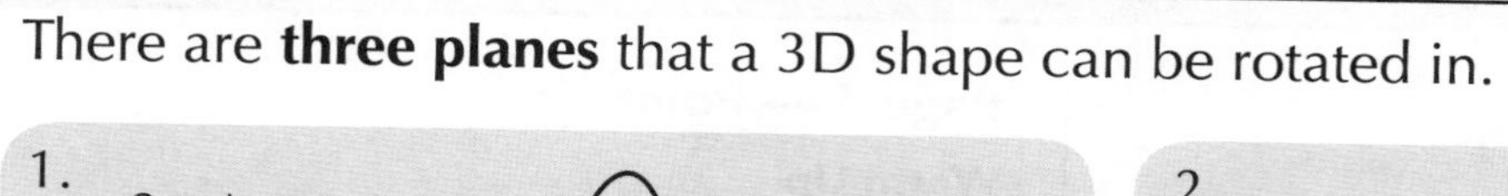

There are **three planes** that a 3D shape can be rotated in.

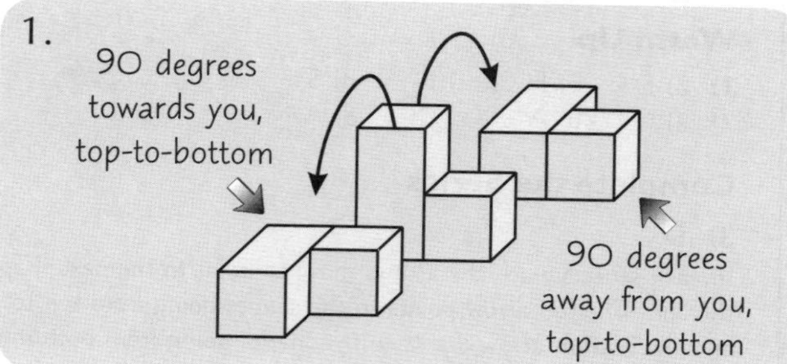

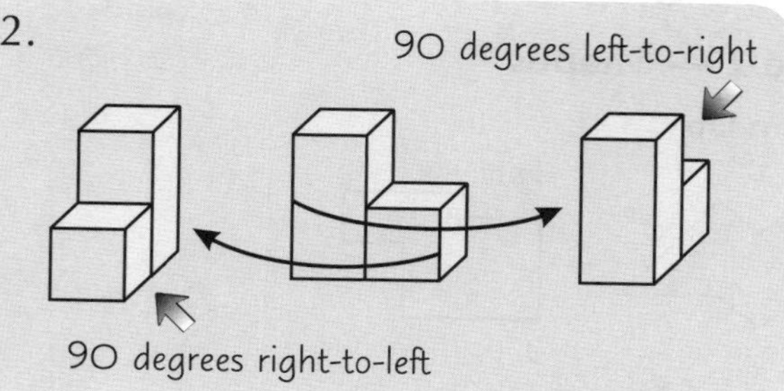

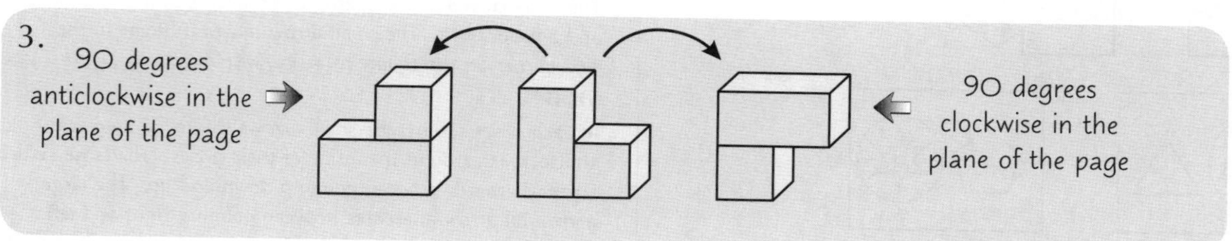

Other terms

Line Types:

Shading Types:

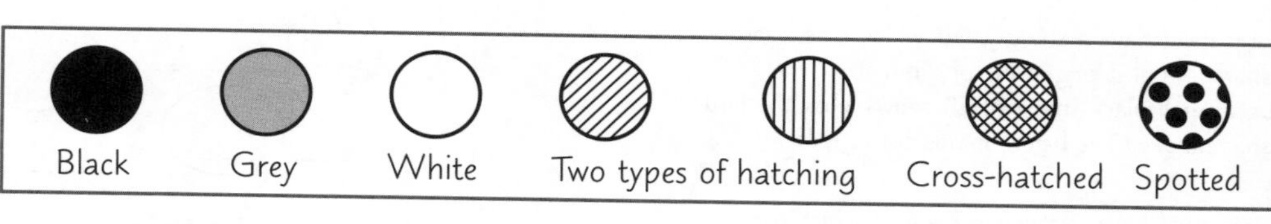

Layering — when a shape is in front of or behind another shape, or where two or more shapes overlap each other.

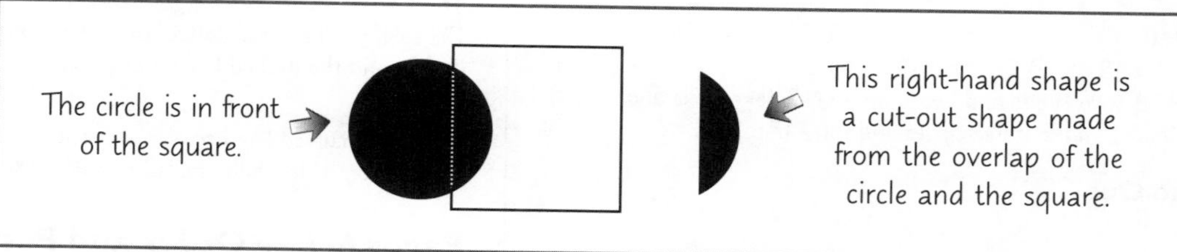

The circle is in front of the square.
This right-hand shape is a cut-out shape made from the overlap of the circle and the square.

Line of Symmetry — a line which splits a shape into halves that are reflections of each other.

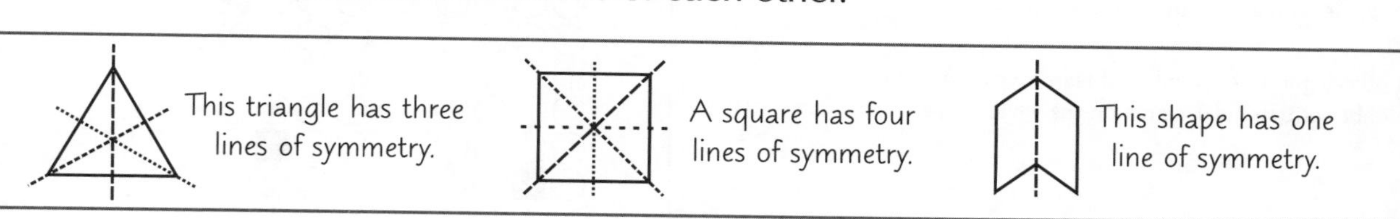

This triangle has three lines of symmetry.
A square has four lines of symmetry.
This shape has one line of symmetry.

Answers

Spotting Patterns

Page 2 — Shapes

Warm Up

1) a) 7 b) 8

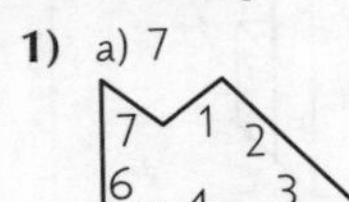
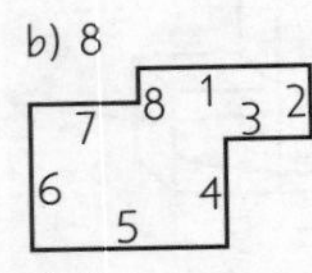

c) 6 d) 9

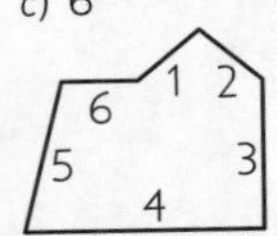
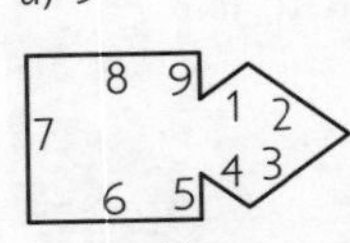

2) a) b)

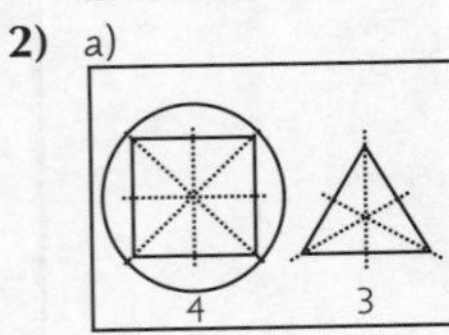
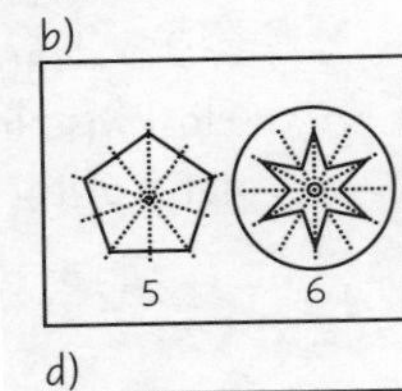

c) d)

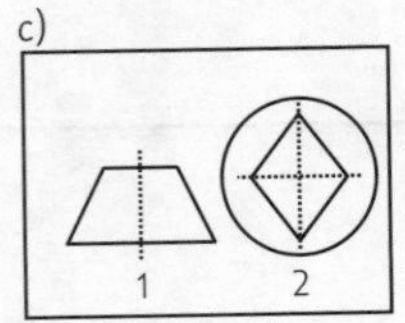
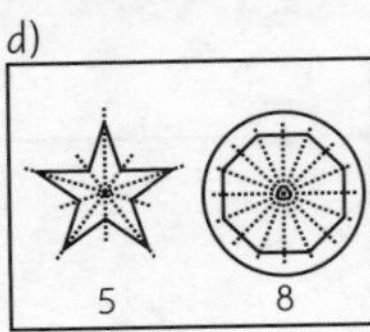

Find the Figure Like the First Two

3) A
All figures must have a small black circle on each straight side of the dashed shape.

4) C
All figures must have a straight line which cuts a large white shape in half along a line of symmetry. There must be a small black shape which shows what the large white shape looked like before it was cut in half.

5) E
All figures must have two pairs of shapes which are joined together by a straight line. In each pair, one shape must have one more side than the other shape.

Page 3 — Counting

Warm Up

1) a) C b) S c) C d) C e) S
2) Options B (two circles and two triangles), C (one circle and one triangle) and E (three circles and three triangles).

Odd One Out

3) B
In all other figures, three of the small shapes have a thick outline.

4) E
In all other figures, there are two lines connecting the larger shape and the smaller shape by their corners and two lines connecting them by their sides.

5) D
In all other figures, the number of teardrops is equal to the number of triangular points on the white shape.

Page 4 — Pointing

Warm Up

1) a) S b) H c) H d) S
2) a) C b) A c) C d) A

Complete the Series

3) D
In each series square, the arrows move to point to the next shape on the line. The top arrow points to the shapes going from top to bottom, and the bottom arrow points to the shapes going from bottom to top.

4) B
The large curved arrow alternates between pointing clockwise and anticlockwise. The small arrow moves to point to the next corner on the square in a clockwise direction.

5) B
In each series square, the small arrows rotate 90 degrees anticlockwise around the inside of their circles. The large vertical arrow alternates between pointing down and up. The large horizontal arrow alternates between pointing right and left.

Page 5 — Shading and Line Types

Warm Up

1) a) white b) spotted c) black d) hatched
2) a) b)

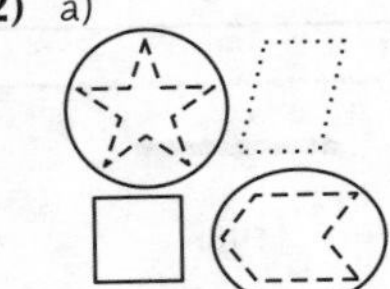
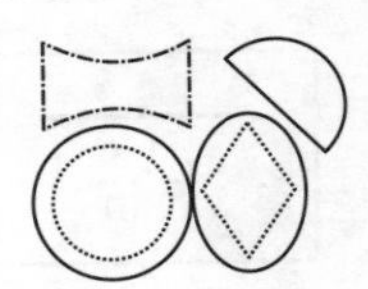

c) d)

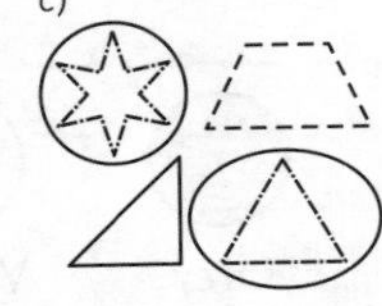
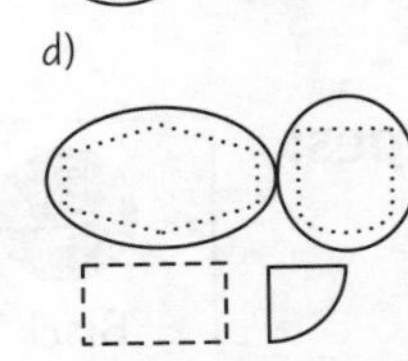

Complete the Pair

3) E
Any white shading becomes black and any black shading becomes white.

4) A
The solid line becomes dotted, the dotted line becomes dashed and the dashed line becomes solid.

5) C
The dotted curved line becomes straight. The small shapes change from being fully shaded to half shaded.

Pages 6-7 — Order and Position

Warm Up

1) a) b)

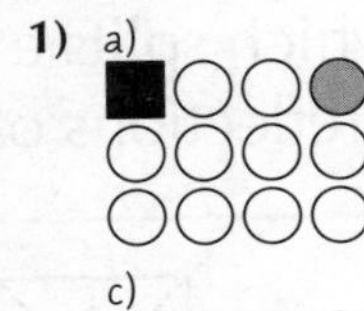
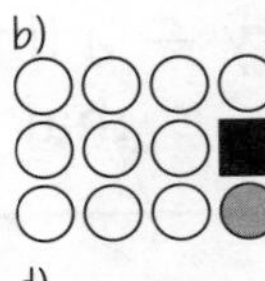

c) d)

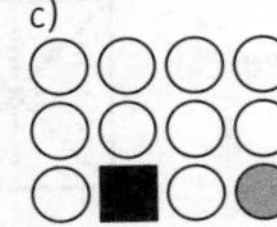
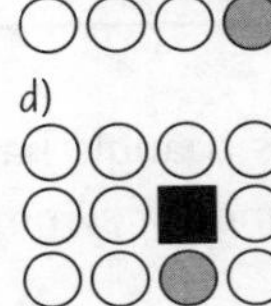

2) a) grey b) black c) white d) grey
3) a) C b) A c) A

Changing Bugs

4) B

The shapes in the bug's body move one place up, except for their shadings. When a shape reaches the top of the bug's body, it moves back to the bottom.

5) D

The shadings of the small shapes on the bug's body move one place clockwise. The bug's eyes move from the top of the bug's head to the ends of the bug's antennae.

6) B

The bug's wings move down to the nearest corner on its body. The small shaded shapes inside the bug's body move to corners of the white shape inside the bug's body.

7) B

The bug's eyes move to the top of its head. The bug's head moves upwards. Each of the bug's feet moves one place to the right. When a shape reaches the right-hand side, it moves back to the left-hand side.

Complete the Square Grid

8) E

Working from left to right, another smaller version of the large shape appears on one of its points. The shapes are added in a clockwise direction around the large shape.

9) A

Working from top to bottom, the two shapes at the start and end of the line stay where they are, but all the other shapes move two places down. When a shape reaches the bottom, it moves back to the top.

10) B

Working from top to bottom, the black shape and the white shape move one place up. The grey shape moves one place to the right.

Page 8 — Rotation

Warm Up

1) a) anticlockwise b) clockwise
c) clockwise d) anticlockwise
2) You should have circled the first, third, fourth and seventh figures.

Rotate the Figure

3) C

The figure is rotated 90 degrees clockwise. Option A is a downwards reflection. In option B, the grey shape is in the wrong place. Option D is a rotated reflection.

4) D

The figure is rotated 180 degrees. Option A is a rotated reflection. Option B is the wrong shape. Option C is a reflection across.

5) C

The figure is rotated 45 degrees anticlockwise. In option A, the black and grey circles shouldn't be on points of the star that are next to each other. Options B and D are rotated reflections.

Page 9 — Reflection

Warm Up

1) a) RE b) RO c) RO d) RE e) RE f) RO
2) You should have circled:
a) the black rectangle b) the small white five-sided shape
c) the straight lines d) the black circle

Reflect the Figure

3) D

In option A, the hearts have swapped places and shadings. Option B is a rotated reflection. In option C, the hearts have swapped shadings.

4) B

In option A, the black segment and one of the white segments have swapped places. Option C is a rotation. Option D is a rotated reflection.

5) B

Options A and D are rotated reflections. Option C is the wrong shape.

Pages 10-11 — Layering

Warm Up

1) You should have circled options B and C.
2) a) 2 b) 3 c) 1 d) 2 e) 3 f) 0
3) a)

b)

c)

Horizontal Code

4) E (DG)

C = heart with the dashed outline is at the front,
D = heart with the dotted outline is at the front.
E = black heart is on top of the heart with the dotted outline,
F = black heart is on top of the heart with the dashed outline,
G = black heart is on top of the heart with the solid outline.

5) A (QU)

P = black shape at the front, Q = grey shape at the front,
R = white shape at the front.
U = shape at the front is overlapping a side of the shape underneath,
V = shape at the front is overlapping a corner of the shape underneath.

6) B (OZ)

M = the square is at the front, N = the ellipse is at the front,
O = the circle is at the front.
Y = the shape at the front is black, Z = the shape at the back is black.

7) C (GX)

G = the small grey shape is a cut-out of the overlap of the two white shapes,
H = the small grey shape is a cut-out of the part of the white shape on the right-hand side that is not overlapping the other white shape.
V = the grey shape is at the top of the figure,
W = the grey shape is at the bottom of the figure,
X = the grey shape is on the left-hand side of the figure.

Complete the Hexagonal Grid

8) D

Going in a clockwise direction, the arrow and hatched pentagon rotate 60 degrees clockwise. The pentagon alternates between being behind and in front of the arrow.

9) D

Going in a clockwise direction, the rectangle, diamond and triangle move one place backwards, except for their shading. The shape that was at the back moves to the front. The circle alternates between being at the top of the white shape and at the bottom of the white shape.

10) B

Going in an anticlockwise direction, a new grey circle is added on top of the next point of the star, moving round the star in an anticlockwise direction. The grey circle that was on top of the star in the previous hexagon moves behind the star. The circle that moved behind the star in the previous hexagon turns black.

3D Shapes and Spatial Reasoning

Pages 12-13 — Rotating 3D Shapes

Warm Up

1) a) Yes b) No c) No d) Yes e) Yes
2) You should have circled options B and E. Option B shows the figure rotated 90 degrees away you, top-to-bottom. Option E shows the figure rotated 90 degrees anticlockwise in the plane of the page, then 90 degrees left-to-right.

3D Building Blocks

3) A
The bottom block in A moves to the back of the figure. The top block in A rotates 90 degrees in the plane of the page to become the block at the front of the figure.

4) D
One of the bottom two blocks in D moves to the back of the figure at the bottom. The other bottom block in D rotates 90 degrees in the plane of the page to become the block at the front-left of the figure. The top block in D rotates 90 degrees left-to-right and moves on top of the block at the back.

5) C
The T-shaped block in C rotates 90 degrees right-to-left, then 90 degrees away from you, top-to-bottom, to become the block at the back of the figure. The bottom left block in C moves in front of the T-shaped block, on the left of the figure. The bottom right block in C moves to the front right of the figure.

3D Rotation

6) C
Shape C rotates 90 degrees towards you, top-to-bottom. It then rotates 90 degrees right-to-left.

7) A
Shape A rotates 180 degrees towards you, top-to-bottom.

8) D
Shape D rotates 90 degrees towards you, top-to-bottom. It then rotates 90 degrees left-to-right.

9) B
Shape B rotates 90 degrees anticlockwise in the plane of the page. It then rotates 90 degrees left-to-right.

Pages 14-15 — 2D and 3D Shapes

Warm Up

1) a) 2 b) 1 c) 3 d) 0 e) 1 f) 2
2) Option F cannot be made from the net because the hatched triangle should be pointing away from the grey star.

2D Views of 3D Shapes

3) B
There are four blocks visible from above, which rules out options C and D. There are three blocks visible on the bottom row, which rules out option A. There are two blocks visible on the right-hand side, which rules out option E.

4) C
There are five blocks visible from above, which rules out options A and B. There are two blocks visible on the right-hand side, which rules out option E. There are two blocks visible on the left-hand side, which rules out option D.

5) A
There are three blocks visible on the bottom row, which rules out options D and E. There are four rows of blocks visible, which rules out option C. There are two blocks visible on the right-hand side, which rules out option B.

Cubes and Nets

6) C
Option A is ruled out because the star has the wrong number of points. Option B is ruled out because the black shapes and the three-quarter circle must be on opposite sides. Option D is ruled out because the white star and the white arrow shapes must be on opposite sides.

7) D
Option A is ruled out because if the teardrop cross was on the top and the white and grey square was on the front, the face on the right would be the black triangle with the black circle. Option B is ruled out because the white and grey square and the grey shield must be on opposite sides. Option C is ruled out because the face with the black triangle and black circle has been rotated.

8) B
Option A is ruled out because the white oval and the white circles must be on opposite sides. Option C is ruled out because the face with the white, grey and black rectangle has been rotated. Option D is ruled out because if the white oval was on the top and the grey triangles with the white circle was on the front, the face on the right would be the white, black and grey rectangle.

Pages 16-17 — Folding

Warm Up

1) Options A, B, E and F
2) a) 2
b) 4
c) 3
d) 2
e) 4

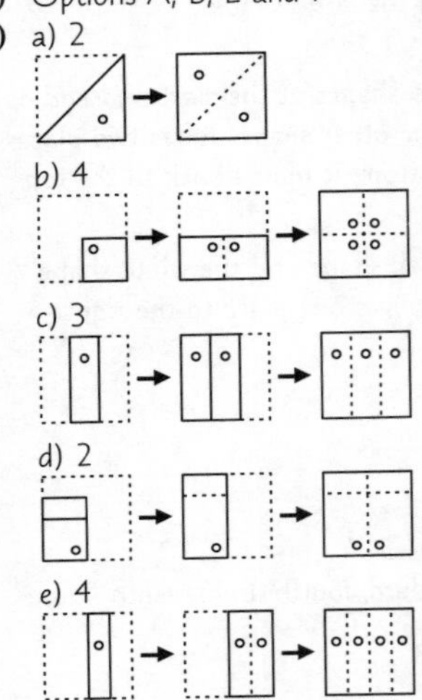

Fold Along the Line

3) A
Options B and C are ruled out because the fold line has moved. Option D is ruled out because the part of the figure that has been folded is the wrong shape. Option E is ruled out because the part of the figure originally below the fold line is the wrong shape.

4) E
Option A is ruled out because the part of the figure that has been folded is the wrong shape. Option B is ruled out because the figure has been broken apart along the fold line. Option C is ruled out because the part of the figure originally to the right of the fold line is the wrong shape. Option D is ruled out because the fold line has moved.

5) B
Option A is ruled out because the part of the figure originally to the right of the fold line should still be visible. Option C is ruled out because the part of the figure originally to the right of the fold line is the wrong shape. Option D is ruled out because the part of the figure that has been folded is the wrong shape. Option E is ruled out because the fold line has moved.

Fold and Punch

6) B

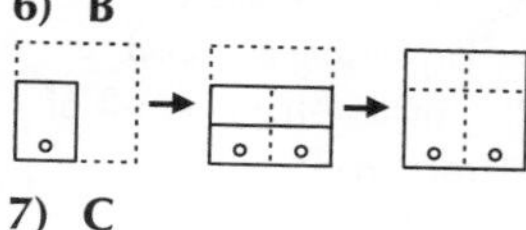

7) C

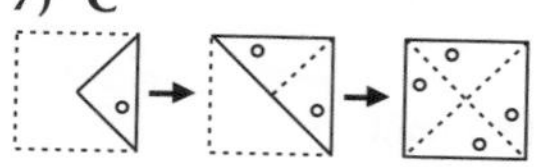

8) C

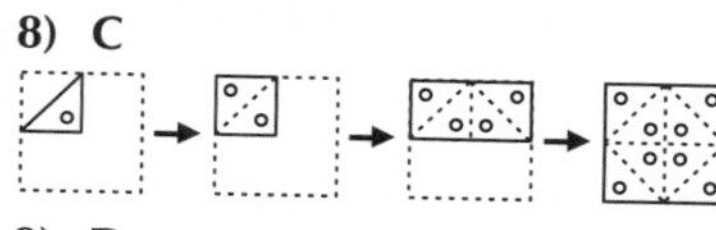

9) D

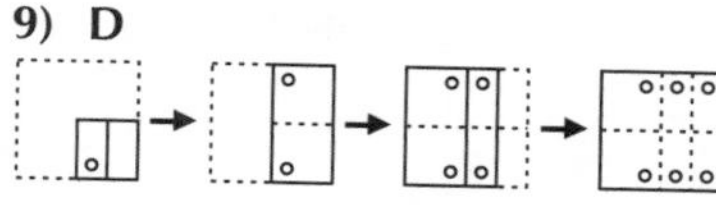

Page 18 — Hidden Shape

Warm Up

1) You should have circled options B, C, E, F and I.

2) a) b) c)

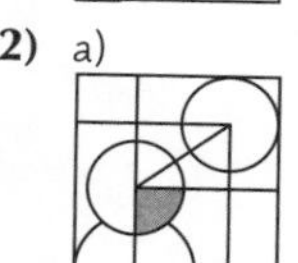

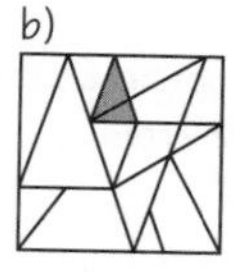

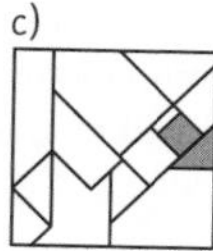

Hidden Shape

3) E

4) B

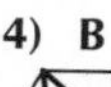

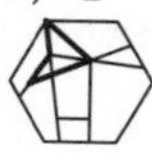

Page 19 — Connecting Shapes

Warm Up

1) a) b)

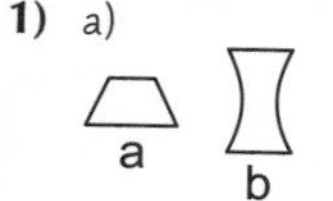

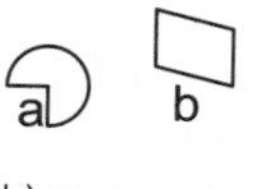

2) a) b)

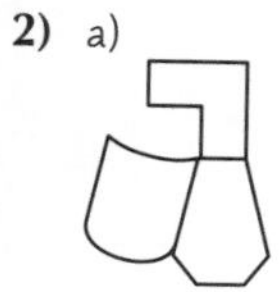

Connecting Shapes

3) B

Option A is ruled out because the T-shape is connected to the wrong side of the five-sided shape. Options C and E are ruled out because the wrong side of the T-shape is connected to the five-sided shape. Option D is ruled out because the wrong side of the curved shape is connected to the five-sided shape.

4) C

Option A is ruled out because the wrong side of the six-sided shape is connected to the four-sided shape. Option B is ruled out because the triangle is connected to the wrong side of the four-sided shape. Option D is ruled out because the triangle and the hexagon are connected to the wrong sides of the four-sided shape. Option E is ruled out because the wrong side of the triangle is connected to the four-sided shape.

Pages 20-29 — Assessment Test 1

Section 1 — Complete the Series

1) E

The figure rotates 90 degrees clockwise in each series square.

2) D

The next square to the right in the top row is shaded grey in each series square. When the shading reaches the right-hand side, it starts on the left-hand side on the next row down. The black star moves one square to the left in each series square. When it reaches the left-hand side, it starts to move to the right.

3) B

The circles move to the next clockwise corner in each series square. The figure alternates between showing two raindrops at the top and bottom, and a single raindrop in the centre.

4) B

In each series square, the next clockwise section of the circle is shaded in. The shading alternates between black and grey. The star moves between the top right and bottom right corner.

5) D

The shape alternates between a circle and an oval in each series square. The hatching rotates 45 degrees clockwise.

6) C

The number of sides on the grey shape decreases by one in each series square. The number of points on the white star increases by one in each series square.

7) B

The black triangle rotates 90 degrees anticlockwise about the centre of the octagon in each series square. The grey triangle rotates 90 degrees clockwise about the centre of the octagon in each series square.

8) E

All of the diamonds move one space down the lines in each series square. When they reach the bottom, they go back to the top in the next series square. The circles all move one space down and one line to the right in each series square. When a circle reaches the right-hand side, it moves to the left-hand side in the next series square.

9) B

In each series square, the next shape up moves to the front. Each shading moves to the next shape up in each series square. When a shading reaches the top shape, it moves to the bottom shape in the next series square.

10) D

The outer shape alternates between a square and a circle in each series square. The outer shape also gets smaller in each series square. The inner shape alternates between a white circle and a black square in each series square. The line alternates between being on the left-hand side of each series square and being at the top. The shading of the circle on the end of the line alternates between white and black.

Section 2 — Find the Figure Like the First Two

1) D

In all figures, there must be one black circle that overlaps a side of the large shape.

2) B

All figures must have a black shape at the front, a white shape in the middle, and a diagonally hatched shape at the back.

3) E

All figures must include a dashed line. All the shapes in the figure must be reflected over this dashed line.

4) A

All figures must have one upwards and one downwards pointing arrow. There must be one less circle than the number of raindrops.

5) A

All figures must have a smaller shape overlapping the straight side of a larger shape. The part of the smaller shape that overlaps with the larger shape must be shaded black.

6) C

All figures must have one line with a black circle on its left-hand end and one line with a white circle on its left-hand end. The two shapes on either side of the lines must be shaded in black an equal amount.

7) C

All figures must have a smaller shape inside a larger shape. The larger shape must have one less side than the smaller shape. There must be a black copy of the smaller shape on the left of the figure.

8) E

All figures must have a diagonally hatched small shape at the front, and a large white shape at the back. The arrow must pass behind the small shape and in front of the large shape.

9) D

All figures must have a small shaded shape inside a larger white version of the same shape. There must be an arrow coming out of the midpoint of each side of the larger shape.

10) C

All figures must have a line with a small black shape on the end. This shape must be the same shape that is inside the rectangle (not the circles). There must be an equal number of circles as sides on the shape inside the rectangle.

Section 3 — 2D Views of 3D Shapes

1) B

There are four blocks visible from above, which rules out options C and D. There are two blocks visible at the back of the figure, which rules out option A.

2) D

There are four blocks visible from above, which rules out options A and B. There are two blocks visible at the front of the figure, which rules out option C.

3) B

There are four blocks visible from above, which rules out options A and C. There are two blocks visible on the right-hand side of the figure, which rules out option D.

4) A

There are five blocks visible from above, which rules out options B and D. There are three rows of blocks, which rules out option C.

5) D

There are five blocks visible from above, which rules out options A and C. There is one block visible at the front of the figure on the left-hand side, which rules out option B.

6) B

There are six blocks visible from above, which rules out options A and D. There are two blocks visible at the front of the figure, which rules out option C.

7) A

There are eight blocks visible from above, which rules out options C and D. There is one block visible at the back of the figure, which rules out option B.

8) C

There is one block visible at the back of the figure from above, which rules out options A and D. There are two blocks visible on the right-hand side of the figure, which rules out option B.

Section 4 — Vertical Code

1) B (PV)

P = arrow pointing up, Q = arrow pointing down.
U = hatched circle, V = grey circle, W = white circle.

2) C (AZ)

A = arrow pointing anticlockwise, B = arrow pointing clockwise.
Y = arrow inside circle, Z = arrow inside square.

3) A (KL)

J = shapes in the boxes are grey, K = shapes in the boxes are black.
L = left-hand box is empty, M = right-hand box is empty,
N = neither box is empty.

4) C (FT)

D = the outline of the larger shape is dotted, E = the outline of the larger shape is dashed, F = the outline of the larger shape is solid.
T = smaller shape at top of larger shape, U = smaller shape on left of larger shape, V = smaller shape on right of larger shape.

5) E (BGO)

A = 2 arrows, B = 3 arrows.
G = arrows pointing left, H = arrows pointing right.
N = no lines inside the arrows, O = one line inside the arrows,
P = two lines inside the arrows.

6) D (NX)

M = line on the right-hand side, N = line on the left-hand side.
X = bottom shape at the front, Y = middle shape at the front,
Z = top shape at the front.

7) A (CT)

A = dot in the top corner, B = dot in the bottom-right corner,
C = dot in the bottom-left corner.
T = black arrowhead, U = white arrowhead.

8) A (ER)

E = no cross in the top-right box, F = a cross in the top-right box.
Q = 2 black dots, R = 1 black dot, S = no black dots.

Section 5 — Reflect the Figure

1) C

In option A, the oval hasn't been reflected. In option B the triangle hasn't been reflected. In option D, the triangle has been rotated instead of reflected.

2) D

In options A and C, there is a grey stripe inside the wrong shape. In option B, the grey shape has been reflected but the white shapes haven't.

3) B

Option A is a 180 degree rotation. In option C, the circles have swapped shadings. Option D is the wrong shape.

4) C

Options A and B are rotations. Option D is a downwards reflection.

5) A

Option B is a 90 degree anticlockwise rotation. In options C and D, the shading of some of the triangles is wrong.

6) D

Option A is a 180 degree rotation. In option B, one of the white segments is in the wrong place. Option C has the wrong shading.

7) C

In option A, the top heart has not been reflected.
In option B, neither of the hearts have been reflected.
In option D, the figure has been rotated 180 degrees.

8) A

In option B, the hatching of the oval is wrong.
In option C, the pentagon and star have swapped shadings. Option D has the wrong layering.

9) B

In option A, the line through the white parts of the circle has not been reflected. Option C has the wrong shading. In option D, only the line through the white parts of the circle has been reflected.

10) D

In option A, the parallelogram hasn't been reflected. In option B, the semicircles have swapped shadings. In option C, the shapes inside the parallelogram haven't been reflected.

Pages 30-39 — Assessment Test 2

Section 1 — Odd One Out

1) D

In all other figures, the grey shape is above the white shape.

2) C

In all other figures, each shape has one curved side.

3) D

All other figures are identical apart from rotation.

4) A

In all other figures, there is one square and one circle overlapping.

5) E

In all other figures, the left shape is the same as the right half of the black shape.

6) B

All other figures have one vertical line of symmetry.

7) A

In all other figures, the shortest line is pointing at the black circle.

8) D

In all other figures, the colours go from top-to-bottom in the order: black, grey, grey, white. When the bottom circle is reached, the pattern continues with the top circle.

9) D

In all other figures, the small shapes increase in number of sides going clockwise round the large circle.

10) C

In all other figures, there are two squares of the same colour joined by a line.

Section 2 — 3D Rotation

1) D

Shape D rotates 90 degrees left-to-right.

2) F

Shape F rotates 90 degrees clockwise in the plane of the page. It then rotates 90 degrees away from you, top-to-bottom.

3) A

Shape A rotates 90 degrees anticlockwise in the plane of the page.

4) C

Shape C rotates 90 degrees towards you, top-to-bottom. It then rotates 90 degrees left-to-right.

5) E

Shape E rotates 90 degrees away from you, top-to-bottom.

6) B

Shape B rotates 90 degrees anticlockwise in the plane of the page.

7) A

Shape A rotates 90 degrees clockwise in the plane of the page.

8) F

Shape F rotates 90 degrees away from you, top-to-bottom. It then rotates 90 degrees right-to-left.

9) C

Shape C rotates 90 degrees right-to-left. It then rotates 180 degrees in the plane of the page.

10) D

Shape D rotates 90 degrees away from you, top-to-bottom. It then rotates 180 degrees left-to-right.

Section 3 — Complete the Pair

1) A

The shape rotates 90 degrees clockwise.

2) D

The shape and the line swap line types.

3) C

The figure is reflected across. The two shapes in the middle swap shadings.

4) A

The grey shape moves to the opposite side. The striped shape is reflected downwards.

5) A

The shape formed by the overlap between the grey shape and the unshaded shape is shown on its own, and it is shaded black.

6) B

The figure rotates 90 degrees anticlockwise. The white shape moves to the back and the grey shape moves to the front.

7) B

Any white shapes move one square down.
Any grey shapes move one square to the right.

8) D

The small shape moves to the next anticlockwise corner of the square. The number of sides on the small shape increases by one. The large shape and the small shape swap shadings.

Section 4 — Find the Figure Like the First Three

1) D

In all figures, the small white shape must be a smaller copy of the large grey shape that has been reflected downwards.

2) C

All figures must have one long white rectangle and two short grey rectangles.

3) A

All figures must be identical apart from rotation.

4) B

In all figures, the longest side of the shape must be dotted. All the other sides must be solid.

5) A

All figures must have exactly three sections of the shape shaded.

6) C

All figures must have an arrow crossing the curved side of the shape. If the curved side curves inwards, the arrow must point into the shape. If the curved side curves outwards, the arrow must point away from the shape.

7) D

All figures must have a black shape at the front. There must be the same number of lines as there are shapes.

8) B

In all figures, the dotted shape is a 90 degree clockwise rotation of the solid shape.

9) C

All figures must show the same type of shape on each side of the pair of solid and dashed lines. The shapes on the side of the dashed line must be white. The shapes on the side of the solid line must be black.

10) B

All figures must show a number of raindrops that is one more than the number of grey rectangles.

Section 5 — Fold Along the Line

1) C

Options A, B and D are ruled out because the fold line has moved. Option E is ruled out because the part of the figure that has been folded is the wrong shape.

2) D

Option A is ruled out because the part of the figure that has been folded is the wrong shape. Options B and C are ruled out because the fold line has moved. Option E is ruled out because the figure has been broken apart along the fold line.

3) B

Option A is ruled out because the part of the figure originally to the right of the fold line should still be visible. Option C is ruled out because the part of the figure that has been folded is the wrong shape. Option D is ruled out because the part of the figure originally to the right of the fold line is the wrong shape. Option E is ruled out because the fold line has moved.

4) D

Option A is ruled out because the part of the figure that has been folded is the wrong shape. Option B is ruled out because the figure has been broken apart along the fold line. Options C and E are ruled out because the fold line has moved.

5) B

Option A is ruled out because the part of the figure that has been folded is the wrong shape. Option C is ruled out because the part of the figure originally to the right of the fold line is the wrong shape. Option D is ruled out because the fold line has moved. Option E is ruled out because the figure has been broken apart along the fold line.

6) A

Option B is ruled out because the figure has been broken apart along the fold line. Options C and E are ruled out because the fold line has moved. Option D is ruled out because the part of the figure originally to the left of the fold line is the wrong shape.

7) C

Options A and B are ruled out because the part of the figure originally to the right of the fold line is the wrong shape. Option D is ruled out because the fold line has moved. Option E is ruled out because the part of the figure that has been folded is the wrong shape.

8) B

Option A is ruled out because the part of the figure originally to the left of the fold line is the wrong shape. Option C is ruled out because the part of the figure that has been folded is the wrong shape. Option D is ruled out because the fold line has moved. Option E is ruled out because the figure has been broken apart along the fold line.

Pages 40-49 — Assessment Test 3

Section 1 — 3D Building Blocks

1) A

The block on the top of set A rotates 90 degrees towards you, top-to-bottom, to become the middle block of the figure. One of the cubes in set A moves to the top of the figure, and the other moves to the bottom.

2) B

The block on the top of set B rotates 90 degrees towards you, top-to-bottom, to become the back right block of the figure. The block at the bottom left of set B rotates 90 degrees in the plane of the page to become the block at the front of the figure. The block at the bottom right of set B moves to the top of the figure. (The block on the top of set B could also rotate 90 degrees towards you, top-to-bottom, then 90 degrees right-to-left to become the front block of the figure. The block at the bottom right of set B would go on top of it. The block at the bottom left of set B would rotate 90 degrees towards you, top-to-bottom, to become the back right block of the figure.)

3) D

The block on the left of set D is rotated 90 degrees top-to-bottom to become the top left block of the figure. One of the cubes in set D moves underneath this block. The other cube in set D moves to the top right of the figure, at the back.

4) D

The block at the bottom of set D moves to the bottom of the figure. The block in the middle of set D is rotated 90 degrees left-to-right to become the block on the top left of the figure. The block at the top of set D is rotated 90 degrees left-to-right to become the block on the top right of the figure.

5) B

The block at the top of set B is rotated 90 degrees right-to-left to become the bottom left block of the figure. The block at the bottom left of set B moves to the front right of the figure. The block at the bottom right of set B moves to the top of the figure.

6) C

The bottom block of set C is rotated 90 degrees in the plane of the page to become the left block of the figure. The middle block of set C is rotated 90 degrees left-to-right to become the bottom right block of the figure. The top block in set C moves to become the top block on the right of the figure.

7) A

The top block of set A is rotated 180 degrees right-to-left, and then 90 degrees away from you, top-to-bottom, and moves to the bottom of the figure. The bottom right block in set A moves to the front middle of the figure, at the bottom. The bottom left block of set A rotates 90 degrees towards you, top-to-bottom, to become the top block of the figure.

8) B

The bottom block of set B is rotated 90 degrees away from you, top-to-bottom, to become the top block of the figure. The top left block of set B is rotated 90 degrees left-to-right to become the bottom left block in the figure. The top right block of set B moves to the bottom middle of the figure, at the back.

Section 2 — Complete the Series

1) C

In each series square, the circle alternates between white and grey shading. The line with a circle at the end rotates 45 degrees anticlockwise each time.

2) D

There is one less ellipse in each series square. The area where the ellipses overlap is shaded grey.

3) A

In each series square, the whole figure rotates 90 degrees clockwise. The diagonal line alternates between being solid and being dashed.

4) B

In each series square, the arrow is reflected across. The shape that it is pointing to has one more side in each series square.

5) B

The squares in this series are in two pairs. In each pair, the overlapping area between the two shapes remains white, and the remaining area of each shape turns black.

6) D

In each series square, the grey shape rotates 45 degrees anticlockwise. The two black triangles each move two points clockwise around the star.

7) C

In each series square, the white shape is rotated by 90 degrees around the centre of the figure. A grey copy of the white shape appears where the white shape used to be. The small crosses alternate between x and + orientations.

8) A

In each series square, the triangle containing dots and the triangle containing lines swap. Another line is added to the triangle in each series square. One of the black circles becomes white.

9) A

In each series square, the next shape moves to the front, moving in a clockwise direction around the shapes. The next shape becomes grey, moving in a clockwise direction around the shapes.

10) C

In each series square, the shapes move down to the next line, but they miss out the third and fifth lines down. When a shape reaches the fourth line down, it then moves to the top line. The shapes on the top line are always grey, the shapes on the second line down are always white and the shapes on the fourth line down are always black.

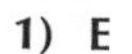

Section 3 — Hidden Shape

1) E

2) A

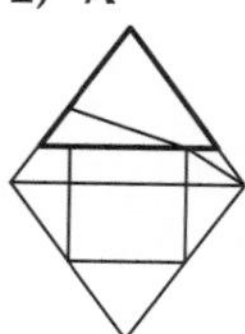

3) C

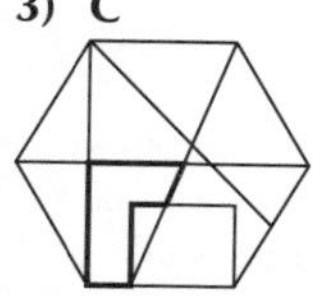

4) B

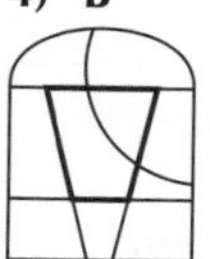

5) D

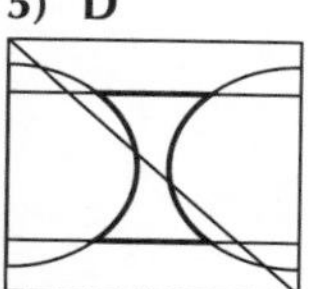

6) C

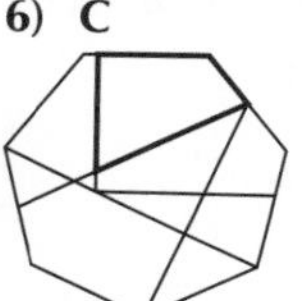

7) E

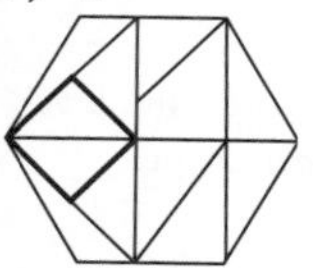

8) A

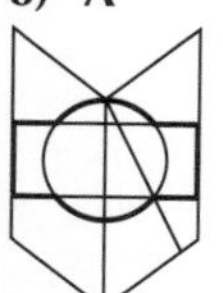

9) B

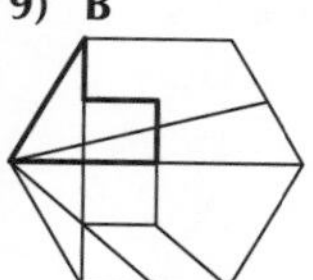

10) B

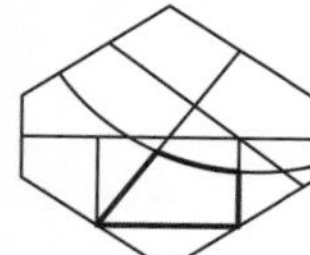

Section 4 — Complete the Square Grid

1) D

Working from left to right, the shape rotates 90 degrees anticlockwise in each grid square.

2) D

The third grid square in each row contains the shape from the second grid square on top of the shape from the first grid square.

3) A

Each type of shading of the large shape (black, grey and white) only occurs once in each row and column. The small shapes are the same in each row.

4) C

The position of the black circle is the same in each row. The position of the circle at the front is the same in each column.

5) B

Working from left to right, the figure rotates 45 degrees clockwise in each grid square. The number of small shapes is the same in each column. The shadings of the small shapes are the same in each row.

6) D

The second grid square in each row shows the shape from the first grid square and a copy of that shape that has been rotated 180 degrees. The third grid square in each row contains the shape formed by the overlap of the two shapes in the second grid square.

7) C

Working from left to right, the figure rotates 90 degrees clockwise in each grid square. The size of the white shape increases in each grid square.

8) A

Each style of outline (dotted, dashed and solid) only appears once in each row and column. Each number of raindrops (2, 3 and 4) only appears once in each row and column. Each shading (black, grey and white) only appears once in each row and column.

Section 5 — Rotate the Figure

1) B

The figure has been rotated 90 degrees clockwise. In option A, the black square is positioned incorrectly. In option C, the curved line and the square are positioned incorrectly. In option D, the black shape is a pentagon instead of a square.

2) D

The figure has been rotated 180 degrees. In options A and B, the black bar is positioned incorrectly. In option C, the grey square is positioned incorrectly.

3) A

The figure has been rotated 90 degrees anticlockwise. In option B, the dotted line is the wrong shape. In option C, the dotted line is solid. In option D, the two halves of the small ellipse have swapped shadings.

4) D

The figure has been rotated 135 degrees anticlockwise. In option A, the shading of the top two triangles is wrong. In option B, the black shape is incorrectly positioned. In option C, the white triangles and the black arrow shape are incorrectly positioned.

5) B

The figure has been rotated 90 degrees clockwise. In option A, the lines with white shapes have swapped places. In option C, the black and white shapes have swapped shading. Option D is a rotated reflection.

6) C

The figure has been rotated 45 degrees clockwise. In option A, the shape has been reflected across instead of rotated. Options B and D are the wrong shape.

7) C

The figure has been rotated 135 degrees clockwise. In option A, the diamond is incorrectly positioned. In option B, the hatching is wrong. In option D, the heart is incorrectly positioned.

8) B

The figure has been rotated 45 degrees anticlockwise. In option A, the grey shape is incorrectly positioned. In options C and D, the arrow is incorrectly positioned.

9) C

The figure has been rotated 45 degrees anticlockwise. In option A, the grey circle is incorrectly positioned. In options B and D, the shading of the triangles is incorrect.

10) A

The figure has been rotated 135 degrees clockwise. In options B and C, the shapes on the ends of some of the lines are incorrect. Option D is a rotated reflection.

Pages 50-59 — Assessment Test 4

Section 1 — Cubes and Nets

1) B

Option A is ruled out because the net doesn't have two identical faces. Option C is ruled out because the grey circle and the droplet must be on opposite sides. Option D is ruled out because the black circle and the cross-hatched face must be on opposite sides.

2) C

Option A is ruled out because the two cube faces with the letter Y must be on opposite sides. Option B is ruled out because the spiral and the grey ring must be on opposite sides. Option D is ruled out because the net doesn't have a grey triangle.

3) A

Option B is ruled out because the three grey triangles and the cross must be on opposite sides. Option C is ruled out because the net doesn't have two identical faces. Option D is ruled out because the dots and the two black triangles must be on opposite sides.

4) C

Option A is ruled out because the paw print and the arrow must be on opposite sides. Option B is ruled out because the star must be on the opposite side to one of the hatched faces. Option D is ruled out because if the paw print is at the front and the grey curved shape is on the top, then the star must be on the right.

5) D

Option A is ruled out because the two quarter-circles and the white circle on a grey circle must be on opposite sides. Option B is ruled out because the heart and the black square must be on opposite sides. Option C is ruled out because the question mark and the grey quadrilateral must be on opposite sides.

6) D

Option A is ruled out because the two black arrows must be on opposite sides. Option B is ruled out because the grey face and the letter M must be on opposite sides. Option C is ruled out because the black arrow should be pointing away from the grey arch.

7) A

Option B is ruled out because if the crescent shape is on the top and the white square on a grey circle is at the front, then the cross-hatched face must be on the right. Option C is ruled out because the white circle on a grey square and the crescent shape must be on opposite sides. Option D is ruled out because if the white square on a grey circle is at the front and the cross-hatched face is on the top, then the white circle on a grey square must be on the right.

8) B

Option A is ruled out because if the smiley face is on the top and the triangle is on the right, then the three lines must be at the front. Option C is ruled out because the grey triangle and the arrows must be on opposite sides. Option D is ruled out because the grey and white T-shape has the wrong rotation.

Section 2 — Complete the Hexagonal Grid

1) D

Going in a clockwise direction, each outer hexagon rotates 60 degrees clockwise. The part-circles nearest the central hexagon alternate between grey and white.

2) A

Going in a clockwise direction, another half of a circle is shaded. The circles are shaded in a clockwise direction around the large circle, starting from the top circle in the top middle hexagon.

3) D

The hexagons on opposite sides of the hexagonal grid are identical.

4) B

All hexagons have two white circles. Going in an anticlockwise direction from the top middle hexagon, each hexagon gains one black circle.

5) A

Going in a clockwise direction, the shape on the right-hand side is the shape on the left-hand side in the next hexagon. The right-hand shape is white and the left-hand shape is black.

6) C

Going in a clockwise direction, each outer hexagon rotates 60 degrees anticlockwise. The hexagons alternate between having the black circle on top of the white circle, and having the white circle on top of the black circle.

7) B

Going in a clockwise direction from the top middle hexagon, the next point on the large star becomes grey, moving in a clockwise direction around the star. The black shading moves to the next point of the small star, moving in a clockwise direction around the star.

8) A

Going in a clockwise direction, the shaded hexagon in the mini-hexagonal grid shows which hexagon is missing from the mini-hexagonal grid in the next outer hexagon.

Section 3 — Find the Figure Like the First Two

1) C

All figures must be identical apart from rotation.

2) B

In all figures, one quarter of the shape must be shaded black.

3) C

In all figures, there must be three arrows pointing in the same direction. There must be a white circle attached to one of the arrows.

4) D

In all figures, all triangles must be on one side of the line and all other shapes must be on the other side.

5) A

All figures must have exactly two shapes with matching shading.

6) A

All figures must have three small squares, shaded white, grey and black. There must be a line though the curved side of the larger shape.

7) D

In all figures, one arrow must be going clockwise and one arrow must be going anticlockwise. There must be a smaller grey copy of the large white shape on each arrow.

8) B

In all figures, the square with the fewest dots must be at the front, and the square with the most dots must be at the back. The square at the front must have one dash, the square in the middle must have two dashes and the square at the back must have three dashes.

9) C

In all figures, each arrow must point from a black circle to the nearest white circle.

10) B

In all figures, the grey star must have the fewest points and the black star must have the most points.

Section 4 — Complete the Pair

1) B

The centre shape and the outer shapes swap shadings.

2) D

The circle moves between the hexagons so that it is second from the back.

3) C

The whole figure rotates 45 degrees clockwise. The two smaller shapes swap shadings.

4) A

The shape rotates 180 degrees. The hatching changes from solid lines to dashed lines.

5) A

A smaller copy of the large shape that has been reflected downwards appears inside the large shape.

6) E

Each shading moves one place downwards. When a shading reaches the bottom, it then moves back to the top.

7) A

The whole figure reflects across. The squares and circles on each white shape swap positions.

8) D

The shape is cut into pieces along each dashed line.

9) C

The number of circles becomes the number of sides of the grey shape. The number of stars becomes the number of circles.

10) C

All squares move to the front of the figure. All triangles move to the back of the figure.

Section 5 — Fold and Punch

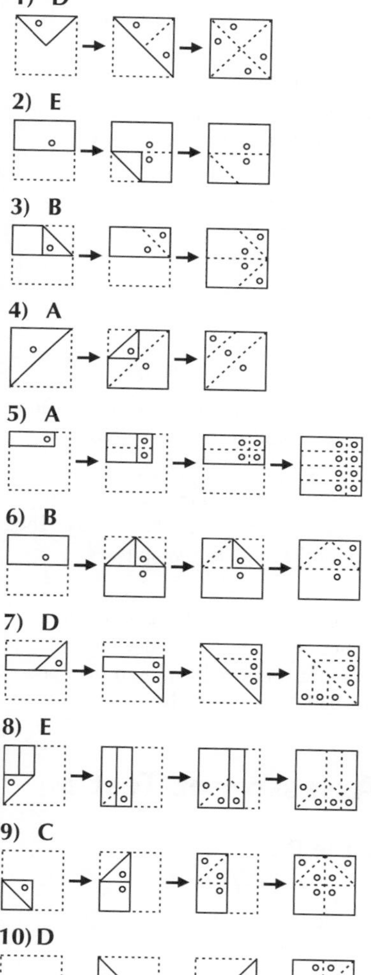

Pages 60-69 — Assessment Test 5

Section 1 — Complete the Square Grid

1) C

Working from top to bottom, the figure is reflected downwards.

2) D

Working from left to right, the hatched shape moves one place clockwise around the large shape. The hatching rotates 45 degrees.

3) A

Working from top to bottom, the shape gets larger and rotates 90 degrees anticlockwise in each grid square.

4) C

Working from left to right, the large star takes on the line type of the bottom line in the top right corner, and the small star takes on the line type of the top line. The two small shapes move on top of the point of the large star that they are closest to.

5) E

Each shape (square, circle and triangle) appears once in each row and column. The three different line arrangements appear once in each row and column.

6) A

Working from top to bottom, the cross moves one place to the left. When the cross reaches the left-hand side, it then moves to the right-hand side. The grey shading moves one shape to the left. When the shading reaches the left-hand shape, it then moves to the right-hand shape. The small white shapes at the back of the figure move to the front one at a time, starting with the left-hand shape.

7) C

Working from left to right, the left-hand and middle grid squares are combined to make the right-hand grid square. The grey shape in the left-hand column moves to the bottom of the figure in the right-hand column, at the back. The black shape moves to the top of the figure, at the back, and is reflected down. The two hatched shapes in the middle column are combined together to make one whole shape.

8) C

On every line where two grid squares meet, the group of three circles on either side are shaded in the same way.

Section 2 — 3D Rotation

1) C

Shape C has been rotated 90 degrees anticlockwise in the plane of the page.

2) F

Shape F has been rotated 90 degrees towards you, top-to-bottom. It has then been rotated 90 degrees left-to-right.

3) B

Shape B has been rotated 90 degrees right-to-left. It has then been rotated 90 degrees away from you, top-to-bottom.

4) D

Shape D has been rotated 180 degrees left-to-right.

5) B

Shape B has been rotated 90 degrees anticlockwise in the plane of the page. It has then been rotated 90 degrees away from you, top-to-bottom.

6) E

Shape E has been rotated 180 degrees left-to-right.

7) A

Shape A has been rotated 90 degrees away from you, top-to-bottom. It has then been rotated 90 degrees right to left.

8) D

Shape D has been rotated 90 degrees right-to-left.

9) F

Shape F has been rotated 90 degrees towards you, top-to-bottom. It has then been rotated 90 degrees anticlockwise in the plane of the page.

10) C

Shape C has been rotated 90 degrees away from you, top-to-bottom. It has then been rotated 90 degrees clockwise in the plane of the page.

Section 3 — Horizontal Code

1) E (DY)
C = lines end in circles, D = lines end in squares.
X = one line, Y = two lines, Z = three lines.

2) C (FJ)
D = inner lines go from bottom left to top right, E = inner lines are vertical, F = inner lines go from top left to bottom right.
J = shield is white with black stripes, K = shield is black with white stripes.

3) E (EV)
E = star is at the back, F = star is at the front.
V = the circle is on an inner corner of the star, W = the circle is on a point of the star.

4) E (NU)
M = the white shapes are rotations, N = the white shapes are rotated reflections, O = the white shapes are the same.
T = arrow above the white shapes, U = arrow under the white shapes.

5) D (GQ)
F = all dots are black, G = half the dots are black,
H = all dots are white.
Q = solid line, R = dashed line, S = dotted line.

6) B (AY)
A = vertical hatching, B = horizontal hatching, C = diagonal hatching.
X = three arrowheads, Y = four arrowheads, Z = five arrowheads.

7) A (MU)
K = teardrop in top square, L = teardrop in middle square,
M = teardrop in bottom square.
U = line is at the front, V = line is at the back.

8) C (JS)
H = the shapes have curved sides only, I = the shapes have straight and curved sides, J = the shapes have straight sides only.
S = spiral starts on the bottom, T = spiral starts on the left.

Section 4 — Find the Figure Like the First Three

1) B
All figures must contain a large white shape that has a line inside it with three loops. The small shape must be the same as the large white shape.

2) A
All figures must have a star and three circles. Two of the circles must be on two points of the star. The remaining circle must be on an inner corner of the star.

3) B
All figures must have two straight lines with a teardrop at both ends. There must be a pair of arrows which point out on either side of the white teardrop.

4) B
All figures must have a large shaded shape on the right-hand side of the figure. There must be two small white shapes that are joined together.

5) C
In all figures, the two shapes that are joined by a line must be reflections across of each other.

6) C
All figures must have a shape with three lines inside it. There must be three triangles around the outside of the shape which have the same line types as the lines inside the shape.

7) D
In all figures, there must be a small white shape inside a large white shape. There must be more triangles on top of the smaller shape than behind it.

8) A
In all figures, the white shapes must rotate 90 degrees clockwise each time, starting with the top shape and moving along the line.

9) E
All figures must have a line with a circle on the end which points to the shape with the most sides, a double-headed arrow which points to the four-sided shape and a diamond-headed arrow which points to the grey shape.

10) E
In all figures, there must be two shapes that overlap. Copies of the shape created by the overlap (including its shading) must be on the end of lines coming out from the overlapping shapes. The number of copies must match the number of sides of the overlapping shapes.

Section 5 — Changing Bugs

1) D
The bug gains an extra pair of legs and its eyes are reflected downwards.

2) C
The bug is reflected downwards and it loses an eye.

3) A
The bug's head rotates 45 degrees anticlockwise. The white shape and the spotted shape swap positions, but the layering remains the same.

4) B
The line types of the small shapes inside the bug's body move one place to the left. The small shape on the left moves above the middle shape and the small shape on the right moves below the middle shape.

5) C
All the teardrop shapes in the bug's body become circles. The legs with arrowhead feet change from pointing away from the bug's body to pointing towards it.

6) A
The bug's head gains a side and the hatching inside the bug's wings rotates 45 degrees anticlockwise.

7) C
The shape of the bug's wings swap with the shapes on the ends of the bug's antennae. The bug's antennae change from solid lines to dotted lines.

8) B
The shadings in the bug's body move two places up. When a shading reaches the top of the bug's body, it moves back to the bottom.

9) D
The bug's eyes move from the outer edge of the bug's head to inside the bug's head. The bug's wings move in front of the bug's body. The shapes at the top and the bottom of the bug's legs swap places.

10) B
The shadings of the bug's body, except for the hatching, move one place down. The shading at the bottom of the bug's body moves to the top. The shapes at the back of the bug's body move to the front, and the shapes at the front of its body move to the back.

Pages 70-79 — Assessment Test 6

Section 1 — Complete the Pair

1) C
The number of points on the star decreases by one.
The white circles become black.

2) D
The figure reflects across and the dashed line becomes solid.

3) A
The entire figure rotates 90 degrees clockwise.

4) C
The shading on each segment moves one place clockwise.

5) A
The spiral is reflected downwards and the grey shape becomes hatched.

6) B
The parts of the line that are outside the large shape disappear. The small shape and the shaded part of the large shape swap shadings.

7) D

Each rectangle moves to the other side of the line. The square rotates 45 degrees.

8) C

The square at the front moves to the back. The hatching is reflected across.

Section 2 — Odd One Out

1) B

All other figures have two black dots.

2) D

In all other figures, the top triangles have the same shading and the bottom triangles have the same shading.

3) A

In all other figures, the line inside the smaller square runs from corner to corner.

4) E

In all other figures, there is one diamond shape on the end of a dashed line and one diamond shape on the end of a solid line.

5) D

All other figures are identical apart from rotation.

6) D

In all other figures, the small, dashed shape is a reflection across of the larger shape.

7) A

In all other figures, the number of sides on each small shape is equal to the number of lines inside the circle.

8) C

In all other figures, the black circle is higher up than the white circle.

9) E

In all other figures, three of the stars have the same shading as the shape at the front, two of the stars have the same shading as the shape in the middle and one star has the same shading as the shape at the back.

10) B

In all other figures, the dashed line goes from one corner of the large shape to the next corner on the large shape.

Section 3 — 3D Building Blocks

1) C

The block at the top of set C moves to the back of the figure. One of the two remaining identical blocks in set C is rotated 90 degrees clockwise in the plane of the page to become the block at the front of the figure on the left-hand side. The final block in set C moves to the front of the figure on the right-hand side.

2) D

The block at the bottom of set D is rotated 90 degrees left-to-right to become the block on the left-hand side of the figure. The block in the middle of set D is rotated 90 degrees clockwise in the plane of the page to become the block on the right-hand side of the figure at the front. The block at the top of set D moves to the top right of the figure, at the back.

3) B

The block at the top of set B is rotated 90 degrees anticlockwise in the plane of the page, then 90 degrees left-to-right, to become the block on the right-hand side of the figure. The block at the bottom of set B is rotated 90 degrees clockwise in the plane of the page to become the block on the left-hand side of the figure at the front. The block in the middle of set B moves to the left-hand side of the figure at the back.

4) A

The block at the top of set A is rotated 90 degrees clockwise in the plane of the page, then 90 degrees away from you, top-to-bottom, to become the block at the bottom of the figure at the front. The block at the bottom left of set A is rotated 90 degrees clockwise in the plane of the page and moves on top of the previous block. The remaining block in set A moves to the back of the figure.

5) D

The block at the top of set D is rotated 90 degrees away from you, top-to-bottom, then 90 degrees left-to-right, to become the block at the back and bottom of the figure. The block at the bottom left of set D then moves on top of it. The remaining block in set D is rotated 90 degrees clockwise in the plane of the page to become the block at the front of the figure.

6) C

The block at the top of set C moves to the front of the figure at the top. The block at the bottom left of set C rotates 90 degrees right-to-left and moves behind and below the previous block, on the right-hand side of the figure. The remaining block in set C moves to the left-hand side of the figure, at the back.

7) B

The block at the bottom of set B is rotated 180 degrees towards you, top-to-bottom, then 90 degrees right-to-left to become the block at the bottom of the figure on the left-hand side. The middle block in set B then moves on top of it. The block at the top of set B is rotated 90 degrees left-to-right to become the block on the right-hand side of the figure.

8) C

The block at the top of set C is rotated 90 degrees clockwise in the plane of the page to become the block at the back of the figure on the right-hand side. The block at the bottom right of set C is rotated 90 degrees left-to-right to become the block at the back of the figure on the left-hand side. The remaining block in set C is rotated 90 degrees clockwise in the plane of the page to become the block at the front of the figure.

Section 4 — Complete the Series

1) A

The entire series square rotates 90 degrees anticlockwise each time. The circle gets smaller.

2) A

In each series square, the cube moves one corner anticlockwise and reveals a different face. The grey square stays on the right-hand side of the cube.

3) D

In each series square, the top horizontal rectangle and the bottom star disappear.

4) C

The entire series square rotates 90 degrees clockwise each time. The squares swap shadings.

5) B

The grey shapes are reflected across in each series square, and the white arrow rotates 90 degrees clockwise. The shape at the front moves to the back.

6) D

In each series square, the arrows move one corner clockwise and swap shading. The black dot moves up and to the left, along the diagonal of the series square.

7) E

The triangles swap shadings in each series square. The shading on the trapeziums becomes the same as the shading on the rectangle from the previous series square.

8) A

In each series square, each circle moves down to the next bend in its line. When a circle reaches the bottom bend, it starts again at the top bend. Each line alternates between solid and dashed.

9) B

In each series square, the black line starts from the next corner of the square, moving round in a clockwise direction. Moving anticlockwise around the circles, one more circle turns black and the curved line passes through it. The line finishes at the next corner of the pentagon, moving anticlockwise around the pentagon.

10) E

In each series square, one more dashed line is added across the centre of the heptagon. The new lines are added clockwise from the corners of the heptagon. The square moves to be on top of the new dashed line. The circle moves to where the square was in the previous series square.

Section 5 — Connecting Shapes

1) A

Options B and C are ruled out because the wrong side of the rectangle is connected to the triangle. Option D is ruled out because the square should be connected to the triangle. Option E is ruled out because the rectangle is connected to the wrong side of the triangle.

2) D

Option A is ruled out because the T-shape is connected to the wrong side of the five-sided shape. Option B is ruled out because both the triangle and the T-shape are connected to the wrong sides of the five-sided shape. Option C is ruled out because the triangle is connected to the wrong side of the five-sided shape. Option E is ruled out because the wrong side of the T-shape is connected to the five-sided shape.

3) C

Option A is ruled out because the wrong side of the trapezium is connected to the arrow shape. Option B is ruled out because the wrong side of the C-shape is connected to the arrow shape. Option D is ruled out because the trapezium is connected to the wrong side of the arrow shape. Option E is ruled out because the C-shape is connected to the wrong side of the arrow shape.

4) A

Option B is ruled out because the wrong side of the seven-sided shape is connected to the L-shape. Option C is ruled out because the seven-sided shape is connected to the wrong side of the L-shape. Option D is ruled out because the five-sided shape is connected to the wrong side of the L-shape. Option E is ruled out because the wrong side of the five-sided shape is connected to the L-shape.

5) E

Option A is ruled out because both the triangle and the cross shape are connected to the wrong sides of the seven-sided shape. Options B and D are ruled out because the wrong side of the triangle is connected to the seven-sided shape. Option C is ruled out because the cross shape is connected to the wrong side of the seven-sided shape.

6) E

Options A and C are ruled out because the semicircle is connected to the wrong side of the large shape. Option B is ruled out because the five-sided shape is connected to the wrong side of the large shape. Option D is ruled out because the wrong side of the five-sided shape is connected to the large shape.

7) C

Options A and D are ruled out because the wrong side of the L-shape is connected to the five-sided shape. Option B is ruled out because both the square and the L-shape are connected to the wrong sides of the five-sided shape. Option E is ruled out because the square is connected to the wrong side of the five-sided shape.

8) B

Option A is ruled out because the quarter circle is connected to the wrong side of the large shape. Option C is ruled out because the wrong side of the quarter circle is connected to the large shape. Option D is ruled out because the wrong side of the triangle is connected to the large shape. Option E is ruled out because both the triangle and the quarter circle are connected to the wrong sides of the large shape.

9) D

Options A and B are ruled out because the wrong side of the seven-sided shape is connected to the eight-sided shape. Option C is ruled out because the trapezium is connected to the wrong side of the eight-sided shape. Option E is ruled out because the wrong side of the trapezium is connected to the eight-sided shape.

10) E

Options A and D are ruled out because the wrong side of the arch shape is connected to the cross shape. Option B is ruled out because the wrong side of the triangle is connected to the cross shape. Option C is ruled out because the triangle is connected to the wrong side of the cross shape.

Pages 80-89 — Assessment Test 7

Section 1 — 2D Views of 3D Shapes

1) A

There are five blocks visible from above, which rules out options D and E. There are three blocks on the right-hand side of the figure, which rules out options B and C.

2) E

There are five blocks visible from above, which rules out options A and D. The figure is made up of three rows of blocks, which rules out option B. There are three blocks in the middle row of the figure, which rules out option C.

3) C

There are six blocks visible from above, which rules out options A, B and D. There is one block on the right-hand side of the figure, which rules out option E.

4) A

There is only one block on the left-hand side of the figure, which rules out option B. There is only one block at the front of the figure, which rules out options C, D and E.

5) B

There are three blocks visible in the middle column of the figure, which rules out options A, D and E. There are two blocks at the front of the figure, which rules out option C.

6) D

There are six blocks visible from above, which rules out options A and B. There is one block at the front of the figure, which rules out option C. There are two blocks on the right-hand side of the figure, which rules out option E.

7) E

There is one block visible on the left-hand side of the figure, which rules out option A. There are two blocks visible on the right-hand side of the figure, with a gap in the middle, which rules out options B and C. There are two blocks visible at the back, which rules out option D.

8) D

There are eight blocks visible from above, which rules out option A. There is only one block at the back of the figure, which rules out option B. There is a gap between two of the blocks in the row before the back block, which rules out options C and E.

Section 2 — Find the Figure Like the First Two

1) B

All figures must have three small shapes that are the same as the large white shape, including rotation. The small shapes must have different shadings. One small shape must be positioned on a side of the large shape and the other two shapes must be completely inside the large shape.

2) E

In all figures, the two outer shapes must be half-shaded black. The shape in the middle must be fully shaded black.

3) C

All figures must have five black shapes which are positioned on the outside of the large shape or spiral. There must be three of one type of shape and two of another type of shape.

4) B

In all figures, the combined number of lines and circles must match the number of sides on the shape.

5) E

All figures must have a large four-sided shape. All figures must have the same number of stars as there are lines inside the four-sided shape.

6) E

All figures must have a row of shapes at the top and a downward reflection of those shapes at the bottom.

7) A

All figures must have three shapes. The top two shapes must have half the number of sides of the shape at the bottom.

8) D

In all figures, the shapes must alternate shadings from front to back. The hatching furthest towards the back must be a 45 degree clockwise rotation of the hatching closest to the front.

9) D

All figures must have five arrows which have the same arrowhead. The arrows must all be pointing in the same direction (either clockwise or anticlockwise).

10) B

All figures must have a line with four ellipses. The ellipses that appear at the front of the figure must have lines on the left-hand side of the line. The ellipses that appear at the back of the figure must have lines on the right-hand side of the line.

Section 3 — Vertical Code

1) C (CF)

B = quarter circle, C = semicircle, D = three-quarter circle.
E = white shape with black spots, F = black shape with white spots.

2) A (IX)

H = arrow pointing at the heart on the right, I = arrow pointing to the heart on the left.
X = white shapes in the order: circle, square, triangle, Y = white shapes in the order: square, triangle, circle, Z = white shapes in the order: triangle, circle, square.

3) B (ST)

R = the shape is rotated 90 degrees across the line, S = the shape is reflected across the line.
T = the shapes are black and grey, U = the shapes are white and black, V = the shapes are grey and white.

4) A (MTV)

M = curved line, N = straight lines.
S = top half of the circle is shaded black, T = bottom half of the circle is shaded black.
V = two short lines on the main line, W = one short line on the main line.

5) E (EJ)

E = top row of hexagons on top, F = bottom row of hexagons on top, G = hexagons alternate being on top and at the back.
I = the line starts in the bottom left-hand corner,
J = the line starts in the top left-hand corner.

6) E (LOV)

K = large spiral, L = small spiral.
N = the trapezium at the front is on the right, O = the trapezium at the front is in the middle, P = the trapezium at the front is on the left.
U = the trapezium in the middle of the stack has a solid outline,
V = the trapezium in the middle of the stack has a dashed outline,
W = the trapezium in the middle of the stack has a dotted outline.

7) D (ARY)

A = the rectangle on the left is the tallest, B = the rectangle in the middle is the tallest, C = the rectangle on the right is the tallest.
Q = the arrow is on the right, R = the arrow is on the left.
Y = rectangles are white and grey, Z = rectangles are white and black.

8) C (EKO)

D = the dotted line is a line of symmetry of the large shape,
E = the dotted line is not a line of symmetry of the large shape.
J = the small grey shapes are on top of the large shape,
K = the small grey shapes are behind the large shape,
L = one of the grey shapes is on top of the large shape and the other is behind the large shape.
O = the small shape in the centre of the large shape is a rotation,
P = the small shape in the centre of the large shape has the same orientation.

Section 4 — Reflect the Figure

1) C

Option A is a rotation. Option B is the wrong shape.
Option D is a rotated reflection.

2) C

In option A, the line inside the white diamond is in the wrong place.
In option B, the white diamond has become a parallelogram.
In option D, the line inside the diamond has not been reflected.

3) A

In option B, the octagon has become a pentagon. In option C, the hatching inside the hexagon has been rotated. In option D, the black circle is in the wrong place.

4) D

Option A is a 90 degree clockwise rotation. In option B, the teardrop has been reflected downwards. In option C, the straight line inside the three-quarter circle has not been reflected.

5) B

Option A is the wrong shape. Option C is a downwards reflection.
Option D is identical to the original figure.

6) B

In option A, the circles are in the wrong places. Option C is a rotated reflection. In option D, the shading of the shapes is wrong.

7) D

In option A, the small stars at the top of the figure have not been reflected but their shadings have. In option B, the large black hatched star has not been reflected.
In option C, the small stars are in the wrong places.

8) A

In option B, the layering of the small squares and lines is wrong.
Option C has not been reflected and has the wrong shading.
In option D, the hatched square has been rotated.

9) B

In option A, the grey stripes inside the arrow shape have not been reflected. In option C, the two diagonal lines are in the wrong place. Option D is identical to the original figure.

10) C

In option A, the grey trapezium has moved to the back.
In option B, the grey rectangle and the white shield have swapped outlines. In option D, the white shield has not been reflected.

Section 5 — Fold Along the Line

1) B

Options A and D are ruled out because the fold line has moved.
Option C is ruled out because the part of the figure originally below the fold line is the wrong shape.

2) A

Option B is ruled out because the fold line has moved. Option C is ruled out because the part of the figure that has been folded is the wrong shape. Option D is ruled out because the part of the figure originally below the fold line should still be visible.

3) B

Option A is ruled out because the fold line has moved. Option C is ruled out because the part of the figure originally to the right of the fold line should still be visible. Option D is ruled out because the part of the figure originally to the right of the fold line is the wrong shape.

4) D
Option A is ruled out because the part of the figure that has been folded is the wrong shape. Option B is ruled out because the figure has been broken apart along the fold line. Option C is ruled out because the fold line has moved.

5) C
Option A is ruled out because the part of the figure that has been folded is the wrong shape. Option B is ruled out because the fold line has moved. Option D is ruled out because the part of the figure originally to the left of the fold line is the wrong shape.

6) D
Option A is ruled out because the part of the figure originally above the fold line is the wrong shape. Option B is ruled out because the figure has been broken apart along the fold line. Option C is ruled out because the fold line has moved.

7) A
Option B is ruled out because the part of the figure that has been folded is the wrong shape. Option C is ruled out because the fold line has moved. Option D is ruled out because the part of the figure originally below the fold line is the wrong shape.

8) B
Option A is ruled out because the part of the figure originally to the left of the fold line should still be visible. Option C is ruled out because the part of the figure originally to the left of the fold line is the wrong shape. Option D is ruled out because the fold line has moved.

9) C
Option A is ruled out because the part of the figure that has been folded is the wrong shape. Option B is ruled out because the part of the figure originally above the fold line is the wrong shape. Option D is ruled out because the figure has been broken apart along the fold line.

10) C
Option A is ruled out because the fold line has moved. Option B is ruled out because the part of the figure originally below the fold line is the wrong shape. Option D is ruled out because the figure has been broken apart along the fold line.

Pages 90-99 — Assessment Test 8

Section 1 — Find the Figure Like the First Three

1) C
In all figures, there must be a large shape at the back that is the same as the shape inside the white rectangle.

2) A
All figures must have three shapes that are the same apart from size and shading. The largest shape must be connected to the medium-sized shape by a solid line, and the medium-sized shape must be connected to the smallest shape by a dashed line.

3) B
In all figures, there must be two shapes at the front that are downward reflections of each other. The large shape at the back must have one more side than the two shapes in the middle.

4) E
All figures must be identical apart from rotation.

5) B
In all figures, the number of bold lines must be the same as the number of grey shapes.

6) C
In all figures, there must be a small shape at the front that is the same shape as the small white shape formed by the line. The shape at the front must be positioned on a corner of the large shape.

7) A
In all figures, the larger shape must be overlapped by the smaller shape on one of its curved sides. The shape at the front of the figure must be see-through. The larger shape must have a line through one of its straight sides.

8) D
In all figures, there must be a black arrow pointing to the shape that has hatching running in the same direction as the white arrow.

9) B
In all figures, shapes on one side of the line must be attached to the line on one of their points. Shapes on the other side of the line must be attached to the line on one of their sides. The shapes attached by their points must be split in two parallel to the line, and the part closest to the line must be shaded grey.

10) C
In all figures, the number of lines in the middle of the large shape must match the number of corners of the large shape that have a circle on them.

Section 2 — Complete the Square Grid

1) B
Working from top to bottom, the figure gets larger and the shadings swap over.

2) A
Each type of shape and each type of shading only appears once in each row and column.

3) C
Working from left to right, the figure rotates 90 degrees clockwise and one more circle is shaded black.

4) C
Working from left to right, the first grid square is added to the second grid square to make the third grid square. In the third grid square, all the shadings turn black.

5) D
Working from left to right, the whole figure is reflected downwards and each circle moves one place towards the other end of the line.

6) A
Working from top to bottom, each shading moves one place clockwise. Each large shape only appears once in each row and column.

7) B
Working from left to right, the number of arrows in the second grid square is the same as the number of thick black lines in the third grid square. The arrowheads in the second grid square are the same shape as the large white shape in the first grid square. The hatching in the rectangle stays the same.

8) D
Working from left to right, the figure moves diagonally across the square. Going anticlockwise, a new petal is added to the figure each time. The shading of the new petal alternates between black and white. The figure is not rotated.

Section 3 — Cubes and Nets

1) B
Option A is ruled out because the black arrow and the semicircle must be on opposite sides. Option C is ruled out because there aren't two white arrows on the net. Option D is ruled out because there isn't a grey circle on the net. Option E is ruled out because the trapezium and the rectangle must be on opposite sides.

2) E
Option A is ruled out because the circle and the black cube face must be on opposite sides. Option B is ruled out because there isn't a white cross on the net. Option C is ruled out because the grey Z-shape and the black cross must be on opposite sides. Option D is ruled out because the three-pointed star and the triangle must be on opposite sides.

3) D

Option A is ruled out because there isn't a white hexagon with a grey stripe on the net. Option B is ruled out because the hexagon and the spiral must be on opposite sides. Option C is ruled out because the heart has the wrong rotation. Option E is ruled out because the heart and the four-pointed star must be on opposite sides.

4) C

Option A is ruled out because the C-shape has the wrong rotation. Option B is ruled out because the triangles and the parallelogram must be on opposite sides. Option D is ruled out because if the triangles are on the front and the dots are on the top, then the rectangles should be on the right. Option E is ruled out because there aren't two parallelograms on the net.

5) B

Option A is ruled out because the ovals have the wrong rotation. Option C is ruled out because there is no white circle on top of a grey circle on the net. Option D is ruled out because if the circles are on the front and the arrow is on the top, then the ovals should be on the right. Option E is ruled out because the arrow and hatched rectangle must be on opposite sides.

6) D

Option A is ruled out because the heart should be opposite either the ring shape or the two semicircles, so these three faces cannot be seen together. Option B is ruled out because the star shape and the square with a circle inside must be on opposite sides. Option C is ruled out because if the ring shape is on the front and the two semicircles are on top, then the square with the circle inside should be on the right. Option E is ruled out because the square with the circle inside has the wrong rotation.

7) A

Option B is ruled out because there is no cube face with four dots on the net. Option C is ruled out because if the three black lines are on the front and the five dots are on the top, then the arrow should be on the right. Option D is ruled out because the five dots and the triangle must be on opposite sides. Option E is ruled out because the triangle has the wrong rotation.

8) C

Option A is ruled out because the triangle has the wrong rotation. Option B is ruled out because the circle with the line through it has the wrong rotation. Option D is ruled out because if the star is on the front and the circle with the line through it is on the top, then the two arrows should be on the right. Option E is ruled out because the star and the triangle must be on opposite sides.

Section 4 — Odd One Out

1) C

In all other figures, the shapes are transparent.

2) D

In all other figures, the inner shape has a dashed outline and the outer shape has a solid outline.

3) A

All other figures have five shapes.

4) C

In all other figures, the arrow comes out from the sides of the small shape, not the corners.

5) B

In all other figures, small shapes which are the same shape have the same shading.

6) E

In all other figures, the shape in the black box is a 90 degree anticlockwise rotation of the grey shape.

7) A

In all other figures, the shapes on the ends of the spiral are the same.

8) B

In all other figures, the lines are connected to the points on the stars.

9) D

In all other figures, the arrow points to the shape with the same number of sides as the number of dashed lines.

10) C

In all other figures, the number of times the dotted and solid lines overlap is equal to the number of black circles.

Section 5 — Complete the Pair

1) C

The figure is reflected downwards and the shadings swap over.

2) D

The two shapes swap positions and shadings.

3) B

Each arrow changes to point in the opposite direction. The arrowheads change to solid triangles.

4) A

A section is cut out of the top of the large shape. The shape of the cut-out section is the same shape as the bottom half of the small shape. The small shape rotates 180 degrees and its shading changes to match the large shape.

5) E

The arrow from the small, central shape moves to point to where the cross shape was originally. The cross shape moves to where the arrow was originally pointing. The cross shape and the small shape on the edge of the large shape swap shadings with the small central shape.

6) A

The shapes on the left are rotated 90 degrees clockwise and take the shading of the top middle shape. The shapes on the right are rotated 90 degrees anticlockwise and take the shading of the bottom middle shape. The shapes in the middle disappear.

7) C

The entire figure rotates 90 degrees anticlockwise. The rectangles move one corner anticlockwise around the large shape.

8) D

The small shape on the left becomes larger, its outline becomes dotted and the small shape on the right moves inside it. The large shape becomes smaller and moves to the bottom of the figure.

9) B

The whole figured is reflected across. Two straight lines are added to join the existing lines together. The small shapes swap shadings.

10) C

The line becomes horizontal. The bottom part of each of the three shapes disappears. The remaining parts of the shapes are arranged on the line as follows: the shape at the front is above the line, on the left. The shape in the middle is above the line, on the right. The shape at the back is below the line, in the middle.

Progress Chart

Use this chart to keep track of your scores for the Assessment Tests.

You can do each test more than once — download extra answer sheets from cgpbooks.co.uk/11plus/answer-sheets or scan the QR code on the right.

	First Go	Second Go	Third Go
Test 1	Date: Score:	Date: Score:	Date: Score:
Test 2	Date: Score:	Date: Score:	Date: Score:
Test 3	Date: Score:	Date: Score:	Date: Score:
Test 4	Date: Score:	Date: Score:	Date: Score:
Test 5	Date: Score:	Date: Score:	Date: Score:
Test 6	Date: Score:	Date: Score:	Date: Score:
Test 7	Date: Score:	Date: Score:	Date: Score:
Test 8	Date: Score:	Date: Score:	Date: Score:

Look back at your scores once you've done all the Assessment Tests.
Each test is out of 46 marks.

Work out which kind of mark you scored most often:

0-27 marks — Go back to basics and work on your question technique.

28-38 marks — You're nearly there — go back over the questions you found tricky.

39-46 marks — You're a Non-Verbal Reasoning star.